Sola Scriptura in Asia

Davit Hartono
November 6, 1977–September 21, 2017

Sola Scriptura in Asia

EDITED BY
Yongbom Lee
AND
Andrew R. Talbert

☞PICKWICK *Publications* · Eugene, Oregon

SOLA SCRIPTURA IN ASIA

Copyright © 2018 Wipf and Stock Publishers. All rights reserved. Except for brief quotations in critical publications or reviews, no part of this book may be reproduced in any manner without prior written permission from the publisher. Write: Permissions, Wipf and Stock Publishers, 199 W. 8th Ave., Suite 3, Eugene, OR 97401.

Pickwick Publications
An Imprint of Wipf and Stock Publishers
199 W. 8th Ave., Suite 3
Eugene, OR 97401

www.wipfandstock.com

PAPERBACK ISBN: 978-1-5326-4928-8
HARDCOVER ISBN: 978-1-5326-4929-5
EBOOK ISBN: 978-1-5326-4930-1

Cataloguing-in-Publication data:

Names: Lee, Yongbom, editor. | Talbert, Andrew R., editor.

Title: *Sola Scriptura* in Asia / edited by Yongbom Lee and Andrew R. Talbert.

Description: Eugene, OR: Pickwick Publications, 2018. | Includes bibliographical references and index.

Identifiers: ISBN 978-1-5326-4928-8 (paperback). | ISBN 978-1-5326-4929-5 (hardcover). | ISBN 978-1-5326-4930-1 (ebook).

Subjects: LCSH: Theology. | Reformation.

Classification: BR1065 S62 2018 (print). | BR1065 (ebook).

Scripture quotations are from the ESV® Bible (The Holy Bible, English Standard Version®), copyright © 2001 by Crossway, a publishing ministry of Good News Publishers. Used by permission. All rights reserved.

Manufactured in the U.S.A. 11/02/18

In Memory of
Davit Hartono

"Here I Stand, May God Help Me, Amen"

Martin Luther, on April 18, 1521,
before the Diet of Worms

"Christ died for me. Why should I fear death?
I have determined to die for Christ."

Chu Ki-Chol (1897–1944), a Korean Protestant pastor and martyr, who was tortured and killed by the Japanese Empire for refusing to worship the Japanese Emperor

Contents

Preface / ix
Contributors / xi
Introduction / xiii
Abbreviations / xvii

Part 1: Biblical Theology

1 Hermeneutics and Pseudo-Postmodernity in Southeast Asia / ANDREW R. TALBERT / 3

2 Union, Participation, Adoption: A Better Hermeneutics for Holiness / JEFFREY F. SPANOGLE / 19

3 Contextual Biblical Interpretation and Indonesian Readers / MATTHEW R. MALCOLM / 33

4 The Servant and the Jubilee in Matthew's Gospel: Matthew's Christological Reading of Isaiah / DAEHOON KANG / 42

5 *Nomos* in Paul and Philo: A Critique of N. T. Wright's Interpretation of *Nomos* in Paul's Letters / YONGBOM LEE / 63

Part 2: Historical Theology and Philosophy

6 *Theonomous, Autonomous,* and *Heteronomous* Conscience: Conscience in Luther and Kant, and Indonesian Moral Perception / FITZERALD KENNEDY SITORUS / 89

7   *Theologia Crucis* in China / Andrew R. Talbert / 108

8   Calvin's Doctrine of God's Providence in Asian Context: Responses to Recent Critics / Jessica Novira Layantara / 118

Part 3: Christian Worldview

9   Human Rights in Islam and Christianity: Implications for the Pluralistic Society in Indonesia Today / Yonathan Wijaya Lo and Yongbom Lee / 139

10 What *The 7 Habits of Highly Effective People* Missed: A Reflection on Leadership and Christian Worldview / Francisco Budi Hardiman / 162

11 Christian Worldview and the Transformation of Korean Society / Yong Joon (John) Choi / 180

Part 4: Christian Higher Education

12 Athens, Rome, Amsterdam, and Karawaci: Historical and Theological Basis of Christian Worldview-Based Liberal Arts Education / Hendra Thamrindinata / 201

13 True Knowledge, Faith in Christ, and Godly Character: Christian Worldview-Based Liberal Arts Education at UPH / Gunawaty Tjioe / 217

Scripture Index / 237

Preface

IN HIS 1546 PREFACE to the second volume of Martin Luther's Latin writings, Philipp Melanchthon comments that Luther publicly posted the *Ninety-Five Theses* at the *Schloßkirche* in Wittenberg on the eve of All Saints' Day in 1517. The year 2017 marked the 500th anniversary of this event, which inaugurated what is known as the Protestant Reformation. It is needless to say that the Reformation affected every dimension of European society in its day, setting the stage for the Enlightenment and modernity, and undoubtedly transforming the world.

In celebration of the continuing legacy of the Protestant Reformation, on May 5, 2017, an eclectic group of scholars held an academic conference titled *Sola Scriptura in Asia* at the Universitas Pelita Harapan (UPH—"University of Light and Hope") just outside of Jakarta, Indonesia. The conference was an international effort, with presenters from Indonesia, the United States, South Korea, and Australia. At the time of the conference, most were faculty members of UPH, with our plenary speaker representing Handong Global University (Pohang, South Korea), and topics addressing biblical theology, historical theology, and Christian worldview studies. Along with the seven conference papers, we include six additional studies in this volume.

We dedicate this book to Davit Hartono (November 6, 1977–September 21, 2017), who was a beloved colleague at UPH, where he served as the Course Coordinator for the Department of Religion and Theology. Coming from Sukabumi in West Java, he conducted theological studies at Sekolah Tinggi Teologi in Bandung, Indonesia, where he focused on systematic and pastoral theology. Alongside his work at the university, he devoted himself to church ministry and served as the General Secretary in the Synod of his denomination, Gereja Sidang Kristus. It was while he was en route to a denominational meeting that Davit died suddenly. He is survived by his wife, Yulia, and his young son, Gilbert, who were shocked by Davit's sudden death and are still grieving their great loss. Davit was one of the most positive and enthusiastic persons we have ever met. We still remember his gregarious grin and his unique, amusing laugh. Davit gave so much of himself to the mission of the university that all of his colleagues and students have suffered a great loss. We are all, however, deeply grateful to God for the privilege to have been in relationship with such a wonderful human being, a passionate follower of Christ, and a dedicated educator as Davit Hartono.

Hendra Thamrindinata, the former Executive Dean of the Faculty of Liberal Arts (2013–2017) and a current postgraduate researcher at Evangelische Theologische Faculteit (ETF) in Leuven, Belgium, notes, "Davit Hartono was my colleague and friend, since August 2011, with whom I had a good and warm relationship. He was incredibly jovial, but he was also a responsible, gentle, and trustworthy person with a heart for the Lord. He faithfully and excellently fulfilled his ministry as a lecturer and the Coordinator of theological courses in our faculty before his departure to the Lord. I am deeply saddened at his departure, but I am comforted to know that he is with our Lord now."

Dr. Matthew Malcolm, the current Liberal Arts Dean at UPH, writes, "It was a pleasure to have such a reliable and competent person as Course Coordinator in the area of theology. Davit was not only theologically astute; he also had a love of people—which makes such a difference in an educational setting. He was loved and appreciated by his students and colleagues alike. His presence always brightened our academic and social occasions, because of his cheerfulness, humor, diligence, and humility. He continues to be sadly missed." We would like to remember and honor his lasting legacy as a teacher, a colleague, a friend, and a brother in Christ, by dedicating this book to him.

In closing, we would like to express our gratitude to the Faculty of Liberal Arts at UPH for sponsoring the conference that resulted in this volume, especially the Administrative Director, Adriani Gunawan, and Hendra Thamrindinata. We hope and pray this book will inspire other Christian theologians, scholars, and teachers working in Asia to share their insights and experiences with the rest of the world. For God is surely working in mighty ways in their continent through the Word of God, the Holy Spirit, and the Church, the body of Christ.

Soli Deo Gloria

Trinity Sunday 2018
Yongbom Lee
Andrew R. Talbert

Contributors

Yong Joon (John) Choi (PhD, Potchefstroom University, South Africa) is teaching as the Professor of Graduate School of Education and working as the Director of Handong Institute of Learning and Faith at Handong Global University.

Fransisco Budi Hardiman (PhD, Hochschule für Philosophie München, Germany) is teaching as a Faculty of Liberal Arts lecturer at Universitas Pelita Harapan in Indonesia.

Daehoon Kang (PhD, the University of Bristol, UK) is teaching as the Assistant Professor of New Testament at Reformed Graduate School in Seoul, South Korea.

Jessica Novira Layantara (MDiv, Amanat Agung Theological Seminary, Jakarta, Indonesia) is teaching as a Faculty of Liberal Arts lecturer at UPH.

Yongbom Lee (PhD, University of Bristol, UK) taught as a Faculty of Liberal Arts lecturer at UPH from 2015 to 2017 and currently is ministering as English Ministry pastor at Korean Bethel Presbyterian Church in Fayetteville, North Carolina, USA, and teaching as an adjunct professor at the University of North Carolina at Pembroke.

Yonathan Wijaya Lo (DMin, Reformed Theological Seminary, USA) is teaching as a part-time lecturer at Amanat Agung Theological Seminary, Jakarta, and UPH.

Matthew R. Malcolm (PhD, University of Nottingham, UK) is working as the Dean of the Faculty of Liberal Arts at UPH.

Fitzerald Kennedy Sitorus (PhD, Johann Wolfgang Goethe-Universität, Germany) is teaching as a Faculty of Liberal Arts lecturer at UPH.

Jeffrey F. Spanogle (PhD, Trinity International University, USA) is teaching as a lecturer in International Teachers College at UPH.

Andrew R. Talbert (PhD, University of Nottingham, UK) taught as a Faculty of Liberal Arts lecturer at UPH from 2014 to 2017, and is working as the Upper School Humanities and Rhetoric teacher at Cedar Tree Classical Christian School in Ridgefield, Washington, USA.

Hendra Thamrindinata (MDiv, Reformed Evangelical Seminary, Jakarta, Indonesia) worked as the Execute Dean of the Faculty of Liberal Arts at UPH from 2013 to 2017 and, currently, is a postgraduate researcher at Evangelische Theologische Faculteit (ETF) in Leuven, Belgium.

Gunawaty Tjioe (PhD, Biola Univeristy, USA) is working as the Provost of UPH and the Coordinator of Sekolah Dian Harapan (SDH) and Sekolah Lentera Harapan (SLH) in Indonesia.

Introduction

―――― Yongbom Lee and Andrew R. Talbert

When Paludanus van den Broek held the first Protestant Church service in Indonesia (1612) only five years short of the centenary of the Reformation, it is doubtful he had any notion of the scale of the effect that Protestantism would have in the archipelago. He carried forward the legacy of Luther and his Ninety-Five Theses, Zwingli's *Wurstessen*, and, perhaps more closely, Calvin's Reform of Geneva. Developing out of the *Sola Scriptura in Asia Conference* held at Universitas Pelita Harapan (Indonesia) in 2017, this volume explores the impact of the Reformation in Asia, as well as influences from the region on Protestant-shaped practices and modes of thinking 500 years hence.

The scope of this project reflects the breadth and diversity of Asia and its relationship to the Reformation. Though not representing every nation, it provides a rich sampling from both regionally native and expatriate scholars, who have given themselves, in some form or fashion, to engaging with their context in dialogue with the Reformational principles. In this sense, these chapters reflect truly "incarnational" research, for they are conducted within and for Asia—though with considerations and ramifications extending beyond—not in abstraction by external observers.

Admittedly and purposefully eclectic, given that Asia constitutes nearly 60 percent of the world population, the various chapters, nevertheless, fit under four major parts that reflect their maturation in Christian academic contexts: (1) Biblical Theology, (2) Historical Theology and Philosophy, (3) Christian Worldview, and (4) Christian Higher Education. The first five chapters belong to biblical theology, majoring on hermeneutics and exegesis, with particular regard for reading Scripture in an Asian context. Andrew R. Talbert's essay on "Hermeneutics and Pseudo-Postmodernity in Southeast Asia" sets the stage by exploring Luther's unfortunate severing of faith and reason, and the broader impact this has made on epistemology and ontology in the Southeast Asian classroom in a global age. Advocating a return to pre-Reformation realist metaphysics, he targets three topics for engaging this return: meaning, morality, and epistemology. Establishing this realism leads to a foundational hermeneutics characterized by openness, concern for truth, awareness of "being," and an eye for "beauty," all the while maintaining the essential, cross-centered theology of Martin Luther, which redeems reason.

Jeffrey F. Spanogle's chapter "Union, Participation, Adoption: A Better Hermeneutics for Holiness" evolves from engagement with the Laotian *bacci* ritual that offers a better context for understanding biblical "holiness" against modern iterations in Protestantism. He suggests a paradigm of union, participation, and adoption more comprehensively accounts for the command to "be holy" and to be ascribed the attribute of "holiness," which alone belongs to the transcendent God of Israel. Spanogle concludes with practical implications of this approach for teaching Christian theology in Asia today.

In "Contextual Biblical Interpretation and Indonesian Readers," Matthew R. Malcolm gives voice to the "ordinary" Indonesian reader of Scripture and compares it with modern, Western interpretive trends. He draws out two contextual, interpretive impulses that contour such reading and contribute to the hermeneutical enterprise: an orientation of respect and a non-secular interpretive milieu.

As another exegetical endeavor, "The Servant and the Jubilee in Matthew's Gospel: Matthew's Christological Reading of Isaiah" (Daehoon Kang) offers an *intratextual* reading of Isaiah and Matthew, as well as an *intertextual* reading of the same books to show decisively how Jesus takes on the role of the Suffering Servant (Isa 52:13—53:12) and extends this role to his disciples in the same pattern as the Suffering Servant (Isa 65:8-9) in connection with the eschatological Jubilee. Kang then connects this with the need for servant-leadership in Korean churches, which have been plagued by scandals in recent years and, thereby, lost the level of positive influence it once exerted in the country. He anticipates exegetically what Yong Joon Choi advocates in terms of worldview in chapter 11.

The final chapter under "Biblical Theology" serves as a capstone to Part I, because Yongbom Lee deftly brings together exegetical rigor, like Kang, and reflection on warranted interpretive *Vorurteile*, as we see in Malcolm's essay. "*Nomos* in Paul and Philo: A Critique of N. T. Wright's Interpretation of *Nomos* in Paul's Letters" demonstrates careful attention to Paul's use of *Nomos* and reveals that, at least in certain instances, this term should be understood as a "universal principle" over against the vehement claims of N. T. Wright and scholars from the New Perspective that this rendering is impossible. Lee marshals Philo in his defense of a Jewish figure, who interprets *Nomos* as both "Jewish law" and "universal principle," depending on the context in which it is used.

Each of the three chapters in Part II focus on concepts developed in the Reformation and their impact in contemporary Asian contexts. Fitzerald Kennedy Sitorus begins with an examination of the idea of "conscience" in Luther, Kant, and modern Indonesia. Whereas Luther operates from a *theonomos* idea of conscience, Kant develops an *autonomos* concept of the same. Yet the Indonesian moral perception must be, somewhat distinctly, identified as *heteronomous*. Though beneficial in certain respects, Sitorus suggests the heteronomous conscience of Indonesians would benefit from engagement with Luther's construction, particularly when it relates to issues of justice.

Moving geographically north, Talbert's second chapter ("*Theologia Crucis* in China") develops from his experience with the Chinese House Church movement (CHC) in Wenzhou, China. He compares Luther's *theologia crucis* (theology of the cross) with the current persecution of the aforementioned church that centers on the removal of crosses from churches by the Chinese government. Though generally grounded in the *theologia crucis* of Luther, the *theologia crucis* of the CHC is more practical in its considerations of how to be the church in an oppressive context.

Turning from Wittenberg to Geneva in chapter 8, Jessica Novira Layantara looks at the doctrine of providence in the theology of John Calvin in dialogue with modern detractors. Advocating first its biblical endorsement, then its soundness with regard to the attributes of God, she then posits its unique vantage for dialogue with other Asian religions, given its continuity and discontinuity with their perspectives on providence and determinism.

Opening the third part of this volume on Christian worldview, Yonathan Wijaya Lo and Yongbom Lee consider "Human Rights in Islam and Christianity: Implications for the Pluralistic Society in Indonesia Today." Examining first the concept of "human rights" in both Islam and Christianity, and, in the latter case, carrying forward engagement with Calvin's theology as in Layantara, the authors turn their attention as to how Indonesians might uphold human rights, while being faithful to their respective traditions.

At first glance, Fransisco Budi Hardiman's chapter, "What *The 7 Habits of Highly Effective People* Missed: A Reflection on Leadership and Christian Worldview," might sound helpful, but out of place to this volume. Yet this study flows from an Indonesian liberal arts environment in which "leadership" is a course belonging to the core curriculum.

Hardiman shows how "leadership" models generally lack foundation, *telos*, and a structuring metanarrative to give it true fullness, all of which a Christian worldview ably provides.

As noted above, Yong Joon (John) Choi's essay, "Christian Worldview and the Transformation of Korean Society," accomplishes with a worldview study what Kang inaugurates with his chapter on the Suffering Servant. First outlining a Christian worldview, Choi then details the broadly benevolent influence of this worldview in Korean society, though it has recently fallen into disrepute after a number of scandals involving churches and their influential leaders. He concludes with recommendations for the revivification of the church and its influence in Korea.

Part IV connects Christian worldview with Christian higher education via Hendra Themrindinata's essay "Athens, Rome, Amsterdam, and Karawaci: Historical and Theological Basis of Christian Worldview-Based Liberal Arts Education." He looks at the historical development of the liberal arts alongside the concept of "worldview" and unites the two via Herman Bavinck's holistic understanding of Christian education, concluding with a summons to Christian educational institutions that have strayed from this foundation to return to their robust theological heritage.

Our final chapter, "True Knowledge, Faith in Christ, and Godly Character: Christian Worldview-Based Liberal Arts Education at UPH," comes from a leader of an Indonesian university and brings all of the previous research to a practical conclusion, examining the impact of a contemporary, Reformation-inspired education. Gunawaty Tjioe outlines the Christian Worldview liberal arts curriculum at Universitas Pelita Harapan and then summarizes her findings from interviews with alumni and current students that assess their recognition of the benefits and shortcomings of such an education. Though the institution needs continued "reforming," this study revealed an overall affirmative perspective of a Christian Worldview-Based Liberal Arts Education.

These essays concentrate not on a single point of influence by the Reformation on Asia, but rather on the collective, powerful, ongoing impact of this historical event on the majority of the world population. They demonstrate how the Reformation shapes hermeneutical principles, the positive role of cultural dispositions and context for understanding, and the redeeming of culture by way of Christian theology and worldview.

Abbreviations

AB	Anchor Bible
ABS	*American Behavioral Scientist*
AJT	*Asian Journal of Theology*
AMMTC	Ancient Mediterranean and Medieval Texts and Contexts
AYB	Anchor Yale Bible
AYBC	Anchor Yale Bible Commentary
AYBRL	Anchor Yale Bible Reference Library
BBR	*Bulletin for Biblical Research*
BBRS	Bulletin for Biblical Research Supplement
BECNT	Baker Exegetical Commentary on the New Testament
BETL	Bibliotheca Ephemeridum Theologicarum Lovaniensium
BFCT	*Beiträge zur Förderung Christlicher Theologie*
BI	*Biblical Interpretation*
BibIntSer	Biblical Interpretation Series
BNTC	Black New Testament Commentary
BTS	Biblical Tools and Studies
CBQ	*Catholic Biblical Quarterly*
CC	Concordian Commentary
CEV	Contemporary English Version
CNTC	Calvin's New Testament Commentaries

CNTUOT	G. K. Beale and D. A. Carson, eds. *Commentary on the New Testament Use of the Old Testament*. Grand Rapids: Baker, 2007
CSIS	Center for Strategic and International Studies
CSRT	Columbia Series in Reformed Theology
DOTP	T. Desmond Alexander and David Baker, eds. *Dictionary of the Old Testament: Pentateuch*. Downers Grove, IL: InterVarsity, 2010
DPC	Dover Philosophical Classics
EAPR	*East Asian Pastoral Review*
ESV	English Standard Version
EvQ	*Evangelical Quarterly*
FAT	Forschungen zum Alten Testament
FEG	Forschunge zur europäischen Geistegeschichte
GNT	Good New Translation
GP	Grundkurs Philosophie
HNT	Handbuch zum Neuen Testament
HTKNT	Herders theologischer Kimmentar zum Neuen Testament
HTS	*Hervormde Teologiese Studies*
ICC	International Critical Commentary
IEJ	*International Education Journal*
IJST	*International Journal of Systematic Theology*
JAOS	*Journal of the American Oriental Society*
JBL	*Journal of Biblical Literature*
JRT	*Journal of Reformed Theology*
JSOT	*Journal for the Study of the Old Testament*
JSOTSup	Journal for the Study of the Old Testament Supplement Series
JSNT	*Journal for the Study of the New Testament*
JSNTSup	Journal for the Study of the New Testament Supplement Series
JSSH	*Journal of Social Science and Humanities*
LCC	Library of Christian Classics
LNTS	Library of New Testament Studies
LW	Jaroslav Pelikan, Helmut T. Lehmann, and Christopher Boyd Brown, eds. *Luther's Works*. 75 vols. Philadelphia: Fortress, 1955

LXX	The Septuagint
MT	The Masoretic Text
NAC	New American Commentary
NCV	New Century Version
NICOT	New International Commentary on the Old Testament
NICNT	New International Commentary on the New Testament
NIDOTTE	Willem VanGemeren, ed. *New International Dictionary of the Old Testament Theology and Exegesis*. Grand Rapids: Eerdmans, 1997
NIGTC	New International Greek Testament Commentary
NIV	New International Version
NLT	New Living Translation
NovT	*Novum Testamentum*
NovTSup	Novum Testamentum Supplements
NSBT	New Studies in Biblical Theology
NTL	New Testament Library
NTS	*New Testament Studies*
NTSI	New Testament and Scripture of Israel
OTL	Old Testament Library
PBM	Paternoster Biblical Monographs
PNG	Paulus new Gelesen
PNTC	Pillar New Testament Commentary
SBM	Stuttgart biblische Monographien
SCM	Student Christian Movement
SJT	*Scottish Journal of Theology*
SNTSMS	Society for New Testament Studies Monograph Series
SP	Sacra Pagina
SPA	Studies of Philo of Alexander
SPCK	Society for Promoting Christian Knowledge
SPEP	Studies in Phenomenology and Existential Philosophy
SRT	*Studies in Reformed Theology*
STW	Suhrkamp Taschenbuch Wissenschaft

TDOT	G. Johannes Botterweck, Helmer Riggren, and Heiz-Josef Fabry, eds. *Theological Dictionary of the Old Testament*. 16 vols. Grand Rapids: Eerdmans, 1974–2018
THL	Theory and History of Literature
TLOT	Ernst Jenni and Claus Westermann, eds. *Theological Lexicon of the Old Testament*. Translated by Mark E. Biddle. Peabody, MA: Hendrickson, 1997
TynBul	*Tyndale Bulletin*
VT	*Vetus Testamentum*
VTSup	Vetus Testamentum Supplements
WA	*D. Martin Luthers Werke*. Kritische Gesamtausgabe. 73 Vols. Weimar: Böhlaus, 1883–2009
WBC	Word Biblical Commentary
WUNT	Wissenschaftliche Untersuchungen zum Neuen Testament
ZECNT	Zondervan Exegetical Commentary on the New Testament
ZNW	*Zeitschrift für die neutestamentliche Wissenschaft*

Part 1

Biblical Theology

1

Hermeneutics and Pseudo-Postmodernity in Southeast Asia

—————————————— Andrew R. Talbert

Introduction

In 1984, Allan Bloom opened his infamous book, *The Closing of the American Mind*: "There is one thing a professor can be absolutely certain of: almost every student believes, or thinks he believes, that truth is relative,"[1] be that moral, epistemological, ontological, etc. Given that more than thirty years have elapsed since he wrote, it is worth revisiting this contention. But more than this, it is worth considering whether this cliché and corrosive *Weltanschauung* has spread abroad from the American context in which Bloom wrote in the rapid globalization of the twentieth and twenty-first centuries.

The short response is: yes, most professors in the U.S. will affirm that this is still the case (and some will revel in that). As to the second point, educators in our area of interest, Southeast Asia, will respond likewise in an insipid and soporific canon echoing across this relative world. Like their Western counterparts, students make vague references to "postmodernism" and "sociological" discoveries that put "truth" in question.

The fact of the matter, however, is that though many students pledge allegiance to the fading fashion of postmodern relativity (which students often interchangeably refer to as "subjectivism"), few have the sophistication

---

1. Bloom, *Closing of American Mind*, 25. With the exceptions of the immediate influences of historical developments in America (e.g., the GI Bill), and the situation of race, Bloom's entire work holds true for many university contexts in Southeast Asia.

of Foucault or Deleuze and their diversity, nor could they articulate anything of panopticism, post-structuralism, totality, or *spatium* and *aion*. And in the realm of morality, we have seen a subconscious, paradoxical, and partial shift away from moral relativism toward "values like tolerance and inclusion"[2] (though not a similar shift toward religious belief and an ontological conception of "truth") even in conservative nations, like Indonesia, at universities, cities, and communities engaged in the global exchange ideas—especially the marketplace. Yet while this global interchange formulates a tenuous simulacrum of morality, the relativisms of other arenas remain firmly in place (i.e., cultural, religious, metaphysical). The unfortunate invention of the smartphone—the true opiate of the masses—only perpetuates the problem, because distractedness occludes contemplation of their operative metaphysics: oughtness, beauty, existence, justice, violence, love, etc. So, students and graduates live in a fragmented and inconsistent world, perpetuating the fragmentation to the ensuing generations all the while denying their actual experience of the world with that word "relative."

But our work here is more than a survey of diverse and depressing educational contexts. Instead, our interests lay in the further question invited by the longevity and constancy of this inane and involuntary falsehood so frequently asserted in the classroom: what is one to do? In educational contexts on this side of providence and the Divine Economy the answer is clear: hermeneutics. But by this we mean "hermeneutics" in the big-boned sense of reading texts and the world well in light of theology, philosophy, and the various fields that have contributed to the discovery of truth in recent years. Against the pseudo-postmodern, dogmatic anti-realists we will suggest that the cosmos and its first principles are (at least partially) knowable, and that the fallibilist liturgy fails to offer the best account of our knowledge and experience of the world. This will set the stage for hermeneutical reflections, and it merits further clarification.

A recent trend in theological works suggests, in many ways rightly, a return to ontology, particularly in the vein of Christian Platonism and Thomist Realism.[3] These works generally foreground "being," its

---

2. Merritt, "Moral Relativism." Bloom narrows this to a single moral virtue: openness; Bloom, *Closing of American Mind*, 26. Taylor echoes this sentiment in describing our time as an "age of authenticity" in which "choice" is the singular value, and "tolerance" (excepting intolerance), the remaining virtue; Taylor, *A Secular Age*, 473–84. For the nihilism of modern "virtue," conceived in terms of "freedom," see Hart, *Atheist Delusions*, 19–26, 224–25.

3. E.g., Candler, *Theology, Rhetoric, Manuduction*; Tyson, *Returning to Reality*; Tyson, *De-Fragmenting Modernity*; Machuga, *Life, the Universe, and Everything*. Machuga also picks a different point of entry, namely, what constitutes an argument and scientific knowledge, both of which are good places to begin with the current

relationship to "truth," its priority to "knowing," and then everything that follows in the various realms of metaphysics and human experience. Though in agreement with these perspectives, this particular essay proceeds pedagogically through the entry point of a primary experience of students—meaning and happiness—and then works back in concentric circles to ontology. Such a strategy generally avoids the floundering of students in the sea of *ens, esse, entia, essentia,* and *existentia,* and instead meets students where they are before leading them to the depths, much like Jesus' encounter with the Samaritan woman (John 4:1–42). The sections that follow—morality and epistemology—likewise lead back to "being," with a further consideration of how this project informs a charitable hermeneutics open to the claims of Scripture.

For those of a radical fideism akin to Luther's *theologia crucis* (or, in a different way, to Barth), this may ring of a return to a scholastic marriage of theology and philosophy ("that whore!") that he descried, and counter to a project entitled *Sola Scriptura*. To that, let me say this much: Luther is dead, and with him a universal foundation for reading and knowing the world (i.e., Holy Scripture) in post-Christendom. What has sprung to life in the soil of the Reformation, among many excellent benefits, is the truly "secular" (i.e., a place in which disbelief in the transcendent is viable) and an assumed relativity of all foundations. Though this essay most certainly advocates a return to the biblical witness as the revolutionary source for knowing the world rightly and the absolute necessity of the in-breaking of the Holy Spirit to illuminate Scripture and the world, there are instances in which such radical fideism encounters equally radical hardness toward Christian belief, for any number of reasons. The "biblical" response to such hardness is not abandonment of individuals, but the exploration of tools in a Pauline manner that engage with shared human experience (e.g., Acts 17:16–34) in a global context, differentiating between the conventional and the natural.[4] Furthermore, though Luther correctly focuses on the element of salvation as it has to do with God's *action* in the *crucifixion*, he neglects salvation as it has to do with the redeeming of human nature in the *incarnation* that was a focus of patristic theology, especially in the Trinitarian debates—the *theologia incarnationis* of Orthodox and

---

"knowledge" of students.

4. The appeal to Tertullian's declamation "what has Athens to do with Jerusalem?" as Christian rejection of philosophy in favor of a pure fideism is no longer defensible. Tertullian freely deploys philosophical reflection in his works, but rejects an embodiment entailed by (especially Greek) philosophical systems; see Karlowicz, *Socrates and Other Saints*, 17–25, 67–81.

Catholic thought.[5] This theology concentrates especially on "being" and those topics that flow from it, thereby enabling theological reflection on and appropriation of all things in service to the redeeming *Logos*, including philosophical reflection on ontology and epistemology. The *theologia incarnationis* and *theologia crucis* are complementary, mutually corrective, though not easily synthesized, especially given the historically combative stances of their respective advocates.[6]

Additionally, it is important to remember that (pre-Reformation) Thomas Aquinas' five famous *viae*, regarded as philosophical formulae, lead to "this being we call God,"[7] but that Christ alone is the *via* to the Triune God.[8] Put differently, the *viae* lead one as far as the philosophers in Limbo in Dante's *Inferno*, but only Christ leads people beyond this to salvation and the beatific vision of God. Theology perfects reason that is unaided by revelation. This is precisely the purpose of the organization of the *Summa*, which many have mistaken as a systematic work for the definitive ordering of theology, including the ensuing generations of Thomas Aquinas' "authoritative" interpreters after his death.[9] The point of bringing Thomas Aquinas into the discussion is that the five *viae*, philosophical reflection, are common ground for all people that set the stage for the reception of the gospel, to move in a certain sense from the simply rational to the beautiful (and supra-rational).[10] Similarly, we will follow a common ground approach that positions students to reflect on "being" that has great potential to open students to revelation, and that leads further to faithful hermeneutics located

---

5. Recall Athanasius' famous phrase, "God became man, that man might become God." The Church Father held both dimensions of salvation together in his works; see Athanasius, *On the Incarnation*, 54; Anatolios, *Retrieving Nicaea*, 107–8.

6. Ratzinger, *Introduction to Christianity*, 228–30.

7. Thomas Aquinas, *Summa Theologiae*, 1.2.3.

8. Placher, *The Domestication of Transcendence*, 23–35; Thomas Aquinas notes, "Because the chief aim of sacred doctrine is to teach the knowledge of God, not only as He is in Himself, but also as He is the beginning of things and their last end, and especially of rational creatures, as is clear from what has been already said, therefore, in our endeavor to expound this science, we shall treat: (1) Of God; (2) Of the rational creature's advance towards God; (3) Of Christ, Who as man, is our way [via] to God"; Thomas Aquinas, *Summa Theologiae* 1.2.prol.

9. Candler argues that Thomas Aquinas' project is to lead the reader to his/her good (i.e., God) "by a participation in the movement of the intellect and will whose agent is God alone"; Candler, *Theology, Rhetoric, Manuduction*, 90–107.

10. This is in keeping with Thomas Aquinas' own goal. Candler summarizes, "It is necessary for the rough-minded (*rudis*) . . . to know their true end (*finis*), before they embark on the long apprenticeship of *sacra doctrina*"; Candler, *Theology, Rhetoric, Manuduction*, 126; Thomas Aqunias, *Summa Theologiae* 1.1.1.

deeply in the Divine *Logos*, holding reality together as one, rather than as discontinuous fragments.

This approach has proved fruitful in the context of Indonesian higher education, thus its place in the discussion of Southeast Asia. Different from Thomas Aquinas' starting place with sacred doctrine and his monastic audience, we meet our pseudo-postmodern students at a gateway that descends rather rapidly into the depths of "being": meaning.

Meaning

Though easy enough to assert "everyone does metaphysics"[11] and everyone exhibits a theology at every moment of the day, partnering this with a practical demonstration leads quickly to acknowledgment and an accompanying willingness to explore just how far down the rabbit hole goes. One tool to initiate this exploration is Andy Crouch's reflection on cultural artifacts, which helps students to reflect on the meaningfulness of everyday items that they take for granted.[12] His questions lead to reflection on what people consider meaningful that bring students a step at a time to contemplation of human nature (or its corruption). Alternatively, having students introduce themselves reveals what they assume matters through how they organize the material in their story and the particular information disclosed. For many, though, the quickest way to the heart is through a threat to the beloved: the phone. Problematizing their use of this device, or, God forbid, separating them from it, opens up the realization that they assume meaningfulness in their possession and use of this item. When this is extended to every act of every day, though, students realize they are floundering in a sea of meaning that is common to the experience of all humanity. Setting aside Kant's insistence that the mind "meaningfully" structures our experiences of the world for the present, this shared experience of meaningfulness eventually raises the question of "Why?" Why are we constantly communicating meaning in every action, thought, purchase, conversation, etc.? Put differently, what are we trying to achieve?

---

11. Tyson, *Returning to Reality*, 1.

12. Crouch proposes five questions for considering cultural artifacts: (1) "What does this cultural artifact assume about the way that the world is?"; (2) "What does this cultural artifact assume about the way that the world should be?"; (3) "What does this cultural artifact make possible?"; (4) "What does this cultural artifact make impossible (or at least very difficult)?"; (5) "What new forms of culture are created in response to this artifact?"; Crouch, *Culture Making*, 29–30.

Aristotle and Thomas Aquinas answer this with a single word: happiness;[13] happiness as a life lived well, depending on what it means to be a human person. That is to say, there are definitely some things that are always good, sometimes good, and always bad for human thriving. In seeking happiness, Aristotle and Thomas Aquinas recognize the central place of the coordinated virtues in leading people to where they belong, existentially speaking. The problem for our relativist students with "happiness" is that it assumes (1) there is a common human nature and (2) that there is some goal or final cause of being human.[14] Thomas Aquinas simply called the latter the beatific vision and participation in God.[15]

The fact that people do things detrimental to their existence or that different cultures conceive of what is meaningful or good in different ways does nothing to undermine the contention that there is a human nature (and Good for which it is made). Arguing in such a fashion proves only the subterfuge (or lack of reflection) of pseudo-postmodern metaphysics: religious modes of knowing the world are relegated to opinion in a manner that "scientific" inquiry is not.[16] In other disciplines the pseudo-postmodern never accounts for differing conclusions as incommensurable opinions, with no actual purchase on reality. One conclusion must be true. The difficulty these concepts of meaning, happiness, and human nature create for the pseudo-postmodern is they impinge on the guiding value of late modernity: freedom. Or, to rephrase an expression from Chesterton, "The believers in human nature and the final cause accept them (rightly or wrongly) because they have evidence for them. The disbelievers in human nature and the final cause deny them (rightly or wrongly) because they have

---

13. "To know that God exists in a general and confused way is implanted in us by nature, inasmuch as God is man's beatitude. For man naturally desires happiness, and what is naturally desired by man must be naturally known to him"; Thomas Aquinas, *Summa Theologiae* 1.2.1.

14. MacIntyre notes that denial of a "human nature" only creates further problems in various arenas: "Take away the notion of essential nature, take away the corresponding notion of what is good and best for members of a specific kind who share such a nature, and the Aristotelian scheme of the self which is to achieve the good, of good, and of pleasure necessarily collapses. There remains only the individual self with its pleasures and pains. So metaphysical nominalism sets constraints upon how the moral life can be conceived. And, conversely, certain types of conceptions of the moral life exclude such nominalism"; MacIntyre, *Three Rival Versions of Moral Enquiry*, 138.

15. Eccl 3:11 writes, "[God] has put eternity into man's heart." Augustine states, "You have made us for Yourself, and *our hearts are restless* until they rest in You"; Augustine, *Confessions* 1.1; Thomas Aquinas, *Summa Theologiae*, 1.12.8.

16. On this topic, see Tyson's evaluation and critique of Kuhn's relativism in his unwillingness to consider a transcendent source to reality; Tyson, *Returning to Reality*, 161–63.

a doctrine against them."[17] "Meaning" exceeds the cultural/conventional or the purely evolutionary understanding of the human person because of its universality and where such investigation ultimately terminates. Cultural differences can certainly create points of entry for reflecting on meaning, but, as conventions rather than nature, they point to the plurality of opinions that hover over the natural and the truth of "being" (i.e., foundations that make knowing possible).

This collision with "being" that lies beneath ideas of human nature and happiness—what causes the nature to "be" and that gives it rational purpose—raises a host of difficulties for the pseudo-postmodern. In the realm of "truth" at least, it problematizes the fashionable, positivistic notion of truth as identical with fact[18] that characterizes the modern sciences, but that cannot account for their foundations. Tyson argues further:

> Modern naturalistic materialism—which has no conception of any intellective and non-material foundation of being—is also inherently incoherent. For how could there be any order in a realm of true contingency and radical flux, how could our minds discern any timeless or universal principles in nature, and how could we "see" contingency and change if there was nothing non-contingent, intellective and unchanging undergirding contingency, change, and the order of nature? How could there be an existing material cosmos governed by reasoned universal regularities if mind is not ontologically prior to matter?[19]

Tyson's "modern naturalistic materialism" is simply the positive side of pseudo-postmodernity. The point of pushing on "meaning" is not to show that students are meaning-makers, so much as to reveal that they find themselves already crashing up against meaning in their everyday experiences, because *essential* meaning is already given to existents. This brings forward considerations of human nature and happiness, which are only stages on the road back to "being" and its Cause, the vastness of which now lies before the contemplative eyes of the student.[20]

---

17. Chesterton, *Orthodoxy*, 355.

18. For the historical transformation of "truth" from "being" to "fact" to "what can be made," see Ratzinger, *Introduction to Christianity*, 57–69.

19. Tyson, *De-Fragmenting Modernity*, 33.

20. If we had more space, we could harmonize this perspective with Coakley's emphasis on all human desire as having its root and goal in the Triune God, that desire is easily (and early) corrupted, and that it requires reordering to truly "humanize" us; Coakley, *God, Sexuality, and the Self*, 51–52. Coakley draws deeply from Dionysius on desire: "For those lacking in reason, [desire] is a limitless appetite for material . . . but this has to be interpreted as a divine yearning for that immaterial reality which

Having made contact with "being," it would seem logical that epistemology might follow, but this topic is not immediate to most students. Swinging back out in this concentric circle, we encounter students at the locus of morality.

Morality

Three different avenues bring us through morality to the foundations that render it rational. Setting aside our initial point regarding tolerance and inclusion for the moment, morality (and often with a nod to religion) is the frequent target of the contention "all truth is relative," with suggestions of its existence ranging from "evolution" to "nurture." The latter suggestion opens the discussion of morality because, as a genetic fallacy, it does not constitute an argument. Though moral *acts* are indeed relative to the contexts in which they are performed, the notion that morality is merely *culturally* relative (read "has nothing to do with truth"), and therefore that we must free ourselves of these moral systems, or let them proceed as long as they do not interfere with individual liberty is a self-deluded farce. In one direction, we must recognize that "it is a very common phrase of modern intellectualism to say that the morality of one age can be entirely different to the morality of another. And like a great many other phrases of modern intellectualism, it means literally nothing at all. If the two moralities are entirely different, why do you call them both moralities?"[21] A slightly different consideration to make is, if all moralities are relative, why bother convincing others of this position? This is, in reality, an attempt at proselytizing to another moral system unaware of itself. It is a metaphysical perspective masquerading as though it were not through an ad hoc collection of catchphrases. If moral relativism means something like "do what suits you in any given circumstance," then this is in fact not relativism, but a refurbished categorical imperative—it is a moral perspective. Therefore the pseudo-postmodern acts in accordance with a perceived good, which means: moral relativism does not exist.[22] The reality that all actions assume the actor's "good" again brings us back to considerations of what it means to be a human person, how we are to act in accordance with this knowledge, and what causes such a nature. A weaker argument in the vein of Chesterton's "democracy of the dead" points out that moral relativism has no history, but that morality and

---

is beyond all reason and all intelligence"; Pseudo-Dionysius, *The Celestial Hierarchy* 144a–b.

21. Chesteron, *Heretics*, 167.

22. Kreeft, *A Refutation of Moral Relativism*, 145–49.

its ground in some Absolute has been believed by all cultures at all times in all places until only quite recently.[23]

A second trajectory regarding morality comes from Charles Taylor, who assesses, dissects, and dismisses the Modern Moral Order (our pseudo-postmodernity) as unsustainable. A compressed form of his argument for a Causal-dependent morality goes as follows: (1) human activity of knowing cannot be separated from our interpretation of the world; (2) our identity and knowing are dependent on our conception of the good, around which we order our lives; (3) therefore, all people *must* have a morality, which has a certain structure that connects "values" to the good; and (4) the framework of this morality is based on and leads to an incomparably higher good (hypergood).[24] This progression might call to mind Thomas Aquinas' argument from gradation[25] or the events leading to the conversion of C. S. Lewis,[26] but, for our purposes of establishing a hermeneutic for the recovering pseudo-postmodern, the point of this venture is Taylor's forcefully repeated challenge as to "whether one's ontology is adequate to support a sense of fullness."[27] That is to say, can the pseudo-postmodern view of morality account for the depths of human experience and bear the weight of "being," in all the density of that term?

A third, and our final option, for forcing a confrontation between the moral relativist and "being" is through the revelation that pseudo-postmodern metaphysics operates under an ontology of violence. Proceeding from the premise "all moral truth is relative" calls into question the majority of human acts. For, most actions we voluntarily perform most of the time are "good" in the sense of coinciding with natural goods for what it means to be human, and they are not items that one can reduce to "values."[28] Including

---

23. Lewis, like Chesteron, makes the historical appeal to the universality of morality (including ubiquitous "goods") that coheres with human existence from within a reality he terms the "Tao"; Lewis, *The Abolition of Man*, 39–63.

24. For Taylor, the best account of this structure of morality and the hypergood is Christian theism; Baker, *Tayloring Reformed Epistemology*, 190.

25. Thomas Aquinas, *Summa Theologiae* 1.2.3.

26. "My argument against God was that the universe seemed so cruel and unjust. But how had I got this idea of just and unjust? . . . What was I comparing this universe with when I called it unjust? . . . Of course I could have given up my idea of justice by saying it was nothing but a private idea of my own. But if I did that, then my argument against God collapsed too"; Lewis, *Mere Christianity*, 38.

27. Smith, *How (Not) to Be Secular*, 105.

28. Bloom describes the modern shift to language of "'value,' meaning the radical subjectivity of all belief about good and evil, serves the easygoing quest for comfortable self-preservation." This terminological preference holds until one includes all voluntary acts in a definition of "moral"; Bloom, *Closing of American Mind*, 141–42, 194–216.

all moral acts (e.g., eating and drinking) in the scope of this inquiry presses forcefully against the Darwinian inclination to reduce all such acts to survival of the fittest or altruism and draws us to the boundaries of believability for accounting for our experience of the world. Further, it impinges on the assumption lying further behind the claim of relativity that there is no ordering cause or meaningfulness, but simply chance occurrences on repeat that bring the cosmos into existence, for example. And here we encounter "being" again, yet here as an amoral, indifferent horror. Humanity arises out of chaos and disorder. The pseudo-postmodern, by imposing any order through the rituals of secular life (i.e., pursuits of meaningfulness—work, education, marriage, politics, etc.) commits repeated acts of violence against the violence of chaotic being. They are attempts to stabilize that which knows no stability, knows nothing at all—pure becoming—because their moral relativity is only a subheading in the relativity of their metaphysics and theology. Truth is "fact," which means observations about the world that are "eventful," yet not traceable back to or identical with "being." Facts and laws happen to be the case, but have no ontological stability.[29] So, pseudo-postmodern morality and "factual" knowledge of the world are abortive attempts to still chaos: an anthropology of thoroughgoing violence that undermines *every* voluntary act and interpretation.[30]

They may partially hold to some semi-Marxist tenet that they can fashion truth to suit their purposes, but what morality genuinely exhibits is that universal desire for "the good" and "the beautiful" way of life, despite personal confusion about one's *telos*. Here, pseudo-postmoderns find themselves confronted again with Thomas Aquinas' claim that no natural desire can be in vain, and that "conscience" was never synonymous with subjective "feeling." Instead, according to its literal definition, "knowing with," reveals conscience was once regarded as a true form of knowledge about the world, and, with correct, charitable guidance, "conscience" and its morality is able

---

29. Chesterton notes, "But as I put my head over the hedge of the elves and began to take notice of the natural world, I observed an extraordinary thing. I observed that learned men in spectacles were talking of the actual things that happened—dawn and death and so on—as if *they* were rational and inevitable. They talked as if the fact that trees bear fruit were just as *necessary* as the fact that two and one trees make three. But it is not . . . You cannot *imagine* two and one not making three. But you can easily imagine trees not growing fruit; you can imagine them growing golden candlesticks or tigers hanging on by the tail. These men in spectacles spoke much of a man named Newton, who was hit by an apple, and who discovered a law. But they could not be got to see the distinction between a true law, a law of reason, and the mere fact of apples falling"; Chesterton, *Orthodoxy*, 1:254.

30. Hart, *Beauty of Infinite*, 35–43; Milbank, *Theology and Social Theory*, 278–79.

to know the world rightly.[31] Therefore, the fact that most human acts are naturally "good" betrays a "truer" ontology characterized not by violence, but by a natural harmony between human acts, their (often subconscious) desire for good, and a common *telos* for humanity. Our existence within "being" and whatever causes it is *disrupted by violence*, not defined by it.

The fullness of this picture may lead some to accept the "good" alternative simply to escape the violent in a way akin to Pascal's wager. At the same time, the classical (and Christian) metaphysics of beauty, truth, and goodness is also a more comprehensive account for human experience of the world. Having now broached the topic of knowledge, we turn to epistemology in the pseudo-postmodern age.

Epistemology

As this essay has hinted throughout, knowledge, conceived of by the pseudo-postmodern student (and popular culture), is currently reducible to positivist-materialism. That is, observable "facts" are "true" and restricted to the material world. But, dear God, please do not apply any pressure to these assumptions, lest we discover knowledge is more complex, touches humanity more deeply, and problematizes our consumerist drive. As research repeatedly shows, "Modern secular reason is grounded in epistemological foundationalism typically traced back to Descartes. Here, truth sits within the confines of what the autonomous human mind can indubitably know and those confines are defined by what can be validly demonstrated by human logic and/or perception."[32] This vision of knowledge has gone through different iterations over the centuries, but the quoted essence remains in place. Obviously, this relegates religious beliefs (and the morals above) to the subjective realm, not relative to a particular culture, but belonging to the internal preferences, or coping mechanisms of the individual. Survey the classroom—most heads nod in agreement.

But this perspective is the feeblest of attempts at epistemology; a willed ignorance of what lies beneath the shallow surface. As we have discussed above, "Modern naturalistic materialism—which has no conception of any intellective and non-material foundation of being—is also inherently incoherent. . . How could there be an existing material cosmos governed by reasoned universal regularities if mind is not ontologically prior to matter?" Descartes performs a philosophical shift that the pseudo-postmodern, a philosophy dilettante, fails to recognize, when he

31. Thomas Aquinas, *Summa Theologiae* 1.79.12–13.
32. Tyson, *Faith's Knowledge*, 13.

prioritizes epistemology over ontology. Put differently, in order to determine what "being" is and what can be known, Descartes subjects "being" to the scrutiny of radical doubt. Prior to the Frenchman, though, philosophy began with ontology and moved to epistemology, because knowledge depends on what is and radical doubt is merely parasitic on knowledge. If all that exists is material, then all that matters is material knowing, and morality, etc. should develop along materialistic lines. Yet, as noted, this epistemology fails to account for the foundations and non-materiality of knowledge and Tyson's other contentions.

A better (read "truer") account of reality proceeds from ontology grounded in human experience and leads to a reflective epistemology. All people experience existence within the given context of "being." Relying on the most powerful of Thomas Aquinas' *viae*, we discover that this "being" both pre-exists to and does not belong to us. We have "being" on loan in our existence and we do not cause "being."[33] Our experience of the world, though, dictates that all things that begin to exist must have a cause, and the cosmos cannot cause itself, because the cosmos is merely the interconnected chain of causes. Furthermore, whatever causes "being" must transcend "being" and itself be without cause, because causes cannot regress indefinitely. Whatever this First Cause may be has united all of the cosmos by "being" and intelligibility—things can be known. Since all things that naturally exist participate in "being" (an ongoing act performed by the First Cause), our knowledge of anything in the cosmos is "first and foremost a function of its ontological relation to this [First Cause] and its reception of the intelligible form from [the First Cause] that gives that thing its specific attributes."[34] Whatever we know depends on it being made known to us; every rational moment is a prodigy. And, it turns out, the pseudo-postmodern belief about knowledge was completely upside-down all along. Knowing the Cause, the dependence of knowledge on "being," and the immateriality of mind and knowledge lead to the realization that "moral, aesthetic, and spiritual qualitative meanings are real, and are more primary than material quantitative facts. This does not make the material and the quantitative unreal, but what is apparent to the senses is not understood as intelligible or actual in anything other than a derived relationship to the spiritual realities on which all material manifestations are dependent."[35]

These realities, or "this reality," bring the pseudo-postmodern as far as Limbo, and to face the decision to either embrace "being," and all the depth

---

33. Cunningham, "Being Recalled," 59–80.
34. Tyson, *Returning to Reality*, 69.
35. Tyson, *Returning to Reality*, 69.

and richness this has to illuminate everyday experience, or they can deny the world and return to *The Matrix*. So positioned with an introductory metaphysics, the question remains as to the relation between this foundation and (especially biblical) hermeneutics.

Hermeneutics

Given the plurality of perspectives on the scope and aim of hermeneutics, we ought to define that term in advance. Anthony C. Thiselton provides us with a comprehensive definition worth adopting: "Whereas *exegesis* and *interpretation* denote the *actual process* of interpreting texts, *hermeneutics* also includes the second-order discipline of *asking critically what we are doing when we read, understand, or apply* texts. Hermeneutics explores the *conditions and criteria* that operate to try and ensure responsible, valid, fruitful, or appropriate interpretation."[36] So, hermeneutics is the umbrella discipline under which interpretation falls, but it is primarily concerned with *how* we understand texts.

The realist metaphysical picture we partially sketched above naturally precedes our interpretation and understanding of biblical texts, not in a denial of the doctrine of illumination, but as an assumption about the reality and intelligibility of the cosmos, about how knowing "works," about the type of knowledge that matters most to our essential nature (and that there is such a nature), about how knowledge of truth leads us back to "being," that language is our primary means of communicating truth, that the fullness of "being" exceeds our experience of it, and that the boundaries of "immanent" and "transcendent" are not so easily demarcated. These items naturally precede interpretation because they either constitute best-account foundations of knowledge, or noetic structures that logically derive from them,[37] and they will both determine our understanding of biblical texts (to a degree), as well as come under the influence of those texts. This is not to claim that these philosophical grounds exert restrictive control over interpretation, but rather they are Gadamerian *Vorurteile* ("prejudices") that make understanding possible.[38] With exceptions perhaps in Proverbs and John, Scripture generally exhibits little concern for the *how we know*. Scripture assumes this, and, is in many ways complementary to these philosophical *Vorurteile* because, as Spanogle's essay demonstrates, the Scriptures already assume a participatory ontology.

36. Thiselton, *Hermeneutics*, 4; italics original.
37. Fiorenza, *Foundational Theology*, 285–86.
38. Gadamer, *Truth and Method*, 289–96.

Furthermore, proceeding from this metaphysical horizon to Scripture is a movement from the tradition-influenced self to the other—a hermeneutical movement that should be characterized by charity and genuine openness to the other and their claims. And a return to "being" often initiates a wonder that renders readers more open.[39] Scripture makes claims on the reader that may satisfy, surpass, disappoint, or refute the horizon of expectation[40] from which the reader encounters Scripture. So, the philosophical foundations are subject to revision and transformation by biblical claims, much like Paul's Jewish, apocalyptic eschatology became reconfigured (not utterly destroyed) by the revelation of Jesus Christ.

The complementarity of our first principles and biblical hermeneutics increases on two levels because (1) biblical texts are not primarily concerned with positivistic facts (though certain "facts" are essential), but with "truth" in relation to human nature and the First Cause (e.g., the Good, morality, meaning, knowledge, etc.), and (2) the evanescent transcendental: the beautiful. Our first principles hinted at the Good of humanity and the inconsistency of pseudo-postmodernity's ontology of violence assumed in its moral relativism that runs contrary to the majority of humanity's moral acts. In addition to the Good, this philosophical foundation opens up hermeneutical consideration of the beautiful as a form of life, an epistemology in which we are knowers and *known*, and an ontology that does not devolve into violence. The form of Christ, as one in whom Christians participate, and the place of peace and love as attributes of God as well as defining themes of the biblical narrative give substance to that transcendental.[41] Considering all of this together, our first principles establish a philosophical hermeneutics, positioning students for openness to baptism into a theological hermeneutics.

Conclusions

At the outset, we concluded that Bloom's contention is not only the case for American universities, but that it has spread like a plague in this global age even to Southeast Asia. Like Bloom, we recognize the need for educational environments that foster the desire to seek the truth, to inquire about human nature, and to consider the nature of the good in a realist fashion. Three points of entry (meaning, morality, and epistemology) set the stage for leading students back to these foundations—philosophical first principles. Luther was right to repudiate the late scholastic vision

---

39. Tyson, *De-Fragmenting Modernity*, 12–13.
40. Jauss, *Toward an Aesthetic*, 25.
41. Hart, *Beauty of Infinite*, 1–5, 15–28.

of a unified philosophic-theological program and, instead, to center his theology on the cross and the in-breaking revelation of truth by God in a manner unanticipated and even contrary to the "wisdom" of world. Yet his work set in motion the complete severing of faith and reason in the modern age that has led to the subjectivization of religious belief, the positivistic notion of truth, and morality dislocated from its Source, among other things. A revival of philosophy as the "handmaiden of theology" is not an attempt to position theology with philosophy and therefore dictate its parameters. Rather, it is a recognition of our experience of the world and those *Vorurteile* that make understanding possible, which we then bring to the hermeneutical enterprise, and that may likewise be redeemed and refined in faithful, charitable reading of Scripture.

Bibliography

Anatolios, Khaled. *Retrieving Nicaea*. Grand Rapids: Baker, 2011.
Athanasius. *On the Incarnation*. Translated by John Behr. Yonkers, NY: St Vladmire's Seminary Press, 2014.
Augustine. *Confessions*. Translated by Henry Chadwick. Oxford: Oxford University Press, 2008.
Baker, Deane-Peter. *Tayloring Reformed Epistemology: Charles Tayper, Alvin Plantinga and the de Jure Challenge to Christian Belief*. London: SCM, 2007.
Bloom, Alan. *Closing of the American Mind*. New York: Simon & Schuster, 1988.
Candler, Peter M., Jr. *Theology, Rhetoric, Manuduction: Or Reading Scripture Together on the Path to God (Radical Traditions)*. Grand Rapids: Eerdmans, 2006.
Chesterton, G. K. *Heretics*. Collected Works of G. K. Chesterton, vol. 1. San Francisco: Ignatius, 1986.
———. *Orthodoxy*. Collected Works of G. K. Chesterton 1. San Francisco: Igna-tius, 1986.
Coakley, Sarah. *God, Sexuality, and the Self: An Essay "On the Trinity."* Cambridge: Cambridge University Press, 2013.
Crouch, Andy. *Culture Making: Recovering Our Creative Calling*. Downers Grove, IL: InterVarsity, 2013.
Cunningham, Conor. "Being Recalled: Life as Anamnesis." In *Divine Transcendence and Immanence in the Work of Thomas Aquinas*, edited by Harm J. M. Goris, Herwi Rikhof, and Henk J. M. Schoot, 59–80. Leuven: Peeters, 2009.
Fiorenza, Francis Schüssler. *Foundational Theology: Jesus and the Church*. New York: Crossroad, 1984.
Gadamer, Hans-Georg. *Truth and Method*. Translated by Joel C. Weinsheimer and Donald G. Marshall. 3rd ed. New York: Continuum, 2004.
Hart, David Bentley. *Atheist Delusions: The Christian Revolution and Its Fashionable Enemies*. New Haven, CT: Yale University Press, 2009.
———. *The Beauty of the Infinite: The Aesthetics of Christian Truth*. Grand Rapids: Eerdmans, 2004.

Jauss, Hans Robert. *Toward an Aesthetic of Reception.* Translated by Timothy Bahti. Theory and History of Literature, vol. 2. Minneapolis: University of Minnesota Press, 1982.

Karlowicz, Dariusz. *Socrates and Other Saints: Early Christian Understandings of Reason and Philosophy.* Translated by Arthur Rosman. Eugene, OR: Cascade Books, 2017.

Kreeft, Peter. *A Refutation of Moral Relativism: Interviews with an Absolutist.* San Francisco: Ignatius, 2016.

Lewis, C. S. *The Abolition of Man.* New York: Macmillan, 1955.

———. *Mere Christianity.* C. S. Lewis Classics edition. London: HarperCollins, 2012.

Machuga, Ric. *Life, the Universe, and Everything: An Aristotelian Philosophy for a Scientific Age.* Eugene, OR: Cascade Books, 2011.

MacIntyre, Alasdair. *Three Rival Versions of Moral Enquiry: Encyclopaedia, Geneaology, and Tradition.* Notre Dame: University of Notre Dame Press, 1994.

Merritt, Jonathan. "Moral Relativism Is a Thing of the Past." *Politics* (blog), *Theatlantic.com*, March 25, 2016, https://www.theatlantic.com/politics/archive/2016/03/the-death-of-moral-relativism/475221/.

Milbank, John. *Theology and Social Theory: Beyond Secular Reason.* Oxford: Wiley, 2006.

Placher, William C. *The Domestication of Transcendence: How Modern Thinking about God Went Wrong.* Louisville: Westminster John Knox, 1996.

Pseduo-Dionysius. "The Celestial Hierarchy." In *Pseudo-Dionysius: The Complete Works*, translated by Colb Luibheid, 143–92. New York: Paulist, 1987.

Ratzinger, Joseph. *Introduction to Christianity.* San Francisco: Ignatius, 2004.

Smith, James K. A. *How (Not) to Be Secular: Reading Charles Taylor.* Grand Rapids: Eerdmans, 2014.

Taylor, Charles. *A Secular Age.* Cambridge: Harvard University Press, 2009.

Thiselton, Anthony C. *Hermeneutics: An Introduction.* Grand Rapids: Eerdmans, 2009.

Thomas Aquinas. *Summa Theologiae.* New York: Catholic Way Press, 2014.

Tyson, Paul. *De-Fragmenting Modernity: Reintegrating Knowledge with Wisdom, Belief with Truth, and Reality with Being.* Eugene, OR: Cascade Books, 2017.

———. *Faith's Knowledge: Explorations into the Theory and Application of Theological Epistemology.* Eugene, OR: Pickwick Publications, 2013.

———. *Returning to Reality: Christian Platonism from Our Times.* Kalos 2. Eugene, OR: Cascade Books, 2014.

2

Union, Participation, and Adoption
A Better Hermeneutic for Holiness in Leviticus

JEFFREY F. SPANOGLE

Introduction

THE MAIN THESIS OF this essay is that holiness and God's command for us to be holy in the Book of Leviticus have often been fundamentally misunderstood and wrongly interpreted. I hope to show how a better paradigm arises from the text through union, participation, and familial language. By examining typical paradigms for interpretation, I highlight how holiness has been flattened as a concept and how the command has been divested of both context and grace. When properly understood, holiness is both a command and a promise within the context of grace. I will close with implications for teaching and for the Asian context.

I want to make two introductory remarks here concerning my own journey in understanding holiness in Leviticus, enriched by my cross-cultural teaching and ministry experiences. First, this topic arose in part through dialogue between my experiences in the country of Laos and through reflection on my own church background, which was largely in the Christian and Missionary Alliance, which has elements of the Holiness Movement and, particularly, the Wesleyan concept of Christian perfection for sanctification. Holiness, in my background, was largely emphasized as something to strive toward as a moral achievement showing true faith. My own understanding of holiness at that time was primarily a moral imitation of God and purity in love for God and motives in serving others. As I studied in a Reformed seminary, however, I began to reflect on holiness in the Scriptures, particularly, the Book of Leviticus. After graduating from the seminary, I lived in Laos and made important crosscultural observations which helped spur a deeper analysis in Leviticus and, especially, on the concept of holiness. One particular experience was the Lao church as an offshoot of the Christian and Missionary Alliance and its emphasis on sanctification through rules and separation.

Second, my experiences in Laos were crucial in developing a deeper understanding of Leviticus and the category of ritual. From my background, ritual was often eschewed as an empty formality that enabled hypocrisy and false worship. In contrast, Lao culture was strengthened through rituals and formalities. One particular ritual called the *bacci* helped me to see the deeply interwoven nature of belief and practice through ritual acts. This ritual was done on many different kinds of occasions for several purposes. Primarily, it was done in order to prepare someone for a life change (marriage or going away) or restore a situation back to an ordered state (illness or funeral). The ritual consisted of a gathering device (for drawing the proper number of spirits back into a person) that was often an enormous arrangement of flowers and plants. The people who were being restored sat next to the arrangement with a person who reads prayers or ritual words to call the spirits back to the people or person. The rest of the people participating in the ceremony sat around in a circular arrangement. After the spirits were called back to the person, everyone would bless the people being restored and others around them who participated. This blessing is done by taking strings from the centerpiece, taking the hand of the one who was to be blessed, stroking thrice under the forearm away from the person while pronouncing evil to come "out," then stroking thrice toward the person while pronouncing good to stay "in," and, lastly, tying the strings around the wrist to bind the good spirits in the person being blessed. This ritual was intended to restore all the good spirits normally living in a person. Not participating in the *bacci* ritual was parallel to pronouncing a curse or inviting evil spirits. My analysis of Leviticus and its rituals in particular was enhanced by my crosscultural experiences in Asia. I began to perceive the rituals of Leviticus as more potent for their holistic view of humanity consisting of both body and spirit. As we will see in this study, voices from Asian contexts can enrich our understanding of what holiness is in Leviticus.

There are four sections in this study. First, I will discuss some problems of understanding holiness and, in particular, the holiness command in Leviticus. Second, I will introduce several widely accepted paradigms for understanding the call to holiness. Third, I will propose a new paradigm and argue that it captures the sense of holiness in Leviticus more precisely than existing paradigms. Lastly, I will elaborate on some practical implications for this new paradigm.

The Problems of Understanding the Holiness Command in Leviticus

There is a paradox in the Torah regarding the concept and command of holiness.[1] While the Torah does not carefully define what holiness is, the Torah emphatically commands Israel to be holy and integrate holiness within its cultic system. I perceive two particular problems in understanding holiness in the Torah in general and in Leviticus in particular. First, there seems to be an inherent contradiction in the concept of holiness in the Torah in that God is holy, because he is separate from anything else and anyone else, yet, Israel is expected to be holy as well, even while Israel does not share the same kind of separateness from the other nations. One may question, "If God alone is holy, how could God expect Israel to be holy?" Holiness separates God from everything and everyone one else, and it can be dangerous, even deadly in some cases. For instance, Moses alone and no other Israelite can approach God in establishing the covenant between God and Israel (Exod 19:12–13, 21–24). However, even Moses is unable to see the face of God (Exod 33:18–23). Those who approach God have more precise and strict commandments because of their proximity to God's holiness (Lev 16; 21–22). From this arises a paradigm of holiness as proximity to God using gradations of holiness according to distance from God's presence.[2] However, the concept of holiness is still described in terms of something unique to God alone (Exod 15:11).[3] Proximity does not capture holiness as divine essence that only describes God and his qualities (Lev 11:43–44; 19:2; 20:3; 22:2, 32).[4]

Second, it is difficult to define what holiness is in the Torah. The etymology of the word is not certain. Sometimes it has been argued that holiness refers to (1) a form of separation from the ordinary, or (2) shining brilliance, or (3) purity.[5] The equivalents in the ancient Near East contain

---

1. Exod 19:5–6, 10–13, 21–24; Lev 16:2–3; Anderson, "The Holy One of Israel," 3–19.

2. Jenson, *Graded Holiness*.

3. 1 Sam 2:2; Josh 24:19; Rev 15:4.

4. Isa 6:3, 57:15. Hartley relatedly notes, "Because key names were intricately tied to the bearer's identity in the ancient Semitic world, this means that holiness is the quintessential nature of God"; Hartley, "Holy and Holiness, Clean and Unclean," 420.

5. Müller, "קדש‬," 1103–18; Naude, "קדש‬," 877–87; Kornfeld and Ringgren, "קדש‬,"

ideas of purity, cleanness, radiance, clearness, or generally something from or attached to the divine realm.[6] The two common definitions—"separated out" and "pure, shining, glorious"—do not define holiness, rather they describe the outward look or effect that holiness produces from something that is made holy or experiences holiness.[7] Holy objects are separated by their nature of being made holy, but this is a corollary to their being made holy. An object is not necessarily holy because it is separated from ordinary use, but it has to be joined to God.[8] Likewise, some things that are holy are described as effulgent or glorious, yet this is an outward appearance rather than what holiness is. On the one hand, both definitions correctly describe the uses of holiness in the Biblical text. Holy things are separated out by nature of their status (Israel in Lev 20:22–26; Levites in Num 16:9) and the glory of God as the physical manifestation of God's holiness is often a consuming fire—bright, purifying, and glorious (Lev 9:24, 10:2; Num 9:15–16; Deut 4:24; 9:23). On the other hand, however, these two definitions only work as the pointers toward the reality that holiness is unique to God himself in describing God's self-revealing activity and the subsequent response within the material realm. Missing is the explanation of causation—what makes something holy—alongside a positive description of holiness. The two definitions above point to a manifestation of holiness or the result something made holy.

Let me return to the paradox of holiness. All the people of Israel are commanded to be holy and even promised that God has made them holy and he would continue to sanctify them. Some important questions arise.

521–45; Bamberger, *The Torah*, 201. Vriezen concludes that holiness is brilliant unapproachable radiance that cannot be witnessed by humanity; Vriezen, *Outline of Old Testament Theology*, 149. In contrast, Eichrodt stresses holiness through the cognates in other languages as something distinguished, separated out, or marked against the definition of brilliance; Eichrodt, *Theology of Old Testament*, 1:270–72.

6. Eichrodt, *Theology of Old Testament*, 1:271–72. Eichrodt notes that within the Ancient Near Eastern uses, holiness is rarely used as a predicate for the deities themselves and more often used for objects or people related to the cult; but within the biblical usage, holiness takes on a personal effect by its use to predominantly describe God as the Holy One.

7. Hartley, "Holy and Holiness, Clean and Unclean," 420.

8. Müller makes this point about separation as the definition of holiness when he writes, "The often-accepted basic meaning 'set apart' [e.g., Eichrodt 1:270–72] may only be inferred: the holy is set apart from the profane in a *temenos*, for example, to protect it and to protect against it as soon as the corresponding need for protection is perceived; the experience of the holy as the 'wholly other' presupposes, for the most part, a point of departure in an understanding of the profane that has been suggested only by the absence of the numinous in modern concepts of normalcy"; Müller, "קדש," 1104–5. See also Hartley, "Holy and Holiness, Clean and Unclean," 420.

How could God command someone to be "holy" or attain holiness that is unique to himself and deadly to the average Israelite? How does God make someone or something holy? What does it mean for Israel to be commanded holiness? Several extensive works have been written to answer this question. However, they do not appear to have fully reconciled the concept of holiness with the application and evidence of Leviticus. Many interpretations see the holiness command pointing to a set of characteristics—moral, cultic, and legal as described in the laws—that emulate the character of God—commonly known as *imitatio Dei*.[9] This does not, however, do justice to the depth of the holiness command nor the unique characteristics of being described as a holy people.[10] Another proposed paradigm to explain the holiness command is based on separation from the ordinary and dedication to God.[11] Yet, this does not explain how the moral laws allow imperfect or sinful people to be attached to God without redefining the purity and transcendence of holiness. While both paradigms are important to understanding the holiness command, a tension arises between holiness as God's consuming perfection and holiness as attachment or relationship to God, which requires the need for continual atonement through sacrifice.

Leviticus presents this paradox through several means. A clear example is the first instance of the holiness command in Lev 11. This chapter follows the deaths of Nadab and Abihu in Lev 10 where they inappropriately approached the altar and offered incense to God. Yet, the chapter commands various food laws and holiness within the framework of the high priest approaching the Holy of Holies in Lev 16. The food laws define what is clean and what is unclean to eat, and they are ultimately related to holiness and Israel's participation in the tabernacle. The remaining question is what purpose the food laws serve concerning holiness and how they explain why the two priests were killed, when they approached God.

Survey of How to Understand the Call to Holiness

There are a few widely accepted views concerning holiness. The most common interpretation is the *imitatio Dei*, where holiness is primarily a moral or behavioral pattern to follow from God's moral character. Jacob Milgrom, the

---

9. Nihan, *From Priestly Torah to Pentateuch*; Milgrom, *Leviticus 1–16*, 687; Milgrom, *Leviticus 17–22*; Hartley, *Leviticus*; Gorman, *Divine Presence and Community*.

10. Wells, *God's Holy People*, 94–96; Rooker, *Leviticus*, 47; Morales, *Who Shall Ascend the Mountain?*, 215–16; Kleinig, *Leviticus*, 11.

11. Wenham, *The Book of Leviticus*, 22; Balentine, *Leviticus*, 154–55.

seminal figure for Levitical studies, comments on Lev 19:2, "Thus the *imitatio dei* [sic] implied by this verse is that just as God differs from human beings, so Israel should differ from the nations (20:26), a meaning corroborated by the generalization that encloses this chapter (v. 37): Israel is holy only if it observes YHWH's commandments."[12] God is infinitely separated and perfect and Israel is called to a similar separation and emulation of God's ethical perfection.[13] Most importantly, Milgrom argues that, by pursuing holiness, humanity will be able to enter the presence of God and achieve God's "providence and protection."[14] Hence, for Milgrom, the goal of the commands is to earn God's blessings by becoming worthy of holiness and God's presence through imitation, and more importantly, the concept of holiness in this approach is filtered through a primarily moral lens.

Gordon J. Wenham has a more complex notion of holiness at the beginning of his Leviticus commentary but he remains within the *imitatio Dei* paradigm. Wenham describes holiness in the beginning of his commentary as "a state of grace to which men are called by God, and it is attained through obeying the law and carrying out rituals such as sacrifice."[15] This state of grace is from God's redemption of Israel from Egypt and a proper response to God's covenant. Wenham continues, "Man is expected to respond to God's grace. But how? This is the role of the law. The law explains how men are to imitate God."[16] Wenham proceeds to summarize the holiness command by saying, "Man's highest duty is to imitate his creator."[17] Here, while holiness is described as a "state of grace," the primary meaning for the Israelite is still behavioral. The problem with the *imitatio Dei* paradigm in Leviticus is that they do not account for the context of the command and the concept of holiness is limited to behavioral or moral issues.

We can find several descriptions of holiness in Leviticus that move beyond imitation and reflect more complexity. Samuel Balentine writes, "the summons to holiness can be fulfilled only when fidelity to God is embodied

---

12. Milgrom, *Leviticus 17–22*, 1604.

13. Milgrom, *Leviticus 17–22*, 1714–15. Milgrom also bases the idea of holiness on separation: "Israel is enjoined to be holy because YHWH is holy (19:2). This does not mean that Israel can achieve or even imitate YHWH's holiness. There is an unbridgeable gap between them. Holiness implies separation, distinction"; Milgrom, *Leviticus 17–22*, 1397.

14. Milgrom, *Leviticus 17–22*, 1606.

15. Wenham, *Leviticus*, 23; see also Wenham's discussion of attribution of holiness to priests and nation; Wenham, *Leviticus*, 18–25.

16. Wenham, *Leviticus*, 32.

17. Wenham, *Leviticus*, 180–81.

with equal passion by both ethical and religious commitments."[18] Balentine also argues that the holiness command must be read in tandem with God's promise of sanctification:

> For all their considerable emphasis on the command to *be holy*, these chapters affirm that the One who issues the command is the same One who empowers its recipients to obey it. "You shall be holy. . . I YHWH am holy. . . and I will make you holy." Without the last promise, the command would be heavy indeed. From the human perspective—perhaps from God's as well—and even Israel's history, the command would likely buckle under the weight of its own futility.[19]

This affirmation of both command and divine action more accurately reflects both the holiness command in Leviticus and its context.[20] Furthermore, Balentine reflects a dynamic relationship between God and Israel, which moves beyond a framework of law and obedience toward a framework of redemption.[21]

Jo Bailey Wells also develops a more complex view of holiness for Israel by examining how the text uses holiness to describe Israel's relationships with God, other nations, and itself. She starts with an analysis of Exod 19:5–6 and argues that holiness means four things for Israel: "Israel is unique. . . Israel belongs to God. . . Israel must live for God. . . Israel must relate to others."[22] Wells further describes a uniquely multifaceted exposition of holiness when used with respect to Israel as, "This rather ambivalent state, whereby Israel is declared holy yet equally called to be holy, I describe as 'the call to holiness.' 'Holy' describes a status and a standard and a function."[23]

---

18. Balentine, *Leviticus*, 160.

19. Balentine, *Leviticus*, 168.

20. Kleinig makes similar statements regarding the holiness command, "The purpose of God's revelation to Moses in Leviticus is summed up well by his call to the congregation of Israel: 'You are/will be/shall be holy (קדשים תהיו), as I the Lord your God am holy.'. . . First, it is a statement of fact by God, a Gospel declaration: 'You are holy.'. . . Second, this is a promise of God: 'You will be holy.'. . . Third, the call to holiness is a demand from God: 'You shall be holy'"; Kleinig, *Leviticus*, 11–12.

21. Balentine writes concerning how "I YHWH your God" bookends the Holiness Command in Lev 22:31–33, "the phrase 'I sanctify you' (v. 32) provides the coupling that promises God will not ultimately allow the call for a holy people to fail. As the seventh of seven occurrences (20:8; 21:8, 15; 21:23; 22:9, 16, 32), the words 'I sanctify you' bring into full view God's inviolable commitment to be at work in Israel's midst, sanctifying them in their obedience, forgiving them their failures, and restoring them to new possibilities for attaining the holiness God requires"; Balentine, *Leviticus*, 172.

22. Wells, *God's Holy People*, 55–57.

23. Wells, *God's Holy People*, 56.

Wells goes on to explain that holiness must be a relational term for people and things, because holiness is unique to God alone:

> First and foremost, holiness represents the essential characteristic of God, as revealed by the name Yhwh. The term קדשׁ is associated with Yhwh alone, though it is first used in the Hebrew Scriptures of certain things in close relation to him, rather than directly of Yhwh himself . . . Israel is declared holy at the point where it makes a covenant with Yhwh (Exod. 19.6); but this holiness is related to the nation living faithfully for him within the unique relationship of covenant . . . The use of קדשׁ and its derivatives is extended to all places, things and persons, in so far as they belong, or have come to belong, *to* Yhwh. Thus their holiness is relational and directional.[24]

In other words, holiness is a description for those things that uniquely belong to God or are distinctively joined to God and point to his holiness. She adequately captures the difficulties inherent within the paradox of the holiness command and particularly, the relational nature in the holiness command to Israel.

Balentine and Wells, in my opinion, more accurately capture the complexity of the holiness command in Leviticus than Milgrom and Wenham. However, we need to dig deeper to further understand how Israel is commanded to be holy and how we can understand holiness more holistically and multidimensionally, moving forward from its common, monolithic, conceptually-flattened understanding. In the rest of this study, I will discuss two critical questions concerning the holiness command in Leviticus: (1) how Israel can be instructed to be holy and ascribed holiness at the same time, and (2) how God's transcendental attribute, holiness, can be ascribed to humanity.

Holiness in the Paradigm of Union, Participation, and Adoption

I want to propose two paradigms and show how they more accurately reflect the complexity of holiness in Leviticus and further allow for a more accurate interpretation of the holiness command. For the first paradigm, I am appropriating the systematic category of union, sometimes referred to as *theosis* or *deification*. Constantine R. Campbell best captures this concept:

---

24. Wells, *God's Holy People*, 96–97.

this theme [of union] is best conveyed through four terms: union, participation, identification, and incorporation. *Union* gathers up faith union with Christ, mutual indwelling, trinitarian, and nuptial notions. *Participation* conveys partaking in the events of Christ's narrative. *Identification* refers to the believers' location in the realm of Christ and their allegiance to his lordship. *Incorporation* encapsulates the corporate dimensions of membership in Christ's body.[25]

I use the terms "union" and "participation" to capture this systematic category. On the one hand, needless to say, we must be cautious to adapt the New Testament Christological concepts in our understanding of holiness in Leviticus. On the other hand, however, as we will see shortly, the themes of union and participation are evident in the Torah itself. In other words, the New Testament writers such as John (e.g., John 15:1–17; 17:6–26) and Paul (e.g., Rom 6:1–14; 8:1–17; Gal 2:20) did not create new concepts in their understanding of who Christ is and who believers are in relation to Christ, but they adopted the Old Testament themes and concepts to explain the Christ-event and its outcomes.

First, union is vital to Leviticus, because it closely follows Exodus with the entire covenant making ceremony. God not only makes a covenant with them but promises to be present with them in the tabernacle. Union from this perspective is most clearly seen in each holiness command by the phrase "your God" (Lev 11:44–45; 19:2; 20:7–8). Second, participation occurs throughout Leviticus through the rituals and festivals, but more pointedly, Israel is made holy as they participate in God's holiness through the cultic system. God participates in Israel through the priesthood and through their presence at the tabernacle. Participation in God's physical presence occurs through the high priest as representative and requires Israel's unique participation. More importantly, alongside the holiness command, God promises a unique participation for sanctification through the repeated reminder of who he is—"I am the Lord who sanctifies you" (Lev 20:8; 21:8, 15, 23; 22:9, 16, 32, ESV). Third, identification is seen through God's election and redemption of Israel. This is found in the holiness commands through the phrase, "to be your God," alongside the reminder of God's redemption of them from Egypt (Lev 11:45; 20:26). Israel belongs to God and the covenant repeatedly calls for their fidelity to him. Fourth and lastly, incorporation is seen in the plural "you" in each call to holiness. This plural call to a community is grounded in the Lord himself—"be holy, for I am holy" (Lev 11:44; 11:45; 19:2; 20:26; 21:8). Hence, the union between

---

25. Campbell, *Paul and Union with Christ*, 413.

God and Israel is the foundation for both the holiness command and the divine act of sanctification. Participation provided by the cultic system is further the means of grace whereby Israel enacts their holy identity and enjoys the benefits of their fellowship with God. Holiness is not simply a call to imitate God but to an identity, fellowship, and blessing.

Union and participation further help explain various phenomena in Leviticus better than other paradigms. I have asked two main questions—(1) how Israel can be instructed to be holy and ascribed holiness at the same time, and (2) how God's transcendental attribute, holiness, can be ascribed to Israel. First, union shows how Israel as the representative of the humanity is mysteriously joined to God and, now, Israel is ascribed holiness through a similar paradigm to the *imago Dei*. Second, union and participation show how Israel is ascribed holiness from their union with God but are called to participate in this holiness through God's prescribed cultic system. Israel is given a means of grace to fellowship with God and enjoy him.

In addition to union and participation, I contend that the relational concepts of adoption and marriage also help better explains holiness and the holiness command in Leviticus. This language is seen partly from the context in Exod 4:22 when God calls Israel "my firstborn son." Also, there is a verbal parallel ("I will be your God") between Exod 6:7 and Lev 26:2. This language mirrors ancient adoption language.[26] However, two further instances indicate a more familial language and relationship for the purpose of holiness. First, in Lev 20:1–8, the offense of giving a child to Molech is described as adultery or harlotry. The positive corollary to this description is that Israel's covenant relationship to God parallels that of marriage and their children uniquely belonging to God alone. Second, in Lev 21–22, rules for holiness are determined in part through familial relationships to the priests. For example, holy portions are only given to those who are directly attached to the family. If a daughter marries outside the family, she no longer receives portions, but if she becomes divorced or widowed without children and returns to her father's house, she once again receives the holy portions (Lev 22:10–13). The idea of holiness as a state of grace is built into the holiness command through adoption and familial language from the phrase "for I am the LORD your God" (Lev 11:44, 45;

---

26. Paul, "Adoption Formulae," 173–85; Weinfeld, "Covenant of Grant in the Old Testament," 184–203. Weinfeld notes, "The formulation of the priestly covenant with Abraham, 'to be unto you a God' (Gen 17:7–8) and the priestly formulation of the covenant with Israel, 'I will be your God and you shall be my people' (Lev 26:12; Ex 6:7; Deut 29:12), is taken from the sphere of marriage/adoption legal terminology like its Davidic counterpart in II Sam 7:14"; Weinfeld, "Covenant of Grant in the Old Testament," 200.

19:2, 10, 25, 34; 20:7; 21:8; 23:22; 24:22; 25:17; 25:55; 26:1), referencing the covenant relationship context. Hence, holiness is not a state of grace that must be achieved, but lived out as an identity. God disciplines Israel but will never utterly forsake them (Lev 26).[27]

Practical Implications of Union, Participation, and Adoption in Asia

I will briefly highlight some implications of this study in the context of teaching in Asia. First, we need to think about how to perceive sanctification and the analogies used to convey how we are made holy. Often sanctification is seen as keeping your salvation, especially when attached to an imitation paradigm for holiness. Once the holiness command is removed from its context within Israel's redemption from their slavery in Egypt—the gracious covenant relationship, God's promises, and the nature of holiness aside from God's union and participation with his people—the void is filled with a moral law that does not accurately reflect the lawgiver or its redemptive nature. Law apart from God's grace and promises is not the gospel but moralism and legalism. In order to properly convey what sanctification means for us today, we need to have a more holistic approach to holiness. I observed that many churches in Laos follow the Holiness movement in the United States in their teaching of sanctification, and, because of their unbalanced understanding, legalism was the resulting church culture. This leads to my next implication for how to bring about a meaningful change of perception for sanctification and theology.

Second, primarily oral cultures transmit information differently from primarily literate cultures that focus on abstraction of ideas. Based on my experience in both Laos and the International Teachers College (ITC) in Indonesia, primarily oral cultures generally tend to thrive on analogies better than abstractions. Many of my Asian students complain about poor translations of the Bible in their own languages. Several had not read the Bible extensively (or at all) until they came to ITC, even though they were active in their home churches; much of this is due to the oral culture around preaching or hearing the word rather than reading it. Many have legalistic understandings and analogies for salvation. The implication for teaching in this context is that we need better analogies and paradigms to communicate a more complete or "thicker" description of the Scriptures and grace in salvation. These analogies, in turn, should further help to drive students to study the Scriptures for themselves. Adoption is a concrete analogy that

27. Calvin, *Institutes*, 2.8.14.

is readily understandable. Union and participation give the students a robust analogy to approach the text and arrive at thicker conclusions and applications. While union and participation might be more abstract, the move from adoption and familial analogies to the paradigm of union and participation is not difficult within these cultures—especially given their deeply familial and relational contexts. In order to bring a meaningful change, we need to drive students to study the Scriptures in their original contexts and lead students through the process of exegesis and hermeneutics for their own cultural applications.

Third, we need more voices from Asia to study and bring out the Scriptures from their contexts. My own study was enriched by my experience in Laos and continues to grow in Indonesia. My students continue to provide new and fresh ways of seeing the Scriptures from their cultural contexts. In my opinion, Leviticus needs other voices beyond those in the developed world, which can enrich our understanding of the book for the global Church of Jesus Christ.

Conclusion

This study offers a new holistic understanding of holiness in Leviticus. In the first section, I discussed various problems of understanding holiness in the Torah in general, and the holiness command in Leviticus in particular. It is difficult to harmonize the fact that God is holy, in part because he is ontologically separate from creation, and the fact that he calls Israel to be holy, even when Israel is not ontologically separate from the other nations. Also, it is difficult to define the essence of holiness apart from the effects or secondary causes of holiness.

In the second section, I criticized the primacy of the *imitatio Dei* paradigm, widely used to interpret and understand the holiness command in Leviticus, in which holiness is essentially a moral or behavioral pattern to imitate who God is. In my opinion, scholars like Balantine and Wells more accurately capture the complexity for the holiness command in Leviticus.

In the third section, I proposed a new holistic paradigm that captures the sense of holiness in Leviticus more precisely than the paradigm of the *imitatio Dei*. Applying Campbell's description of the systematic category of union, I argued that the paradigm of union, participation, and adoption better portrays the concept of holiness in Leviticus than the paradigm of the *imitatio Dei*, based on four considerations. First, union is a crucial theme in Leviticus (Lev 11:44–45; 19:2; 20:7–8). Second, participation with God permeates Leviticus as a means for enjoying and nourishing this union (Lev

20:8; 21:8, 15, 23; 22:9, 16, 32). Third, God has elected and redeemed Israel using familial language of adoption and marriage to describe his relationship with them, and he is the God over Israel (Exod 4:22–23; Lev 11:45; 20:1–8; 20:24–26). Fourth, the theme of incorporation in Leviticus has its basis in who God is (Lev 11:44, 45; 19:2; 20:26; 21:8). Understanding holiness in Leviticus through the paradigm of union, participation, and adoption help us better understand (1) how Israel can be instructed to be holy and ascribed holiness simultaneously and (2) how God's transcendental attribute, holiness, can be ascribed to Israel.

In the fourth section, I elaborated on a few practical implications for this new paradigm, in the context of teaching Christian theology in Asia today. First, Christian theology teachers in Asia need to think about how to understand and convey sanctification more holistically. Second, Christian theology teachers in Asia need to seriously consider the fact that many students from Southeast Asian countries are from predominantly oral cultures that engage scripture better through analogies. Third, Christian theology teachers in Asia need to be more aware of Asian Christian's understanding of the Scriptures in their own cultural contexts, instead of simply importing the traditional Christian theology from the West without any critical engagement, in order that Asian Christian students may be able to apply the Scriptures to their own cultural contexts faithfully and relevantly at the same time.

Bibliography

Anderson, Bernhard W. "The Holy One of Israel." In *Justice and the Holy: Essays in Honor of Walter Harrelson*, edited by Douglas A. Knight, 3–19. Atlanta: Scholars, 1989.
Balentine, Samuel E. *Leviticus*. Interpretation. Louisville: Westminster John Knox, 2003.
Bamberger, B. *The Torah, A Modern Commentary: Leviticus*. New York: Union of American Hebrew Congregations, 1978.
Calvin, John. *Institutes of the Christian Religion*, LCC 20. Edited by John T. McNeil. Translated by Ford Lewis Battle. Louisville: Westminster John Knox, 1960.
Campbell, Constantine R. *Paul and Union with Christ: An Exegetical and Theological Study*. Grand Rapids: Zondervan, 2012.
Eichrodt, Walther. *Theology of the Old Testament*. Vol. 1. Translated by J. A. Baker. OTL 1. Louisville: Westminster John Knox, 1967.
Gorman, Frank H. *Divine Presence and Community: A Commentary on the Book of Leviticus*. Grand Rapids: Eerdmans, 1997.
Hartley, John E. "Holy and Holiness, Clean and Unclean." In *DOTP*, 420–31. Downers Grove, IL: InterVarsity, 2003.
———. *Leviticus*. WBC 4. Waco, TX: Word, 1992.

Jenson, Philip Peter. *Graded Holiness: A Key to the Priestly Conception of the World.* JSOTSup 106. Sheffield: JSOT Press, 1992.

Kleinig, John. *Leviticus.* Concordia Commentary. Saint Louis: Concordia, 2003.

Kornfeld, W. and H. Ringgren, "קדש." In *TDOT* 12:521–45.

Milgrom, Jacob. *Leviticus 1–16.* AB 3. New York: Doubleday, 1991.

———. *Leviticus 17–22.* AB 3A. New York: Doubleday, 2000.

Morales, Michael. *Who Shall Ascend the Mountain of the Lord.* Downers Grove, IL: InterVarsity, 2015.

Müller, H. "קדש." In *TLOT* 1103–118.

Naude, J. "קדש." In *NIDOTTE* 877–87.

Nihan, Christophe. *From Priestly Torah to Pentateuch: A Study in the Composition of the Book of Leviticus.* FAT 25. Tübingen: Mohr/Siebeck, 2007.

Paul, Shalom M. "Adoption Formulae: A Study of Cuneiform and Biblical Legal Clauses." *Maarav* 2 (1980) 173–85.

Rooker, Mark. *Leviticus.* NAC 3A. Nashville: Broadman & Holman, 2000.

Vriezen, Theodor Christiaan. *An Outline of Old Testament Theology.* 2nd ed. Oxford: Blackwell, 1970.

Weinfeld, Moshe. "The Covenant of Grant in the Old Testament and in the Ancient Near East." *JAOS* 90 (1970) 184–203.

Wells, Jo Bailey. *God's Holy People: A Theme in Biblical Theology.* Sheffield: Sheffield Academic, 2000.

Wenham, Gordon J. *The Book of Leviticus.* Rev. ed. NICOT. Grand Rapids: Eerdmans, 1979.

3

Contextual Biblical Interpretation and Indonesian Readers

― Matthew R. Malcolm

Introduction

"I don't want to take part in the Asian theology networks. They're only interested in post-colonial readings!" This comment from an Asian colleague, which was immediately reiterated by others, alerted me to a perception among some Asian academics that certain themes are deemed by the broader academy to be more palatable and publishable from Asian voices than other themes. Voices of protest, it is claimed, are celebrated more than voices of patient respect. Given that I have been struck more than anything by the culture of humble respect among my Indonesian students in comparison to their Western counterparts, I have become all the more interested in hearing the interpretative voices of "ordinary" Indonesian readers. I am intrigued by the question: how do "ordinary" Indonesian accounting, communication science, food technology, and management students interpret the Bible in this Muslim-majority culture, and how do their interpretations relate to the broader academic discussions of which they are largely unaware? In this essay, I attempt to give an overview of the area of "contextual" biblical interpretation, and its relation to hermeneutics more broadly. I then sketch out some ways in which Indonesian readers might offer distinctive contributions to the interpretation of the Bible. These arise initially from the surprises of my own experience as an Australian lecturer based in Indonesia but are also related to anthropological and educational studies. This chapter aims, then, to ponder the distinctive insights of Indonesian interpretative voices.

Contextual Biblical Interpretation

What is contextual biblical interpretation? The phrase may sound ambiguous. It is referring not to the context of the biblical text itself, but to the context of the reader. The context of the biblical text has preoccupied scholars for centuries, but it is in the last several decades that the context of the reader has come to prominence as an important element in interpretation. It seems undeniable that a reader's upbringing, education, community, language, cultural assumptions, and motivations influence their interpretation of a text, for good and for bad. Committed Christian readers may interpret biblical texts differently to the way sceptical atheists read them. Depressed readers may detect different nuances in the Psalms to those who are going through a period of elation. Wives and husbands may differently hear Paul's tone of voice as they attempt to interpret his instructions to wives and husbands.

To deny the influence of the interpreter's context would be naïve. And yet in mainstream biblical interpretation, several factors have often combined to downplay this significant factor: the use of the third person singular in scholarly discourse (mimicking a scientific style), the pervasiveness of certain commonalities of cultural privilege among published interpreters, and a desire to respect divinely given truth have variously contributed to a reticence among many biblical interpreters to consider the impacts of the reader's context on their interpretation.[1] However, the constraints provided by a reader's context need not be denied or seen as a negative thing. Theologically speaking, it is God's gift to humans that they exist in finite bodies, in specific places, at particular moments in time, with the opportunity to share with and learn from people in other locations and times. The "postmodern" reaction against Enlightenment pseudo-objectivity need not be rejected by conservative Christians as anti-truth but can rather be discerningly welcomed as pro-incarnation: humans are, by their God-given, Christ-shared nature, *particular*.

---

1. Related to the third factor (the desire to respect divinely given truth), Piper notes, "Because the Bible alone is the inerrant, infallible authority for what we are to believe about God and how he wants us to live, it is no surprise that we bring a lot of baggage to the text. By nature, we don't like the thought of absolute authority residing in anyone outside of ourselves"; Piper, "Biblical Exegesis," 2.

Two related influential facets of the particularity of the reader are race and culture. The present author is unable to write, except as a white Australian who lives and works in Indonesia. The editors of Text @ Contexts series rightly note:

> Contextual readings of the Bible are an attempt to redress the previous longstanding and grave imbalance that says that there is a kind of "plain," unaligned biblical criticism that is somehow "normative," and that there is another, distinct kind of biblical criticism aligned with some social location: the writing of Latina/o scholars advocating liberation, the writing of feminist scholars emphasizing gender as a cultural factor, the writings of African scholars pointing out the text's and the readers' imperialism, the writing of Jews and Muslims, and so on. The project of recognizing and emphasizing the role of context in reading freely admits that we all come from somewhere; no one is native to the biblical text; no one reads only in the interests of the text itself.[2]

As an example of the impacts of cultural assumptions on interpretation, one could note the fact that a great many English translations of the Bible completely conceal the Gospel of Mark's many references to uncleanness, by referring to "demons" rather than to "unclean spirits."[3] Is it just a coincidence that these translations are largely produced by interpreters who operate in cultures for which there is no important distinction between ritual cleanness and uncleanness? Would translators operating in cultures that feature important categories of clean and unclean produce different translations? There has been a flurry of interest in recent years, then, in giving attention to biblical interpretations that come from a variety of racial and cultural locations (as well as other facets of particularity). But much of this attention has been given to groups within the United States, such as African American readers, Asian American readers, Latina/o American readers, and so on. There has been little attention in internationally published literature given to the particularity of Asian readers who live in Indonesia.[4]

---

2. Kim, *1 and 2 Corinthians*, x.

3. See for example Mark 7:25 in the 1984 NIV, the CEV, the GNT, the *Living Bible*, the *Message*, the NCV, and the NLT. Although this verse comes in the context of Jesus' just having established his provocatively new categorisation of "clean" and "unclean," these translations render the affliction of the Syrophoenician woman's daughter as "an evil spirit," "a demon," or "disturbed."

4. Banawiratma and Müller, "Contextual Social Theology," 1–249; Intan, *"Public Religion"*; Singgih, "Let Me not Be Put to Shame," 71–85.

Likewise, much academic reflection on contextual interpretation is focused on that which is *self-consciously* contextual. That is, attention is given to interpreters whose work openly advocates the liberation of their reading community. This is by no means a bad thing. As an example, Mitzi J. Smith introduces a recent project that gives voice to African American Womanist hermeneutics as a consciously political endeavour, in which the authors "unapologetically confront in their essays issues of oppression such as racism, sexism, classism that impact black women's lives and other women of color and their communities."[5] To reiterate, this is by no means an unimportant endeavour. It results in fresh attention to the constraints of privileged readings, and directly defies particular strategies of marginalisation. However, attention can also profitably be turned to those readers who are less intentionally conscious of contextual parameters and reading projects. This is the interest of the present chapter.

The Place of Contextual Interpretation in Broader Hermeneutical Reflection

Before coming to focus on Indonesian readers in this chapter, however, it may be worth briefly considering the place of contextual interpretation in broader hermeneutical reflection. In short, contextual interpretation is not hermeneutically sufficient, but it is significant nevertheless. Recognising the particular location of the reader is just *one* part of the hermeneutical endeavour. Two other essential parts are recognising the particular contexts of the text, and conducting a process of linguistically rigorous, open, respectful questioning of the text itself.[6] From the comments that follow, then, one should not deduce that I am outlining a comprehensive hermeneutical approach, but rather highlighting one element that should not be ignored.

The Interpretative Impulses and Contributions of Indonesian Readers

I want to suggest two features of twenty first century Indonesian culture, which might result in distinctive interpretative impulses. One is an orientation of respect, the other is a non-secular interpretative milieu. Although the

---

5. Smith, *I Found God in Me*, 4.

6. For a much fuller account of how contextual concerns fit into hermeneutics, see Malcolm, *From Hermeneutics to Exegesis*.

choice of these features arises from my own experience, I will also seek to relate my discussion to relevant anthropological and educational studies.

An Orientation of Respect

As flagged earlier, one of the most striking impressions I gained as soon as I began teaching in Indonesia was the culture of humble respect: students call me "sir," and are very reticent to use my first name, even though this is an entirely normal feature of academic life in my native Australia. If they are found cheating or plagiarising, they are usually devastated and quickly apologetic. Of course, one does not know whether the respect is genuine or skin deep, but the outside observer would do well to defer judgment. I was once told by an Indonesian colleague that international lecturers need to be aware of the need for Indonesians to preserve face in public. The significance of shame in Asian cultures has been well documented.[7] Another Indonesian colleague told me that in a particular setting of workplace conflict, it is "not the Indonesian way" to divide over it "like Americans," but rather to patiently listen for opportunities for long term reconciliation. The loss of face associated with a public falling out would be so catastrophic, according to this colleague, that it would be preferable to patiently wait for heretofore unnoticed possibilities for resolution. Respect for others—especially for teachers—may be an influential feature of an Indonesian reading context. The importance of the avoidance of shame and the expression of respect in Indonesia has been noted by anthropologists and educationalists. It can be seen in such varied cultural practices as the wearing of veils, a strong awareness of relational power structures, obedience to authority, and tolerance of ambiguity.[8]

During my own liberal arts classes in one semester (involving about 140 Indonesian students altogether), my students and I were reading through, and discussing, Mark's Gospel. When we reached the passage about the Syrophoenician woman, I offered two interpretations of Jesus' initial refusal to exorcise her daughter. The first interpretation was that Jesus was testing the woman's faith, and always expected to heal the daughter. The second was that Jesus initially assumed that it was not yet time for Gentile inclusion, but the woman's response changed his mind and redirected his mission. I tried to present both alternatives as plausibly as possible. In recent decades, the second reading above has found traction in non-Asian settings, such as Europe,

---

7. Ha, "Shame in Asian and Western cultures," 1114–31.

8. The latter three points can all be seen in Novera, "Indonesian Postgraduate Students Studying"; Lindquist, "Veils and Ecstasy," 487–508.

Australia, and (overwhelmingly) the USA.⁹ Is it a coincidence that it is largely these cultures that have produced readings of the passage in which the teacher's mission is corrected and adjusted by an unnamed outsider? Perhaps or perhaps not. Either way, it is worth hearing how readers outside of Europe, Australia, and the USA interpret the passage. I gave my students an anonymous survey to find out which interpretation they found more likely, and the results were overwhelmingly (over 90 percent) in favour of the reading in which Jesus the teacher was providing a test for the woman's faith—a test which she took up and passed with relish. The extent to which the students' cultural background attuned them for such a reading may be debated. But it is appropriate to ponder the distinctive interpretative impulses that might arise from the culture of respect in Indonesia. In interpretative situations in which Western readers might be quick to highlight individual resistance, or iconoclastic challenge, might Indonesian readers be more inclined to patiently listen for hints of respect, loyalty, or agreement? Might the awareness of issues of "face" result in discerning readings in which all parties within a dispute are displayed in a favourable light?¹⁰

A Non-Secular Interpretative Milieu

In three different classes, I spent a session working through Paul's first letter to the Corinthians. Given that this is a letter with which I have done a lot of work, I told each class that they could choose for us to explore any part of the book in greater depth, and we would do so. I suggested that they might choose sections relating to: wisdom, sexuality, meat offered to idols, the use of tongues and prophecy in worship, or the resurrection. To my great surprise, the choice in every class was almost instant and unanimous: meat offered to idols. Recently an Indonesian colleague shared a link to a piece of stand-up comedy in which the South East Asian comedian suggested that all Asian people fit into one of two categories: they have either seen a ghost, or they know someone personally who has seen a ghost. Although this was

---

9. Countryman, "How Many Baskets Full?," 643–55; Van den Eynde, "When a Teacher Becomes a Student," 274–79; Cadwallader, "Dog-throttling," 97–124; Alonso, *The Woman Who Changed Jesus*.

10. For an example, Anjajah publishes an article "Asia on Top, Indonesia Lowest in Beer Consumption" on *The Jakarta Post* on February 5th, 2018, in which he writes, "Beer companies claim that beer has many health benefits. But doctors say beer is an alcoholic drink that can be harmful. . . Drinking beer moderately has certain benefits like other alcoholic drinks. Still, one has to be cautious in consuming alcohol, including beer." The author's painstaking effort to please those who are in favor of alcohol and those who are opposed may sound overly indecisive to Western ears.

clearly intended as hyperbolic humour, it is interesting that the depiction of a worldview in which the supernatural world is active and evidently resonated strongly with the Singaporean audience.

While belief in the supernatural is a common feature of life throughout the world, it is not always welcomed as a feature of academic discussion, even of religious texts. However, the reticence to allow belief in God to affect public discussion in the post-Christian West is not a feature of Indonesian life. Unlike the secularising West, and unlike China, Indonesia remains firmly committed to a consciousness of the reality of the divine. This can be seen in such events as well publicised blasphemy trials.[11] However, it can be seen perhaps most clearly in Indonesia's official national worldview, *Pancasila*. The first of its five pillars for Indonesian society is: *Ketuhanan Yang Maha Esa* ("belief in the absoluteness of God"). In 1997, Douglas E. Ramage commented:

> Many visitors to Indonesia notice that references to Pancasila are everywhere—on village-square monuments, on television news, in speeches by officials reported in the press, and if one were to look, even in school textbooks... Pancasila has meaning for Indonesians far beyond stale government propaganda.[12]

Twenty years later, in 2017, the government instituted new requirements, insisting that universities give mandatory classes not only in "civics" (which has been required for some time), but directly on *Pancasila*. Of course, not all Indonesians actually believe in God, but the phenomenon of belief in the divine is an open and influential feature of society.

Again, it is worth pondering: What distinctive interpretative impulses might arise from this feature of Indonesian culture? Just as the theme of "uncleanness" is often disguised by Western English-speaking translators of Mark, might there be nuances of idolatry or worship or supernatural activity that are likewise being glossed over in Western translation or interpretation of the Bible? Whereas interpretations arising in settings of secular learning in the West might shy away from the significance of the divine, and rather suggest the totalising influence of social, political, or other factors, might ordinary Indonesian readers offer a distinctive voice at ease with spiritual or divine influence?

---

11. Cochrane, "Christian Governor in Indonesia."
12. Ramage, *Politics in Indonesia*, ix.

Conclusion

We have seen that contextual biblical interpretation aims to pay attention to features of the reader's context. This is one part of a larger hermeneutical package, and, theologically speaking, it respects the fact that God has gifted all people with particularity of place and time. I have suggested that two features of the present time in Indonesia are a culture of patient respect and a culture of awareness of the reality of the supernatural. The pressure for Asian voices to become either de-localized or Western-palatable in order to participate in academic discussion of the Bible may turn out to be a significant problem. In a post-Babel, post-Pentecost world, we have the opportunity to learn from a rich global assortment of voices as we pay attention to Scripture. Genuinely Indonesian voices must be among them.

Bibliography

Alonso, Pablo. *The Woman Who Changed Jesus: Crossing Boundaries in Mk 7,24–30.* BTS 11. Leuven: Peeters, 2011.

Anjaiah, Veeramalla. "Asia on Top, Indonesia Lowest in Beer Consumption." Food (blog), Thejarkatapost.com, February 5, 2018, http://www.thejakartapost.com/life/2018/02/05/asia-on-top-indonesia-lowest-in-beer-consumption.html.

Banawiratma, J. B., and J. Müller. "Contextual Social Theology: An Indonesian Model." *EAPR* 36 (1999) 1–249.

Cadwallader, Alan H. "Dog-throttling: Nineteenth Century Dogmatic/Cultural Constructions of the Syrophoenician Woman." In *Hermeneutics and the Authority of Scripture*, edited by Alan H. Cadwallader, 97–124. Adelaide: Australian Theological Forum, 2011.

Cochrane, Joe. "Christian Governor in Indonesia Found Guilty of Blasphemy against Islam." *World* (blog), *NYtimes.com,* May 9, 2017, https://www.nytimes.com/2017/05/09/world/asia/indonesia-governor-ahok-basuki-tjahaja-purnama-blasphemy-islam.html.

Countryman, L. William. "How Many Baskets Full? Mark 8:14–21 and the Value of Miracles in Mark." *CBQ* 47 (1985) 643–55.

Ha, Francis Inki. "Shame in Asian and Western Cultures." *ABS* 38 (1995) 1114–31.

Intan, Benyamin Fleming. *"Public Religion" and the Pancasila-Based State of Indonesia.* New York: Lang, 2006.

Kim, Yung Suk. *1 and 2 Corinthians.* Texts @ Contexts. Minneapolis: Fortress, 2013.

Lindquist, Johan. "Veils and Ecstasy: Negotiating Shame in the Indonesian Borderlands." *Ethnos* 69 (2004) 487–508.

Malcolm, Matthew R. *From Hermeneutics to Exegesis: The Trajectory of Biblical Interpretation.* Nashville: B&H Academic, 2018.

Novera, Isvet Amri. "Indonesian Postgraduate Students Studying in Australia: An Examination of Their Academic, Social and Cultural Experiences." *IEJ* 5 (2004) 475–87.

Piper, John. "Biblical Exegesis: Discovering the Meaning of Scriptural Texts." http://cdn.desiringgod.org/pdf/booklets/BTBX.pdf.
Ramage, Douglas E. *Politics in Indonesia: Democracy, Islam, and the Ideology of Tolerance*. Papers on Southeast Asian Subjects 7. London: Routledge, 1995.
Singgih, Emanuel Gerrit. "Let Me not Be Put to Shame: Towards an Indonesian Hermeneutics." *AJT* 9 (1995) 71–85.
Smith, Mitzi J. "Introduction." In *I Found God in Me: A Womanist Biblical Hermeneutics Reader*, edited by Mitzi J. Smith, 1–16. Eugene, OR: Cascade Books, 2015.
Van den Eynde, S. "When a Teacher Becomes a Student: The Challenge of the Syrophoenician Woman (Mark 7.24–31)." *Theology* 103 (2000) 274–79.

4

The Servant and the Jubilee in Matthew's Gospel

Matthew's Christological Reading of Isaiah

DAEHOON KANG

Introduction

AFTER NARRATING THE STORY of Jesus' healing of Peter's mother-in-law, Matthew cites Isa 53:4 and comments, "This was to fulfill what was spoken by the prophet Isaiah: 'He took our illnesses and bore our diseases'" (Matt 8:17).[1] Responding to John's question, "Are you the one who is to come, or shall we look for another?" (Matt 11:3), Jesus responds to John's disciples, "Go and tell John what you hear and see: the blind receive their sight and the lame walk, lepers are cleansed and the deaf hear, and the dead are raised up, and the poor have good news preached to them. And blessed is the one who is not offended by me" (Matt 11:4–6). Here, Jesus is quoting from Isa 35:4–6; 61:1. In this study, I will make three exegetical observations, based on my intratextual reading of the Book of Isaiah and the Gospel of Matthew, and my intertextual reading of the two books—Matthew's use of Isaiah.[2] First, Matthew identifies Jesus with the Suffering Servant in the fourth Servant

---

1. I will be using the ESV as my primary translation, unless otherwise noted.

2. The term "intratexuality" refers to the relationship between a passage and the later passages that refer to it in the same text. The term "intertextuality" refers to the relationship between one passage in a text and those passages in later texts, which quote or allude to or echo the pretext, for various literary purposes.

Song (Isa 52:13—53:12) in Deutero-Isaiah (Matt 8:17; Isa 53:4).[3] Second, Matthew extends Jesus' healing ministry to his disciples (Matt 10:1–42), following the pattern within the Book of Isaiah, as the work of the Suffering Servant in the Deutero-Isaiah is extended to the servants (Isa 65:8–9). Third, Matthew portrays Jesus' healing ministry in the light of the Jubilee (Matt 11:5). After discussing these points, I will reflect on some theological implications of this study for Korean Protestant churches today.

Jesus as the Suffering Servant (Matt 8:17)

Matt 8:1—9:38 has three sets of miracle stories (Matt 8:1–15; 8:23—9:8; 9:18–34). There are three general themes in Matt 8:1—9:38: (1) Christology (Matt 8:1–17); (2) discipleship (Matt 8:18—9:13); (3) the experience of the kingdom of heaven through the Son of David (Matt 9:14–34). In Matt 8:17, Matthew identifies Jesus with the Suffering Servant in Isa 53:4 and sees the fulfillment of Isa 53:4 in Jesus' healing ministry. Scholars have debated whether or not Matthew identifies Jesus with the Suffering Servant in Isa 53:4 in Matt 8:17. For instance, Ulrich Luz comments:

> The formula quotation has often been overinterpreted. Given the context that speaks of the sovereign authority of Jesus the healer, ἔλαβεν and ἐβάστασεν can only mean "to take away" and "to carry away"... There is, therefore, in the Matthean context no talk of the suffering of the servant of God. In contrast to 12:18–21, the word παῖς θεοῦ ("servant of God") does not appear here. Precisely that part of Isa 53:3–5 is used here that does not speak of the suffering of God's servant. Our quotation is an example of the way early Christian exegesis, like the Jewish exegesis of the time, sometimes quotes individual words of scripture without any regard for their context.[4]

While W. D. Davies and Dale C. Allison are open to the possibility that Matthew "understood the healing ministry to be a type of Jesus' redemptive suffering; or may be the association between sin and the distasteful reality of disease was so intimate (John 9.2) that the healing of sickness could be

---

3. It goes beyond the scope of this study to discuss the division of the Book of Isaiah. Regardless of the historical origin(s) of the Deutero-Isaiah (Isa 40–55) and the Trito-Isaiah (Isa 56–66), I see substantial theological coherence between them.

4. Luz, *Matthew 8–20*, 14; Matthew uses the verb βαστάζω in Matt 3:11 in which John the Baptist describes his role as a slave who unties and carries out sandals, which suggests that, in Matt 8:17, Jesus did not simply remove our illnesses and our diseases but he himself "took our illnesses and bore our diseases." Likewise, in Matt 20:12, the workers in the vineyard themselves bear the burden and heat of the day.

conceived of as a taking away of sins," they note, "the lengthy debate on this issue has been inconclusive."[5] I support the common view that Matthew identifies Jesus with the Suffering Servant in Isa 52:13—53:12 in Matt 8:17 for the following three considerations.[6]

First, Matthew's more literal translation of Isa 53:4 than the LXX suggests that he is not citing Isa 53:4 as a proof text, isolated from its literary and theological context (Isa 52:13—53:12). Here are the texts of Isa 53:4 in the MT, the LXX, and Matt 8:17:

Isa 53:4 MT אכן חלינו הוא נשא ומכאבינו סבלם

("Surely he has borne our griefs and carried our sorrows"; ESV)

Isa 53:4 LXX οὗτος τὰς ἁμαρτίας ἡμῶν φέρει καὶ περὶ ἡμῶν ὀδυνᾶται

("This one bears our sins and suffers pain for us"; NETS)

Matt 8:17 αὐτὸς τὰς ἀσθενείας ἡμῶν ἔλαβεν καὶ τὰς νόσους ἐβάστασεν

("He took our illnesses and bore our diseases"; ESV)

Craig L. Blomberg makes a general comment about Matthew's use of the Scriptures, "On many occasions Matthew does as well [use the LXX], particularly when he is largely following his sources—Mark and Q. But at least as frequently he goes his separate way at key junctures, reflecting a more literal translation from the Hebrew text or adopting a Hebrew or Aramaic variant that had developed in Jewish tradition."[7] Maarten J. J. Menken observes that Matthew's citation of Isa 53:4 in Matt 8:17 "differs considerably from the LXX" and suggests that "either the evangelist himself translated from the Hebrew, or he used an existing tradition."[8] Menken notes, "Within the context of Isa 52:13—53:12, the Hebrew verb [נשא] means 'to bear, to take upon oneself' (see also Isa. 53:12); as the Greek verb λαμβάνειν may well have more or less the same meaning (see, e.g., Pindar, *Pythian Odes* 2.93: λαμβάνειν ζυγόν; Matt. 10:38: λαμβάνειν στραυρόν), it is within the Isaian context an adequate translation."[9] Menken also points out, "The verb סבל qal means 'to

---

5. Davies and Allison, *Gospel according to Saint Matthew*, 2:38.

6. E.g., Wilson, *Healing in Gospel of Matthew*, 81–93; Osborne, *Matthew*, 299–300; France, *Gospel of Matthew*, 321–23; Stuhlmacher, "Isaiah 53 in Gospels and Acts," 157; Beaton, "Isaiah in Matthew's Gospel," 70; Betz, "Jesus and Isaiah 53," 81; Hagner, *Matthew 1–13*, 210–11; Harrington, *Gospel of Matthew*, 115; Gundry, *Matthew*, 150; Albright and Mann, *Matthew*, 94.

7. Blomberg, "Matthew," 2.

8. Menken, "Source of Quotation," 314–15.

9. Menken, "Source of Quotation," 317–18.

bear, to carry'; can have the same meaning, and βαστάζειν is thus an adequate translation."[10] Luz's comment that, since there is no mention of the suffering of God's Servant in Isa 53:3–5, Matthew does not have the Suffering Servant in mind in Matt 8:17 is unconvincing. As I will discuss shortly, Matthew identifies Jesus with the Servant of the LORD in the Deutero-Isaiah in Matt 12:18–21 (Isa 40:1–4) and Matt 20:28 (Isa 53:12). It is difficult to think that Matthew has not yet identified Jesus with the Servant of the LORD in Matt 8:17 but, all of sudden, he does in Matt 12:18–21. As we will see in this study, Matthew closely follows the themes of the Servant of the LORD, the servants, and the eschatological Jubilee in the Book of Isaiah, and incorporates them into his Christology, eschatology, and ecclesiology.

While Matthew uses the words ἀσθένεια and νόσος in reference to Jesus' physical healing of Peter's mother-in-law in Matt 8:14–17, Matthew does not go beyond the literary context of Isa 52:13—53:12, for Isa 53:5 specifically mentions, "with his wounds we are healed." Both the Hebrew verb רפא in the MT and the Greek verb ἰάομαι in the LXX frequently refer to physical healing. Many scholars make similar observations. For example, Peter Stuhlmacher points out, "Matthew's summary of Jesus' healing ministry in Matthew 8:16 is expanded by the Evangelist in 8:17 by a retrospective citation of Isaiah 53:4. Matthew presupposes the Hebrew text of this passage; even Jesus' messianic healings should be understood as the work of the Servant."[11] Otto Betz suggests, "Matthew certainly knew the spiritual meaning of Isaiah 53:4: Bearing and taking away our sicknesses actually refers to the vicarious suffering of the Servant because of our sins."[12] Davies and Allison note, "[Jesus'] portion is with lepers and demoniacs, and he identifies himself with humanity in its suffering."[13] R. T. France comments, "It thus seems that for Matthew the figure of the Servant of Yahweh in Isaiah, which other early Christians looked to only for an explanation of Jesus' suffering and death, was a more holistic model for Jesus' ministry as a whole."[14]

Second, Matthew cites Isa 42:1–4 in Matt 12:18–21, in which he identifies Jesus with the Servant of the LORD in the first Servant Song

---

10. Menken, "Source of Quotation," 319.

11. Stuhlmacher, "Isaiah 53 in Gospels and Acts," 157; Gundry similarly notes, "Some think that Isaiah spoke only figuratively in 53:4; i.e., sickness and pains there stand for sins. Along with forgiveness of sins, however, physical well-being was thought to characterize the messianic age (Isa 29:18; 32:3–4; 35:5–6). We therefore do well to follow Matthew's literalism"; Gundry, *Matthew*, 150.

12. Betz, "Jesus and Isaiah 53," 81.

13. Davies and Allison, *Gospel according to Saint Matthew*, 38.

14. France, *Gospel of Matthew*, 322.

in the Deutero-Isaiah.[15] The fact that Matthew cites Isa 42:1–4 in Matt 12:18–21 immediately after he mentions the Pharisees' plot to kill Jesus and his continuing healing ministry supports the contention that Matthew identifies Jesus with the Servant of the LORD in the Deutero-Isaiah. The Pharisees' plot to kill Jesus because of his healing ministry (Matt 12:1–3) echoes the death of the Suffering Servant in Isa 52:13—53:12. Matthew cites Isa 42:1–4 in Matt 12:18–21 and interprets Jesus' healing on the Sabbath (Matt 12:1–13) and its aftermath (Matt 12:14–16). Matt 12:18a reminds the readers of the heavenly voice at Jesus' baptism (Matt 3:17; Isa 42:1a). The Servant's purpose to bring forth justice to the nations (Isa 42:1) is the background of the purpose of Jesus' ministry.[16] Jesus is the chosen and sent Servant as the hope of all nations (Matt 12:21; 28:19–20) in order to establish justice and righteousness through his obedience to God's redemptive will. If Matthew identifies Jesus with the Servant of the LORD in the Deutero-Isaiah in Matt 12:18–21, Matthew must have made that identification already in Matt 8:14–17.

Third, Matthew 20:20–28 follows Mark 10:35–45, in which Matthew alludes to Isa 53:11–12 and identifies Jesus with the Suffering Servant in Isa 53:11–12. Matthew's allusion to Isa 53:11–12 in Matt 20:28 is identical to Mark's citation of Isa 53:11–12 in Mark 10:45. Mark paraphrases Isa 53:11–12 in the second half of Mark 10:45—"[the Son of Man came] to give his life as a ransom for many (δοῦναι τὴν ψυχὴν αὐτοῦ λύτρον ἀντὶ πολλῶν)." Morna D. Hooker expresses her doubt about the common view that Mark identifies Jesus with the Suffering Servant in Mark 10:45, based on her linguistic observation:

> There is, however, not the slightest evidence to show that these two terms [λύτρον in Mark 10:45 and אשם in Isa 53:10] were ever connected: the λύτρον, as we have seen, was the redemption of a person or thing by purchase; the אשם was the repayment of something wrongfully withheld, together with a guilt-offering by means of expiation: the one is a business transaction; the other involves a sacrifice for sin. Some scholars have stressed the substitutionary element implied by the word ἀντί in Mark 10:45.

---

15. Similarly, Osborne, *Matthew*, 465–66; France, *Gospel of Matthew*, 470–71; Harrington, *Gospel of Matthew*, 180–81; Davies and Allison comment on Matt 12:18–21, "Matthew has evidently latched on to Isa 42.1–4 because it serves so remarkably to illustrate the nature of Jesus' ministry in Israel. Jesus is the unobtrusive servant of the Lord"; Davies and Allison, *Gospel according to Saint Matthew*, 2:324; Gundry, *Matthew*, 229–30; Hagner, *Matthew 1–13*, 338–39.

16. Beaton comments on Matt 12:18b, 20b, "Here κρίσις would then be interpreted as the liberation of the oppressed and the renewal of the burdened"; Beaton, *Isaiah's Christ in Matthew's Gospel*, 157.

The אשם, however, was never a substitute: it was payment, together with compensation and a guilt-offering.[17]

As Yongbom Lee notes, "As Hooker observes, אשם in the Hebrew Scripture stands for 'guilt-offering' and is distinct from the concept of λύτρον. Hooker, however, does not make much out of the fact that the LXX translates נפשו אשם אם־תשים (literally, 'if you [singular] lay down his life as a guilt-offering') as ἐὰν δῶτε περὶ ἁμαρτίας (literally, 'if ever you [plural] give [his life an offering] for sin'), which demonstrates the translator's interpretive freedom."[18] In her more recent publication, Hooker points out:

> This redemption of his people is now to be fulfilled, according to Mark 10:45, by the Son of Man surrendering his own life as a "ransom." Isa 53:10–11, however, contains a different idea. This passage speaks of God's Servant being made a "guilt offering," which involved making restitution to the injured party and offering a sacrifice as a means of expiation. This is a very different image [from that in Mark 10:45], and it is taken over in the LXX version, which translates that term [אשם] by the phrase "for sin."[19]

As Lee notes, "The phrase περὶ ἁμαρτίας in Isa 53:10 does not simply 'take over' אשם ('guilt-offering') but reflects an interpretative move that associates אשם with the imagery of תאטה ('sin/purification offering') related to the Day of Atonement."[20] While there is no "ransom" idea in Isa 52:13—53:12, it is present in Isa 43:1–13. Lee identifies a conceptual similarity between

---

17. Hooker, *Jesus and the Servant*, 77. As Collins points out, the term λύτρον (both in the singular and the plural) occur in the LXX (Ex 21:29; 30:11–16; Num 35:31–34; Lev 19:20; 25:24, 51–52; 27:31; Prov 6:35, 13:8; Isa 45:13); Collins, *Mark*, 500–502; Num 3:12 ("I hereby accept the Levites from among the Israelites as *substitutes* [λύτρα] for all the firstborn that open the womb among the Israelites. The Levites shall be mine").

18. Lee, *Son of Man as Last Adam*, 137.

19. Hooker, "Isaiah in Mark's Gospel," 48.

20. Targum Isaiah 53:10 ("Yet *before* the LORD *it was a pleasure to refine and to cleanse the remnant of his people, in order to purify their* soul *from sins* [נפשהון מחובין ולנקאה]; *they* shall see *the kingdom of their Messiah, they shall increase sons and daughters, they* shall prolong days; *those who perform the law of* the LORD *shall prosper in his pleasure* [the innovative wording of the Targum in italics]"; Chilton, *Isaiah Targum*, 104–5). Milgrom challenged the consensus interpretation of as חטאת "sin offering" and argued for "purification offering"; Milgrom, "Sin-Offering or Purification-Offering?" 237–39. It goes beyond the scope of this study to determine the precise meaning of חטאת. What is important for our discussion is the fact that the LXX translator brings in the imagery of חטאת in translating אשם in Isa 53:10.

Mark 10:45 and Isa 43:3–4, and multiple verbal parallels Mark 10:45 and Isa 53:11–12 LXX, which he visualizes in the following table:[21]

Isa 53:11–12 [LXX]	Mark 10:45
δίκαιον εὖ δουλεύοντα πολλοῖς ("[the] righteous one who serves many well"[22])	διακονῆσαι ("to serve")
ἀνθ' ὧν παρεδόθη εἰς θάνατον ἡ ψυχὴ αὐτοῦ ("because his soul was given over to death" [NETS].)	δοῦναι τὴν ψυχὴν αὐτοῦ ("to give his life") Mark 10:33 παραδοθήσεται ("will be handed over")
Isa 43:3–4 λύτρον ("ransom")	λύτρον ("ransom")
Αὐτὸς ἁμαρτίας πολλῶν ἀνήνεγκεν ("he bore the sins of many" [NETS].) διὰ τὰς ἁμαρτίας αὐτῶν παρεδόθη ("because of their sins he was given over" [NETS].)	ἀντὶ πολλῶν ("for many") Mark 10:33 παραδοθήσεται ("will be handed over")

As Matthew follows Mark 10:35–45 in Matt 20:20–28, he could not have missed Jesus' identification with the Suffering Servant in Isa 53:11–12, evident in his own literary source.

Jesus, the Servant of the Lord, and the Servants (Matt 10:1–42)

In this section, at first, I will explore the intratextual connections between the Servant of the Lord in the four Servant Songs in the Deutero-Isaiah (Isa 40–55) and the servants in the Trito-Isaiah (Isa 55–66) and argue that the anointed one in Isa 61:1–3 continues the work of the Servant of the Lord and extends his work to other servants. Then, I will show how Matthew identifies Jesus as the Suffering Servant of the Lord in the Deutero-Isaiah and the anointed one (Isa 61:1–3) and extends Jesus' healing ministry to his disciples in Matt 10:1–42.

---

21. Lee, *Son of Man as Last Adam*, 139.

22. Lee's literal translation; NETS translation "a righteous one who is well subject to many" does not reflect the active voice of the participle δουλεύοντα in Isa 53:11 [LXX].

The Servant of the LORD and the Servants in Isaiah

In the Deutero-Isaiah, the identity of the Servant of Yahweh (עבדי יהוה; παῖς/ δοῦλος κυρίου) is multifaceted. John D. W. Watts lists five possible referents for the Servant of Yahweh in the Deutero-Isaiah: (1) Israel; (2) Cyrus; (3) the city of Jerusalem; (4) the prophet himself; (5) an unnamed individual leader.[23] It goes beyond the scope of this study to discuss in detail the multidimensional identity of the Servant of Yahweh in the Deutero-Isaiah. The precise identity of the anointed one (Isa 61:1–3) is equally unclear in its literary context. Some scholars argue that the anointed one is the prophet Isaiah himself.[24] Others consider the speaker as the offspring of the Servant of the LORD in the Servant Songs.[25] As John N. Oswalt notes, Isa 61 and the Servant Songs in the Deutero-Isaiah have not only "some verbal similarities"—e.g., "Spirit" in Isa 42:1; the first person address in Isa 49:1–3; 50:4–6; "opening" in Isa 42:7; "prisoners" in Isa 49:9)—but also "general tone and function."[26] Others identify the speaker with a royal messianic figure.[27] In the Old Testament, kings were anointed, as they were appointed as kings (1 Sam 10:1; 16:12–13; 2 Sam 2:4; 1 Kgs 1:39; 2 Kgs 11:12; 23:30). J. S. Bergsma argues:

> There are good reasons to view this speaker—the "servant"— as a royal figure. Although prophets (1 Kgs 19:16) and priests (Exod 28:41; 29:7; 40:13–15; Num 35:25; etc.) were anointed in earlier Scriptures, anointing was most often associated with the office of the king. Other elements of the text also point to royal status: as was seen above (chapter 3), the "proclamation of liberty" to the citizens of a nation (vv. 1f–2b) was typical of ancient Near Eastern monarchs in their accession year; and the "binding up" of the broken hearted (v. 1d) is an image taken

---

23. Watts, *Isaiah 34–66*, 652–59.

24. E.g., Westermann, *Isaiah Prophetic Oracles of Salvation*, 188; Juel, *Messianic Exegesis*, 9. According to Hugenberger, the theme of rejection in the Servant Songs was a common experience of many of the prophets like Isaiah himself (Isa 6:10) and other prophets (Ezek 4:4–6; Jer 11:19), and the endowment of the servant in Isa 42:1 is consistent with a prophetic identification (Isa 61:1; Num 11:25–26; Neh 9:30; Zech 7:12); Hugenberger, "The Servant of the Lord in the 'Servant Songs' of Isaiah," 112.

25. E.g., Beuken, "Servant and Herald of Good Things," 438–40; Childs, *Isaiah*, 503; Gregory, "Postexilic Exile in Third Isaiah," 481.

26. Oswalt, *Book of Isaiah*, 562.

27. E.g., Sweeney, "Reconceptualization of Davidic Covenant," 55–56; Koole, *Isaiah III*, 270; Oswalt, *Book of Isaiah 40–66*, 563; Bergsma, *Jubilee from Leviticus to Qumran*, 199–200; Kruger, "Isaiah 61:1–3(4–9) 10–11," 1564; Walton, "Imagery of Substitute King Ritual," 734–43.

from the ubiquitous king-as-shepherd metaphor (Ezek 34:4). Thus, while the idea of anointing does bear overtones of prophetic and priestly status as well, its primary force should be seen as denoting royal office.[28]

John H. Walton observes many verbal parallels in Isaiah and concludes, "the Servant is to be identified as an ideal royal figure to whom messianic-like expectations were connected and who suffered and/or died because of the sins of the people"[29]

I do not intend to attempt to solve the mystery of the identity of the Servant of the LORD or the anointed one within the historical and literary context of the Book of Isaiah. That would be beyond both my expertise and the scope of this study. My goal in this chapter is limited to explore (1) various intratextual links between the Servant of the LORD and the servants within the Book of Isaiah itself, (2) Matthew's perception of Jesus as the Servant of the LORD and the anointed one in Isa 60:1 in his Gospel, and (3) Matthew's extension of Jesus' healing ministry to his disciples (Matt 10:1–42). Therefore, it seems sufficient for me to start from Willem A. M. Beuken's view that the speaker in the first person in Isa 61 identifies himself as a successor to the Servant in Isa 40–55, with "the coordinating themes of being moved by God's Spirit, good tidings and consolation, and ultimately the ascent of a righteous progeny."[30] Although Isa 61:1–3 does not mention rejection or suffering, the anointed one (Isa 61:1–3) incorporates the core features of the Servant of the LORD in the four Servant Songs in the four considerations. First, Isa 61:1 ("The Spirit of the LORD God is upon me") alludes to Isa 42:1 ("My Spirit is upon him") and Isa 48:16 ("And now the Lord GOD has sent me, and his Spirit"). Second, the speaker speaks in the first person in Isa 49:1–3; 50:4–6; 61:1–3. Third, the release of prisoners in Isa 61:1 echoes to Isa 40:9; 42:1, 7; 49:2, 9; 50:4–9; 52:13—53:12. Fourth, the terms "offspring" and "righteousness" (Isa 61:3, 9, 10) allude to Isa 53:10–11.

In the Book of Isaiah, the Servant of the LORD in the Deutero-Isaiah is closely associated with the "servants" (עבדים/δοῦλοι) in Isa 56:6; 63:17; 65:8, 9, 13, 14, 15; 66:14. As Beuken surveys:

---

28. Bergsma, *Jubilee from Leviticus to Qumran*, 200.

29. E.g., "Spirit upon him" (Isa 11:2; 42:1; 61:1); "[he] will bring justice" (11:3–4; 42:1; 61:1–3); "impact on the nations" (11:10; 42:6; 49:6; 61:9–11; 62:1–2); "[he] set prisoner free" (42:7; 61:1); "[he] has message" (49:2; 50:4; 61:1); "reward with him" (49:4; 62:11); "[he] will bring splendor to Israel" (11:10; 49:5–6; 61:3; 62:3); "[he] will restore Israel" (11:11–12; 49:5–6; 61:3–4).

30. Beuken, "Servant and Herald of Good Tidings," 438–40; similarly, Blenkinsopp, *Isaiah 56–66*, 221; Oswalt, *Book of Isaiah 40–66*, 562–63.

While DI only speaks of "the Servant (of YHWH)" (singular), TI only speaks of "the servants (of YHWH)" (plural), but on the understanding that the first mention of the notion in the plural comes precisely *before* the end of DI (54.17). In this way, the reader learns, still within the compass of DI, in which form this cardinal theme will be continued. This connection is not fortuitous. In the last text involving the Servant, he is promised that "he shall see offspring" (53.10), but when and how this will happen remains open. To this the first text about "the servants of YHWH" gives a provisional answer. The city addressed in ch. 54 learns that its children will live as the servants of YHWH on their own heritage (54.17: "This is the heritage of the servants of YHWH and their righteousness from Me"). And so DI leaves the reader with a hint who these servants of YHWH are and what their heritage is like. If we readers want to understand properly how this question is elaborated by TI, then we should also pay attention to two important accompanying notions, which already in DI belong to the semantic field of "the Servant," namely "the offspring, seed" (*zerāʿ*) and "righteous(ness)" (*ṣaddîq, ṣᵉdāqâ, ṣedeq*). The first notion, "the seed," has occasioned the turning of "the Servant" to "the servants" by taking a turn itself in 53.10. Before the fourth Servant Song, Israel is addressed as "the seed" of the patriarchs (Abraham: 41.8, 51.2; Jacob-Israel: 45.19), which will itself have offspring (43.5, 44.3, 49.19), but from 53.10 on the promise of posterity regards the Servant and the new city (54.3). The second notion, "righteous(ness)," occurs connected in a remarkable way with "the seed" (45.25: "In YHWH shall all the offspring of Israel find righteousness and boast"; 48.18f.: "Your righteousness would be like the waves of the sea and your offspring like the sand"), but also with "the Servant" and "the servants." For according to DI, God guarantees that the Servant will excel in "righteousness" and will transfer it to those who belong to him, so that "righteousness" will also become the essence of their life (53.11, 54.17).[31]

Isa 58:8 ("Then shall your light break forth like the dawn") reminds the readers of the Servant in Isa 42:6 ("a light for the nations") and Isa 49:6 ("I will make you as a light for the nations, that my salvation may reach to the end of the earth"). In Isa 60:1—63:6, the promise given to the Servant of the LORD comes true through the servants. Isa 60:1 writes, "Arise, shine, for your light has come, and the glory of the LORD has risen upon you." Isa 60:3 states, "And nations shall come to your light, and kings to the brightness of your rising."

---

31. Beuken, "Main Theme of Trito-Isaiah," 68.

Those who were once oppressed (Isa 61:1–3) become "the offspring of the blessed of the LORD" (Isa 65:23). As Michael A. Lyons observes, "Isaiah 54; 56–66 extends and develops earlier passages in Isaiah 40–55 to argue that Yahweh's righteous servant creates a community (the 'servants'/ 'offspring') who suffer righteously like him and are vindicated like him."[32] As A. T. Abernethy correctly concludes, due to the servant's mission, "a community of 'servants' (54:17; 56:6; 63:17; 65:8, 9, 13, 14, 15; 66:14) will arise to take up Israel's mission of bringing God's justice to the world (56:1; 58)."[33]

The servants follow the way of the Servant of the LORD. Suffering and rejection are the main themes of the four Servant Songs and a core characteristic of the Servant (Isa 42:4; 49:4, 7; 50:6–9; 53:3–12). The first Servant is humble and establishes justice on earth, caring for the weak (Isa 42:1–4). The second Servant suffers from carrying out his mission (Isa 49:4, 7). Like Jeremiah (Jer 11:19–21; 18:18; 20:10), the third Servant is grievously assaulted (Isa 50:4–6). The fourth Servant is humiliated vicariously for others (Isa 52:13—53:12). The suffering and vindication of the servants of the Trito-Isaiah evoke the earlier passages concerning the Suffering Servant (Isa 42:4; 49:4, 7; 50:6-9; 53:3-12). As Lyons sums up, "Isaiah 54; 56–66 extends and develops earlier passages in Isaiah 40–55 to argue that YHWH's righteous servant creates a community (the 'servants'/'offspring') who suffer righteously like him and are vindicated like him. The servant's role of being a 'light to the nations' (Isa 42:6; 49:6) is also passed on to the inhabitants of the restored Zion using the theme of 'light' (Isa 55:5; 60:1-22; 62:1-12)."[34] God promises, "Your people shall all be righteous; they shall possess the land forever, the branch of my planting, the work of my hands, that I might be glorified" (Isa 60:21; 57:1). The mission of the speaker in Isa 61:1–9 is to make his people righteous, which was the mission of the Suffering Servant (Isa 53:10–11). God's favor will be "oaks of righteousness" (Isa 61:3). Righteousness is depicted as the essence of the offspring of the Servant (Isa 62:1–2).

Jesus and His Disciples

Matthew extends Jesus' healing ministry to his disciples in Matt 10, which parallels the relationship between the Servant of the LORD in the Deutero-Isaiah and the servants in the Trito-Isaiah. Matt 9:35—10:4 deals with the purpose of mission (Matt 9:35–38) and Jesus' calling the Twelve

---

32. Lyons, "Psalm 22 and 'Servants' of Isaiah 54," 649.
33. Abernethy, *Book of Isaiah and God's Kingdom*, 156.
34. Lyons, "Psalm 22 and the 'Servants' of Isaiah 54," 649.

(Matt 10:1–4). Jesus has compassion for the crowds who are distressed and downcast "like sheep without a shepherd" (Matt 9:36). Jesus summons his twelve disciples for this restoration and gives them "authority over unclean spirits, to cast them out, and to heal every disease and every affliction" (Matt 10:1). The harvest of restoration echoes the eschatological Jubilee (Matt 11:5–6; Isa 29:18; 35:5; 61:1), which is fulfilled through Jesus' disciples' healing ministry (Matt 10:1–42), following Jesus' healing ministry (Matt 8:1—9:38). It is important to note that Jesus' authority (Matt 9:6, 8) is mentioned at the center of his healing activities (Matt 8:1—9:38), which is given to his disciples in the missionary discourse (Matt 10:1).[35] Jesus' authority in Matt 10:1 brings us back to his activity in Matt 8:16 (4:23; 9:35), which was followed by his identity as the Suffering Servant of the LORD (Matt 8:17). Matt 10:1–2a writes, "And he called to him his twelve disciples and gave them authority over unclean spirits, to cast them out, and to heal every disease and every affliction. The names of the twelve apostles are these." Matthew mentions the word μαθηταί ("disciples") in Matt 10:1 but calls the Twelve ἀπόστολοι ("apostles") in Matt 10:2, which also highlights the fact that Jesus' authority sends (ἀποστέλλω) his twelve disciples to a mission. To reject the one who is sent is, therefore, to reject the one who sends (Matt 10:11–15). F. H. Agnew notes, "It is the relationship between sender and sent, not the content of the commission given, that is primarily important. The šālîaḥ is entirely determined by this relationship, and it is in this respect only that he is empowered to act."[36] Matthew emphasizes that Jesus calls his disciples to join his healing and restoration ministry; in other words, Jesus's disciples' mission is an extension of Jesus' own mission. Jesus give his disciples detailed instruction concerning the lifestyle of his commissioned servants in Matt 10:5–15. They are to preach (Matt 10:7) and heal others (Matt 10:8), following his own example (Matt 3:2; 4:17; 9:35). Jesus extends his ministry to his disciples. They are to follow Jesus' humble lifestyle (Matt 10:9–10; 8:20).

Jesus forewarns his disciples of their future persecution because of him, as they continue Jesus' healing ministry in Matt 10:16–23. As Luz notes, "'Ἕνεκεν ἐμοῦ and εἰς μαρτύριον αὐτοῖς ('for my sake' and 'as a testimony to them') make clear that these persecutions came about only as the result of the proclamation."[37] The disciples' suffering verifies their authentic identity as the followers of Jesus (Matt 10:18b, 24–25, 17:22, 20:18, 19). As Davies and Allison notes:

---

35. Similarly, Davies and Allison, *Gospel according to Saint Matthew*, 2:116.
36. Agnew, "Origin of the NT Apostle-Concept," 81.
37. Luz, *Matthew 8–20*, 90.

That Matthew was conscious of these parallels is clear from two facts. The first is 10.25, which concludes our section: it is enough for the disciple to be like the master. This makes the imitation of Christ explicit. Equally telling is the arrangement of chapters 5–10. Before the apostles are told what to say and do (10), the narrative recounts what Jesus said (5–7) and did (8–9). Thus 5–9 is the hermeneutical key to 10.[38]

Matt 10:24–42 depicts the characteristics of discipleship, focusing on the conviction that the disciples are destined to suffer in proclaiming the kingdom of heaven and to be vindicated in the heavenly court. As France comments, "while they can never aspire to be *above* their teacher, they may hope one day to 'become like' him."[39] Luz correctly states that suffering is "the necessary consequence of the proclamation and the necessary form of discipleship" since suffering and persecution reflect the lifestyle of their Lord and master (Matt 10:24–25).[40]

In Matt 10:34–39, Jesus mentions the purpose and result of his coming, and uses several keywords here—"peace" (Matt 10:34, 13); "family" (Matt 10:36, 25); "worthy" (Matt 10:37–38, 10–13); "I have come" (Matt 10:34 [x2], 35); "whoever..." (Matt 10:37–39). Anyone who follows Jesus and proclaims the good news will be hated by others, and experience persecution, trials, family strife, and martyrdom (Matt 10:34–37). Only those who take the cross are worthy of their master (Matt 10:38–39). Matt 10:38 makes it clear that anyone who follows Jesus must suffer for his sake. Luz states, "All of chap. 10 also makes clear that existence in conformity with Jesus is a part of confessing (10:7–14, 17–22, 24–25, 38–39), that is, poverty, defenselessness, and suffering on behalf of Jesus."[41] John Nolland comments on Matt 10:37, "Though the point is made only indirectly, it now becomes clear how Jesus can say that he is responsible for the coming of the sword and of division in families: he insists on such a fierceness of loyalty to himself the significance of normal bonds and commitments, and specifically family ones, is undercut. The ties that bind are relativized in favour of a newly found, more fundamental tie."[42] In Matt 10:40–42, Jesus encourages his itinerant disciples by promising their vindication and reward. Matt 10:40 is closely connected with Matt 10:1–2 which emphasizes the terms, "authority" and "apostle." Matthew emphasizes that the life of the disciples who become like

38. Davies and Allison, *Gospel according to Saint Matthew*, 197.
39. France, *Gospel of Matthew*, 401.
40. Luz, *Matthew 8–20*, 115.
41. Luz, *Matthew 8–20*, 105.
42. Nolland, *Gospel of Matthew*, 441.

the least in the course of proclaiming the good news is the true confession and testimony for the world. In other words, Jesus calls his disciples not only to proclaim the good news of the kingdom of heaven but also live it out in their lives. As Jindřich Mánek observes, there is no difference between the term οἱ μικροί ("the little ones") in Matt 10:42 (18:6, 10, 14) and the term οἱ ἐλάχιστοι ("the least") of the judge's brothers in Matt 25:40.[43] The little ones, a title of honour for Jesus' true disciples, are identified with Christian messengers or missionaries who are in needs, to carry out the work that Jesus commissioned them.[44] To sum up, the main themes in Matt 10:5–42 have to do with suffering and persecution, which reflect the life of Jesus and his servants. The prophet Isaiah foresaw that the Servant of the LORD fulfills the eschatological Jubilee through his suffering and persecution and extends his work to the servants. In parallel, Matthew identifies Jesus as the Servant of the LORD (Matt 8:17) and portrays that Jesus fulfills the eschatological Jubilee through his healing ministry (Matt 8:1—9:38) and extends his healing and restoration ministry to his disciples (Matt 10:1–42).

Jesus' Healing Ministry in the Light of the Jubilee (Matt 11:5)

Matthew portrays Jesus' healing ministry in the light of the Jubilee (Matt 11:5), in parallel with Isaiah's depiction of the ministry of the Servant in Isa 61:1–4. Lev 25:8–55 describes in detail the legislation of the Jubilee and its basic requirements which include the release of slaves and returning properties to their original owners, because the land ultimately belongs to Yahweh and the Israelites are tenants (Lev 25:10). Every fiftieth year, each Israelite clan' property must be restored to its original owner. The fact that the year of the Jubilee was proclaimed by a sounding trumpet on the Day of Atonement (Lev 25:9) indicates that it centers around the removal of sin which, according to Walter C. Kaiser, "made possible the restored relationship between God and his people."[45] Margaret Barker notes:

43. Mánek writes, "Es besteht kein Unterschied zwischen μικροί und ἐλάχιστοι (vgl. Matt. 10:42, wo das Manuskript D ἐλάχιστος hat, wohingegen andere Manuskripte μικρός anführen. Lateinische Übersetzungen lesen: unus ex minimis istis)"; Mánek, "Mit wem identifiziert sich Jesus?," 22.

44. Similarly, Davies and Allison, *Gospel according to Saint Matthew,* 231; Mánek, "Mit wem identifiziert sich Jesus?" 25.

45. Kaiser, *Toward Old Testament Ethics,* 218. According to Barker, the Jubilee was a practical application of the atonement because the latter implies the restoration of the eternal covenant and the whole creation to the original state; Barker, "The Time Is Fulfilled," 24.

> The Jubilee, the Sabbath of Sabbaths, was proclaimed on the Day of Atonement (Lev. 25.9) and so the custom of the Jubilee must be understood in this context. Since atonement was itself a rite which restored the eternal covenant and enabled the whole creation, not just the community of Israel, to be restored to its original state, the Jubilee was a practical application of the atonement. *The key figure in the rite of atonement was the high priest who was the visible presence of the LORD on earth, and, just as the LORD had ordered the creation at the beginning, so he recreated it on the Day of Atonement at the New Year. The Jubilee recreated society by restoring people to their own land and by removing the burden of slavery and debt.*[46]

Bergsma similarly observes, "From the perspective of the canonical parameters of Leviticus, there is a certain correspondence between Lev 25 as the climax of the largely social regulations in chs. 17–25 ('Holiness Code') and Lev 16 as the climax of the largely cultic regulations in chs. 1–16 ("Priestly Code")."[47] Bradley C. Gregory notes argues that there are good reasons for "seeing an allusion to Leviticus 25 in the ministry of this Trito-Isaianic prophet." Gregory continues:

> First, the word דרור ["release"] in the sense of liberty is a rare word in the Hebrew Bible, appearing only in Leviticus 25, Jeremiah 34, Ezekiel 46, and here in Isaiah 61 . . . The allusion to Leviticus 25 is further strengthened when one considers the larger theological understanding of debt-slavery in Second Isaiah, where the exile is identified with debt-slavery into which Israel was placed because of her sins. "Proclaim to her that her service is completed, that her iniquity has been paid for, that she has received from the hand of YHWH double for all her sins" (Isa 40:2).[48]

In Ezek 40:1, Ezekiel connects the restoration of Israel with the Day of the Atonement and the legislation of the Jubilee (Ezek 46:17; Jer 34:8, 15, 17). As Bergsma notes, "This [Ezek 40] might be characterized as an 'eschatological' reinterpretation of the jubilee, in the sense that the jubilee is understood to be an image of Israel's final and ultimate state of existence. Ezek 46:16–18 assumes the jubilee will be observed in this 'final state,' and makes modifications of it to regulate the land transactions of the monarch."[49] The Jubilee

---

46. Barker, "The Time is Fulfilled," 24; Barker's italicization.
47. Bergsma, *Jubilee from Leviticus to Qumran*, 82.
48. Gregory, "The Postexilic Exile in Third Isaiah," 484.
49. Bergsma, *Jubilee from Leviticus to Qumran*, 203.

release is attested in Isa 49:7–9; 58:6; 61:1–3, which provide the most vivid description of the Jubilee outside of the Pentateuch. As Gregory observes, a series of infinitives in Isa 61:1–3 parallel the features of the year of the Jubilee in Lev 25, such as "proclaiming liberty to the captives," "releasing the prisoners," and "the arrival of the year of the Lord's favour."[50]

In Isa 61:1–3, the Jubilee is associated with the anointed one (משח). Bergsma calls Isa 61 "the first messianic re-interpretation of the Jubilee."[51] Lev 25:25–55 and Num 35:9–34 describe the role of a kinsman redeemer (גאל) in Israel. While Isa 61 does not attest this Hebrew word, the Deutero-Isaiah has portrayed Yahweh as Israel's redeemer in Isa 49:7–13; 52:7–10; 60:16; 62:12. The anointed one carries out the Jubilee release in Isa 61:1–2. As Yahweh comforts Israel (Isa 49:13; 52:9), the anointed one comforts all who mourn (Isa 61:2–3). Yahweh and the anointed one work together to execute the provisions of the Jubilee. The anointed one is equipped to take part in the role of Yahweh, since the Spirit of the Lord is upon him.

It is interesting to note that several Qumran documents such as 11Q13 (11QMelch); 4Q372 and 4Q390—and possibly, 4Q521—cite Isa 61 in association with the eschatological Jubilee. Bergsma notes that the Qumran community understood 490 years as a period of ten Jubilees and expected that in the tenth Jubilee a messianic figure would come to "establish spiritual and social justice for Israel."[52] 11Q13 reinterprets the Jubilee in Isa 61 as an eschatological event through which the righteous will be blessed and the wicked will be judged. 11Q13.2.4–7 writes:

> [Its inter]pretation for the last days refers to the captives, about whom he said: «To proclaim liberty to the captives.» And he will make their rebels prisoners [. . .] and of the inheritance of Melchizedek, for [. . .] and they are the inheri[tance of Melchi]zedek, who will make them return. He will proclaim liberty for them, to free them from [the debt] of all their iniquities. And this will [happen] in the first week of the jubilee which follows the ni[ne] jubilees.[53]

11Q13.2.6 cites Isa 61:1 here, as it describes and verifies the role of the eschatological Melchizedek, who is the messenger who brings the good news and is anointed by the sprit (11Q13.2.18), and who will comfort the afflicted and free those who "establish the covenant, those who avoid

---

50. Gregory, "Postexilic Exile in Third Isaiah," 483; *contra* Collins, "Herald of Good Tidings," 225–40.

51. Bergsma, *Jubilee from Leviticus to Qumran*, 202.

52. Bergsma, *Jubilee from Leviticus to Qumran*, 3.

53. In this study, I am using Martínez' English translation of the Dead Sea Scrolls.

walking [on the pa]th of the people" from the hand of Belial (11Q13.2.24). Timo Eskola points out that the messianic expectation in 11Q13 and 4Q521 indicates that the communities behind these texts held "restoration theology with the idea of a jubilee."[54]

Matthew links Jesus' healing ministry with the eschatological Jubilee (Matt 11:5), where he cites Isa 53:4–6; 61:1. Matthew sums up Jesus' healing ministry in Matt 8:1—9:38 in his citation of Isa 61:1 (Matt 11:5)—the lepers are cleansed (Matt 8:1–4); the lame walk (Matt 9:1–8); the dead are raised (Matt 9:18–26); the blind receive their sight (Matt 9:27–31); the deaf hear (Matt 9:32–34); the poor have the good news (Matt 9:35; 10:7). Matt 11:2 identifies this healing ministry with the works of Christ, the anointed one (Isa 61:1), who inaugurates the kingdom of God.[55] Matt 11:5 represents the fulfillment of the messianic expectation in Isaiah (Isa 26:19; 35:5–6; 61:1–2), which includes the concept of the eschatological Jubilee in Isa 61:1–3.

Theological Implications for Korean Protestant Churches Today

In the 1880s, the Gospel of Luke was translated into the Korean language and brought into the Korean peninsula for the first time in history. Many Koreans became Christian believers by reading the Bible on their own and planted the first Korean Protestant church, without direct help from Western missionaries. At the end of the nineteenth century, the Chosun (or, Joseon) Dynasty, the last Korean monarchy before the Japanese occupation of Korea, was threatened by China, Russia, and Japan. Japanese Empire occupied Korea from 1905–1945, annexing the nation in 1910. During these dark days of Korean national history, it is remarkable that there was a home-grown revival movement in Pyongyang in 1907, which was called "the Jerusalem of the East" at that time, similar to the first and the second Great Awakening movement in American church history. Thousands of people from many neighboring towns and villages gathered in Pyongyang and read the Bible together and repented of their sins and gave their lives to follow Jesus Christ. In midst of their national crisis, Koreans found hope for the restoration of their nation in the gospel of Jesus Christ. In contrast to many other former European colonies all around the world, in which Christianity was associated with the oppressors, for Koreans, Christianity became the spiritual force behind their fight for independence. The Bible

---

54. Eskola, *Narrative Theology of New Testament*, 119; similarly, Snodgrass, "Gospel of Jesus," 37.

55. Similarly, Leske, "Isaiah and Matthew," 154.

provided Koreans God's promise for liberty in the dark chapters of their modern history, including Japanese occupation (1905–1945), the Korean War (1950–1953), many national crises after the War, and the subsequent years under military dictatorships (1960s–1980s).

South Korea's industrialization and rapid economic growth in the 1970s and 1980s brought forth many new suburban areas, in which many churches were planted. Churches grew explosively in membership and influence. Many churches became what we call today "megachurches." Unfortunately, however, many Korean Protestant churches uncritically accepted Confucian culture and shamanism in their church polity, blindly worshipping gifted and charismatic preachers as the "servants" of the Lord. Many megachurch pastors became money and power hungry, with no accountability, and have left numerous tragic examples of what seems to be the opposite of Jesus' model of servant-leadership in the New Testament. Today, unfortunately, many South Koreans consider Protestant churches and church leaders corrupt. However, this is not a fair statement at all, because most Protestant church pastors make huge personal and familial sacrifices to faithfully serve their congregations. A few bad examples of corrupt and dishonest megachurch pastors should not be the stereotype of every Protestant pastor.

God has blessed South Korea incredibly in the past one hundred years. The nation that killed many western missionaries, calling them "white devils," now sends the most number of overseas missionaries to all around the world, after the United States. However, as we see Israel's history in the Hebrew Bible, unfortunately, it seems like Korean Protestant churches are slipping into the trap of worshipping the idols of this world (esp. materialism) and becoming self-sufficient, forgetting who God is and who they are in Christ. The so-called "prosperity gospel" is still popular in Korea, and is now influential in many parts of the world today. Some church leaders exhibit self-serving authoritarianism, rather than Christ-like servant leadership. In the year of the 500th anniversary of the Protestant Reformation, a tragic incident took place in a megachurch in South Korea. On November 12, 2017, Myung Sung Presbyterian Church, with more than 100,000 registered members, decided to proceed with hereditary pastoral succession—the Senior Pastor handing over the leadership of the church to his oldest son—which has been a serious issue in South Korean Protestant churches in the past decades. Most Koreans think that this decision of family succession was motivated by the Senior Pastor's desire to hold onto money and power, in complete contrast to the biblical teaching. Also, Rev. David Yong-gi Choi, one of the world's renown charismatic evangelists once, the emeritus Senior Pastor of Yoido Full Gospel Church—the largest church in the world with more than 480,000 members—was indicted and sentenced for corruption charges, misusing the church's finances. These powerful and charismatic leaders who abuse their authority and influence for their own benefits are not much different from Kim Jung Un, the "Dear Leader" of the Democratic People's Republic of Korea. Despite the explosive numerical growth in the 1970s and the 1980s, Korean Protestant churches still lack hermeneutical and spiritual maturity, and fail to holistically incorporate every aspect of Christian faith into their life as their living sacrifice to God (Rom 12:1–2).

In this study, I present an offering to Korean Protestant churches and pastors, reflecting on Matthew's portrayal of Jesus' healing and restoration ministry—the fulfillment of the eschatological Jubilee—who is the Servant of the LORD in the Deutero-Isaiah. As the servants in the Trito-Isaiah continues the work of the Servant of the LORD in the Deutero-Isaiah, Jesus calls his disciples to carry out his healing and restoration ministry. Now, a century after the Great Pyongyang Revival (1907), Korean Protestant churches desperately need a reformation, renewal, revival, and re-empowerment, by going back to the true teaching of the Bible (*sola scriptura*), just as the Reformers did five hundred years ago. Going back to the Scriptures means to rediscover who Jesus is and follow him in every area of one's life.

Conclusion

In this study, I discussed the intratextual connections between the Servant of the LORD in the Deutero-Isaiah and the servants in the Trito-Isaiah, and that between Jesus and his disciples in the Gospel of Matthew. I also discussed in detail Matthew's use of Isaiah in identifying Jesus with the Servant of the LORD in the Deutero-Isaiah and his disciples with the servants in the Trito-Isaiah. Such intertextuality suggests that Matthew does not use the Book of Isaiah as isolated proof texts here and there, but he has in mind the overall themes of the Book of Isaiah in their literary and theological contexts. I made three exegetical observations in Matthew's use of the Scriptures from the Book Isaiah. First, Matthew identifies Jesus with the Suffering Servant in the fourth Servant Song (Isa 52:13—53:12) in the Deutero-Isaiah (Matt 8:17; Isa 53:4). Second, Matthew extends Jesus' healing ministry to his disciples (Matt 10:1–42), as the Book of Isaiah itself extends the work of the Servant of the LORD to that of the servants (Isa 65:8–9). Third, Matthew portrays Jesus' healing ministry in the light of the Jubilee (Matt 11:5), in parallel with Isaiah's depiction of the ministry of the Servant in Isa 61:1–4. These exegetical observations have many important theological implications for Korean Protestant churches, as they face numerous challenges today.

Bibliography

Abernethy, A. T. *The Book of Isaiah and God's Kingdom: A Thematic-Theological Approach*. NSBT 40. Downers Grove, IL: InterVarsity Press, 2016.
Agnew, F. H. "The Origin of the NT Apostle-Concept: A Review of Research." *JBL* 105 (1986) 75–96.
Albright, W. F., and C. S. Mann. *Matthew*. AB 26. New York: Doubleday, 1971.
Barker, Margaret. "The Time is Fulfilled: Jesus and the Jubilees." *SJT* 53 (2000) 22–32.
Beaton, Richard. *Isaiah's Christ in Matthew's Gospel*. SNTSMS 123. Cambridge: Cambridge University Press, 2002.
———. "Isaiah in Matthew's Gospel." In *Isaiah in the New Testament*, edited by Steve Moyise and M. J. J. Menken, 63–78. NTSI. London: T. & T. Clark, 2005.
Bergsma, J. S. *The Jubilee from Leviticus to Qumran: A History of Interpretation*. VTSup 115. Leiden: Brill, 2007.
Betz, Otto. "Jesus and Isaiah 53." In *Jesus and the Suffering Servant: Isaiah 53 and Christian Origins*, edited by W. Bellinger and W. Farmer, 70–88. Eugene, OR: Wipf & Stock, 1998.
Beuken, Willem M. A. "Servant and Herald of Good Things: Isaiah 61 as an Interpretation of Isaiah 40–55." In *The Book of Isaiah: Les oracles et leurs relectures unite et complexite de l'ouvrage*, edited by J. Vermeylen, 411–42. BETL 81. Leuven: Leuven University Press, 1989.
———. "The Main Theme of Trito-Isaiah: 'The Servants of Yhwh.'" *JSOT* 47 (1990) 67–87.
Blenkinsopp, Joseph. *Isaiah 56–66*. AYB 56. New Haven: Yale University Press, 2003.
Blomberg, Craig L. "Matthew." In *CNTUOT*, 1–109.
Childs, Brevard S. *Isaiah: A Commentary*. OTL. Louisville: Westminster John Knox, 2001.
Chilton, Bruce D. *The Isaiah Targum: Introduction, Translation, Apparatus and Notes*. Aramaic Bible 11. Wilmington, DE: Glazier, 1987.
Collins, Adela Yarbro. *Mark: A Commentary*. Hermeneia. Minneapolis: Fortress, 2007.
Collins, John J. "A Herald of Good Tidings: Isaiah 61:1–3 and Its Actualization in the Dead Sea Scrolls." In *The Quest for Context and Meaning: Studies in Biblical Intertextuality in Honor of James A. Sanders*, edited by Craig Evans and Shemaryahu Talmon, 225–40. BibIntSer 28. Leiden: Brill, 1997.
Davies, W. D. and Dale C. Allison. *The Gospel according to Saint Matthew*. Vol. 2, *Commentary on Matthew VIII–XVIII*. ICC. London: T. & T. Clark, 1991.
Eskola, Timo. *A Narrative Theology of the New Testament: Exploring the Metanarrative of Exile and Restoration*. WUNT 350. Tübingen: Mohr/Siebeck, 2015.
France, R. T. *The Gospel of Matthew*. NICNT. Grand Rapids: Eerdmans, 2007.
Gregory, Bradley C. "The Postexilic Exile in Third Isaiah: Isaiah 61:1–3 in Light of Second Temple Hermeneutics." *JBL* 126 (2007) 475–96.
Gundry, Robert H. *Matthew: A Commentary on His Literary and Theological Art*. Grand Rapids: Eerdmans, 1982.
Hagner, Donald. A. *Matthew 1–13*. WBC 33A. Waco, TX: Word, 1993.
Harrington, D. J. *The Gospel of Matthew*. SP 1. Collegeville, MN: Liturgical, 1991.
Hooker, Morna D. "Isaiah in Mark's Gospel." In *Isaiah in the New Testament*, edited by Steve Moyise and Maarten J. J. Menken, 35–50. NTSI. London: T. & T. Clark, 2005.
———. *Jesus and the Servant*. London: SPCK, 1959.

Hugenberger, Gordon P. "The Servant of the Lord in the 'Servant Songs' of Isaiah: A Second Moses Figure." In *The Lord's Anointed: Interpretation of Old Testament Messianic Texts*, edited by P. E. Satterthwaite, R.S. Hess, and G. J. Wenham, 105–40. Grand Rapids: Baker, 1995.

Juel, Donald. *Messianic Exegesis: Christological Interpretation of the Old Testament in Early Christology*. Philadelphia: Fortress, 1988.

Kaiser, Walter C. *Toward Old Testament Ethics*. Grand Rapids: Zondervan, 1983.

Koole, Jan L. *Isaiah III: Isaiah Chapters 56–66*. Translated by Anthony Runia. Leuven: Peeters, 2001.

Kruger, H. A. J. "Isaiah 61:1–3(4–9) 10–11." *HTS* 58 (2002) 1555–76.

Lee, Yongbom. *The Son of Man as the Last Adam: The Early Church Tradition as a Source of Paul's Adam Christology*. Eugene, OR: Pickwick Publications, 2012.

Leske, A. "Isaiah and Matthew: The Prophetic Influence in the First Gospel: A Report on Current Research." In *Jesus and the Suffering Servant: Isaiah 53 and Christian Origins*, edited by W. H. Bellinger, Jr. and W. R. Farmer, 152–69. Harrisburg, PA: Trinity, 1998.

Luz, Ulich. *Matthew 8–20*. Translated by James E. Crouch. Hermeneia. Minneapolis: Fortress, 2001.

Lyons, Michael A. "Psalm 22 and the 'Servants' of Isaiah 54; 56–66." *CBQ* 77 (2015) 640–56.

Mánek, Jindřich. "Mit wem identifiziert sich Jesus? Eine exegetische Rekonstruktion ad Matt. 25:31–46." In *Christ and Spirit in the New Testament Studies: In Honour of Charles Fransis Digby Moule*, edited by Barnabas Lindars and Stephen S. Smalley, 15–25. Cambridge: Cambridge University Press, 1973.

Martínez, Florentino García. *The Dead Sea Scrolls Translated: The Qumran Texts in English*. Grand Rapids: Eerdmans, 1996.

Menken, Maarten J. J. "The Source of the Quotation from Isaiah 53:4 in Matthew 8:17." *NovT* 39 (1997) 313–27.

Milgrom, J. "Sin-Offering or Purification-Offering?" *VT* 21 (1971) 237–39.

Nolland, John. *The Gospel of Matthew*. NIGTC. Grand Rapids: Eerdmans, 2005.

Osborne, Grant R. *Matthew*. ZECNT 1. Grand Rapids: Zondervan, 2010.

Oswalt, John N. *The Book of Isaiah, Chapters 40–66*. NICOT. Grand Rapids: Eerdmans, 1998.

Snodgrass, Klyne. "The Gospel of Jesus." In *The Written Gospel*, edited by Markus Bockmuehl and Donald A. Hagner, 31–44. Cambridge: Cambridge University Press, 2005.

Stuhlmacher, Peter. "Isaiah 53 in the Gospels and Acts." In *The Suffering Servant: Isaiah 53 in Jewish and Christian Sources*, edited by Bernd Janowski and Peter Stuhlmacher, 147–62. Grand Rapids: Eerdmans, 2004.

Sweeney, Marvin A. "The Reconceptualization of the Davidic Covenant in Isaiah." In *Studies in the Book of Isaiah: Festschrift Willem A. M. Beuken*, edited by J. Van Ruiten and M. Vervenne, 41–61. BETL 132. Leuven: Leuven University Press, 1997.

Walton, John H. "The Imagery of the Substitute King Ritual in Isaiah's Fourth Servant Song." *JBL* 122 (2003) 734–43.

Watts, John D. W. *Isaiah 34–66*. WBC 25. Nashville: Nelson, 2005.

Westermann, Claus. *Isaiah Prophetic Oracles of Salvation in the Old Testament*. Translated by Keith Crim. Louisville: Westminster John Knox, 1991.

Wilson, Walter T. *Healing in the Gospel of Matthew: Reflections on Method and Ministry*. Minneapolis: Fortress, 2014.

5

Nomos in Paul and Philo

A Critique of N. T. Wright's Interpretation of Nomos in Paul's Letters

— YONGBOM LEE

Introduction

N. T. WRIGHT IN *Paul and His Recent Interpreters* (2015) sums up the major developments in Pauline theology from F. C. Baur to the present. Wright highlights the contributions of E. P. Sanders' *Paul and Palestinian Judaism* (1977) and the so-called "New Perspective on Paul," and he defends James D. G. Dunn's identification of the law as a boundary-marker for Jews, arguing:

> When Paul speaks of "the law," he is talking of the Jewish law, the Torah. We cannot, without ruining his arguments, make *nomos* into something universal. It is not a generalized "law," a moral code, a quasi-Kantian "categorical imperative," hanging in the sky over the whole human race, demanding moral obedience and making people feel vaguely guilty. Nor can *nomos* in Paul be flattened out into a generalized principle, as in some translations and many commentaries. It is the law which God gave through Moses to Israel. Part of the point of that law, the prized possession and covenant instrument of Israel in particular, was to keep Israel separate from the Gentiles... More significantly for the present discussion, I suspect that the negative reaction to Dunn's proposal has to do with a deep-seated western protestant reading of the whole question. From the sixteenth century onwards, many have taken it as axiomatic that God made

a "covenant of works" with the first humans: they should obey, and then they would have life. They disobeyed, of course, but God then gave the Torah, which was like the first covenant of works only (so to speak) more so. The human plight, and the divine solution to it, then appears like this: this law, as a general moral code, condemns us all, but Jesus has obeyed it in our place. Thus, to say that "the law" is not after all this general moral code has repercussions on the larger picture of salvation. That is why the issue has generated such heat. Make "the law" in Paul Israel-specific, and you shake a foundation of some branches of Reformed theology.[1]

Paul mentions the word νόμος 118 times in his seven "undisputed" letters.[2] In this study, I will carefully examine Wright's claim that, whenever Paul mentions the word νόμος, he always refers to the Law of Moses and translating the word νόμος in his writings as "a generalized 'law,' a moral code" is due to "a deep-seated western protestant reading." While Paul uses the word νόμος typically to refer to the Jewish Law, the Torah, as we will see in this study, there are important exceptions in Galatians (6:2) and Romans (2:14; 3:27; 7:23, 25; 8:2). At the end of this study, I will briefly introduce a passage from Philo (*On the Creation* 1–3) and highlight the parallel between Paul and Philo, in that, when using the word νόμος, both of them typically refer to the Jewish law, the Torah, however, they at times also refer to the universal law of nature for their rhetorical purposes.

Galatians

Paul mentions the word νόμος thirty-two times in Galatians. While Paul typically uses the word νόμος to refer to the Jewish Law, the Torah, Gal 6:2 is an exception. As Hans Dieter Betz comments, "The concept of ὁ νόμος τοῦ Χριστοῦ ('the law of Christ') is strange, since it occurs only here and seems to advocate what Paul had repeatedly rejected in his letter—that the Christian is obligated to do the Law. . . The problem—one of the most crucial

---

1. Wright, *Paul and His Recent Interpreters*, 94; Dunn, *New Perspective on Paul*, 99–140, 213–26, 339–46, 381–94, 413–28.

2. Rom 2:12 [x2], 13 [x2], 14 [x4], 15, 17, 18, 20, 23 [x2], 25 [x2], 26, 27 [x2]; 3:19 [x2], 20 [x2], 21 [x2], 27 [x2], 28, 31 [x2]; 4:13, 14, 15 [x2], 16; 5:1 [x2], 20; 6:14, 15; 7:1 [x2], 2 [x2], 3, 4, 5, 6, 7 [x3], 8, 9, 12, 14, 16, 21, 22, 23 [x3], 25 [x2]; 8:2 [x2], 3, 4, 7; 9:31 [x2]; 10:4, 5; 13:8, 10; 1 Cor 9:8, 9, 20 [x4]; 14:21, 34; 15:56; Gal 2:16 [x3], 19 [x2], 21; 3:2, 5, 10 [x2], 11, 12, 13, 17, 18, 19, 21 [x3], 23, 24; 4:4, 5, 21 [x2]; 5:3, 4, 14, 18, 23; 6:2, 13; Phil 3:5, 6, 9.

problems in the whole letter—is to explain this seeming contradiction."[3] Based on two facts—"(1) Paul has consistently rejected the idea that the Gentile Christians must accept circumcision and obey the Jewish Torah in order to become partakers in the divine salvation," and "(2) The Christian is now already made a partaker in divine salvation through the gift of the Spirit," Betz suggests that "Paul took over the notion from the opponents."[4] Douglas J. Moo identifies two general directions among the interpretations of this phrase ὁ νόμος τοῦ Χριστοῦ in his recent commentary:[5]

1. The law is the law of Moses, the Torah, as fulfilled by, or interpreted by, or focused on, Christ[6]
2. The law is a law distinct from the law of Moses, either

    a. the love command, singled out by Christ as the center of the law;[7]

    b. the ethical teaching of Christ in general (C. Dodd 1968 [134–48]);

    c. the example of Christ;[8]

    d. or some combination of these.[9]

---

3. Betz, *Galatians*, 299.

4. Betz, *Galatians*, 299–300.

5. Moo, *Galatians*, 376–77.

6. E.g., Chester, *Messiah and Exaltation*, 537–601; Ridderbos, *Paul*, 284–85; Barclay, *Obeying the Truth*, 126–41; Kertelge, "Gesetz und Fereiheit im Galaterbrief," 389–90; Schreiner, *Law and Its Fulfillment*, 158–59; Sanders, *Paul, Law, and Jewish People*, 97–98; Matera, *Galatians*, 219–21; Stanton, "Law of Moses," 115–16; Thompson, *Moral Formation*, 126–27; Thielman, *Paul and Law*, 141; Wilson, *Curse of Law*, 100–104; Dunn points to "that law [the Torah] as interpreted by the love command in the light of the Jesus tradition and the Christ-event"; Dunn, *Epistle to Galatians*, 323; Martyn, *Galatians*, 548–49; Hong, *Law in Galatians*, 122–24.

7. E.g., Furnish, *Theology and Ethics in Paul*, 60–64; Mussner, *Der Galaterbrief*, 399; Schrage, "Probleme paulinischer Ethik," 183–88.

8. E.g., Hays, "Christology and Ethics in Galatians," 268–90; Schürmann, "'Das Gesetz des Christus,'" 282–300; Horrell, *Solidarity and Difference*, 222–31; Fee, *God's Empowering Presence*, 463–64; Witherington, *Grace in Galatia*, 423–25.

9. E.g., Vouga, *An die Galater*, 95; Longenecker, *Galatians*, 275–76; Dülmen, *Die Theologie des Gesetzes bei Paulus*, 66–68; Thurén, *Derhetorizing Paul*, 86–87; Deidun, *New Covenant Morality*, 210; Davies, *Paul and Rabbinic Judaism*, 11–46; Bruce, "Curse of Law," 261; Garlington, *An Exposition of Galatians*, 269; Fung, *Epistle to Galatians*, 287. Winger and Räisänen consider the "law of Christ" simply as a rhetorical counterpart to the Mosaic law with no real content; Winger, "The Law of Christ," 537–46; Räisänen, *Paul and Law*, 77–80. De Boer notes, "To carry one another's burdens (v. 6:2a) is synonymous with to be slaves of one another in love (5:13c), which represents the fulfillment of the promise made in Lev 19:18. The fulfillment of this promise is tantamount to the fulfillment of 'the entire [scriptural] law [containing the promises of God concerning Christ and his Spirit]' (5:14)"; De Boer, *Galatians*, 380.

Acknowledging the support for the first direction, especially the link between Gal 5:14 (Lev 19:18) and Gal 6:2, Moo comments, "Nevertheless, the arguments in favor of the second direction of interpretation are a bit more compelling. First, the genitive qualifier Χριστοῦ most naturally identifies this law as the law 'belonging to' or 'stemming from' Christ . . . Second, τὸν νόμον τοῦ Χριστοῦ has a close parallel in 1 Cor 9:20–21."[10] Paul from the beginning of his letter has contrasted "the works of the law" and "faith [in Christ]" (Gal 2:16; 3:2, 5, 10–12). This consistent antithesis between the Torah and faith in Christ makes it difficult to suppose that Paul in Gal 6:2 instructs his readers to "fulfill the Torah of Christ" as opposed to "the Torah of Moses." Regardless of the precise meaning of the phrase ὁ νόμος τοῦ Χριστοῦ in Gal 6:2, Paul most likely has in mind here the general sense of the word νόμος—"rule, or principle"—rather than the Jewish law, the Torah.[11] As Norbert Baumert points out, "Certainly, the usage of the word *nomos* thus experiences a shift of meaning, as in the course of the whole epistle. From 'the works of law' as a rule or means to a standard or means to 'the Law of Moses with all the regulations altogether' (e.g., 5:3; 3:23; 4;4) now to a single law, in fact, of a new kind."[12]

Romans

In Romans, Paul uses the word νόμος most frequently among his letters—74 times—and he most clearly elaborates the relationship between the law and the gospel. As in Galatians, when Paul mentions the word νόμος in Romans, he typically refers to the Jewish law, the Torah. However, as we will see shortly, there are five significant exceptions to this (Rom 2:14; 3:27; 7:23, 25; 8:2). Before we delve into investigating each of these cases, however, we first need to consider the overall thematic flow of Romans.

10. Moo, *Galatians*, 377.

11. As De Boer notes, "Paul meets the objection from the new preachers that the abandonment of the Mosaic Law has effectively left the Galatians churches morally rudderless, for the fulfillment of the law as Scripture containing divine promises pertaining to Christ has profound moral implications"; De Boer, *Galatians*, 381.

12. My translation of "Gewiß erfährt der Wortgebrauch von 'nomos' damit eine Sinnverschiebung, wie im Laufe des ganzen Briefes. Von 'Werke-Gesetz' als Maßstab oder Mittel zu 'Gesetzeswerk des Mose mit allen Einzelvorschriften insgesamt' (z.B. 5,3; 3,23; 4,4) bus hin nun zu einem Einzelgebot, und zwar von neuer Art"; Baumert, *Der Weg des Trauens*, 153–54. Sanders holds that in Galatians "the reader would not understand that Paul intends by 'law' in 5:14 and 6:2 a law which is entirely distinct from the other one"; Sanders, *Paul, Law and Jewish People*, 96–98. Smiles rightly argues against this, "unless such a distinction is understood the reader will not understand the passages in question at all"; Smiles, *Gospel and Law in Galatia*, 219–20.

The Thematic Flow of Romans

Before investigating each passage that includes the word νόμος in Romans, we must pay close attention to the overall shape of Paul's argument in the letter. Any effective writer begins his or her writing with a thesis statement. Paul is not an exception in Romans. Many commentators note that Rom 1:16–17 is Paul's *propositio* of his letter. For instance, Colin G. Kruse observes a striking similarity in content between 1:8–17 and 15:14–33, and identifies that "1:8–17 functions as a *propositio* setting out the purpose of the letter, and 15:14–33 functions as a *peroratio* summing up what has been the main thrust of the letter."[13] When we take a bird's eye view of Romans, we see that Rom 1:16–17 thematically corresponds with the whole letter. Here is a simple but helpful structural outline of Romans.

I. Introduction (1:1–17)

II. Body (1:18—15:13)

    1. Doctrine (1:18—11:36): Justification by Faith

        a. Desperate Need for God's Righteousness (1:18—3:20)

        b. God's Righteousness through Faith in Jesus Christ (3:21—4:25)

        c. Effects of Justification by Faith (5:1—8:39)

        d. God's Righteousness and Israel (9:1—11:36)

    2. Exhortation (12:1—15:13): Life Required for Those Who Are Justified by Faith

        a. God's Righteousness to be Revealed in Christian Life (12:1—13:14)

        b. God's Righteousness to be Revealed for Roman Churches (14:1—15:13)

III. Conclusion (15:14—16:27)

In the main body, there is a major movement from Paul's doctrinal teachings (1:18—11:36) concerning justification by faith to his pastoral exhortations (12:1—15:13). Obviously, Rom 1:18—11:36 also has exhortations and

---

13. Kruse, *Paul's Letter to Romans*, 58; similarly, Longenecker, *Epistle to Romans*, 154; Jewett, *Romans*, 135; Witherington, *Paul's Letter to the Romans*, 21–22; Schreiner, *Romans*, 58; Byrne, *Romans*, 51; Moo, *The Epistle to Romans*, 65; Stuhlmacher, *Paul's Letter to Romans*, 25; Fitzmyer, *Romans*, 253; Ziesler, *Paul's Letter to Romans*, 67; Dunn, *Romans 1–8*, 36–37; Morris, *Epistle to Romans*, 65; Käsemann, *Commentary on Romans*, 21; Cranfield, *Epistle to Romans*, 1:87.

Rom 12:1—15:13 contains doctrinal teachings too. Nevertheless, Paul at first focuses on his doctrinal teachings and, then, he moves to their practical applications. With this thematic flow of Romans in mind, let us examine now how Paul uses the word νόμος in each section of Romans.

Desperate Need for God's Righteousness (Rom 1:18—3:20)

Paul mentions the word νόμος 23 times in Rom 1:18—3:20 (2:12 [x2], 13 [x2], 14 [x4], 15, 17, 18, 20, 23 [x2], 25 [x2], 26, 27 [x2]; 3:19 [x2], 20 [x2]). We will focus on Rom 2:1–16 in particular, which is a difficult passage to interpret in Romans for two reasons. First, there is a debate concerning to whom Paul refers to in Rom 2:14. Second, Paul seems to contradict himself here with what he writes in Rom 3:9–31. I will discuss these two issues in the following. Paul writes in Rom 2:14, "For when Gentiles, who do not have the law, by nature do what the law requires, they are a law to themselves, even though they do not have the law."[14] Kruse lists three common identifications concerning to whom Paul refers in Rom 2:14:

> (i) pagan Gentiles who observe some of the moral precepts of the Mosaic law without being acquainted with law itself; (ii) godly Gentiles referred to in the OT upon whose hearts the work of the law had been written by the Spirit of God; and (iii) Christian Gentiles on whose hearts the law of God has been written in accordance with the new covenant promise of Jeremiah 31:33.[15]

Glen N. Davies concludes that Rom 2:12–16 refers to "pre-Christian Gentiles, who are not only doers of the law but who are also justified before God."[16] Davies points to Old Testament figures like the citizens of Nineveh, Job, Melchizedek, Rahab, Ruth, and Naaman as examples. While this is an interesting suggestion, there is no explicit statement that God justified these individuals in the Old Testament and there is no hint in Rom 2:1–16 that Paul refers to them. After refuting the third identification, I will explain the reasons why I support the first option. I argue against the view that Paul refers to Gentile Christians for the following reasons.

First, Paul has not yet discussed God's righteousness apart from the Torah through faith in Jesus Christ. We can trace four stages of Paul's

---

14. I use ESV as my primary English translation of the text, unless I indicate otherwise.
15. Kruse, *Paul's Letter to Romans*, 136–37.
16. Davies, *Faith and Obedience in Romans*, 60–67.

argumentation in Section A (1:18—3:20) and B (3:21—4:25) in the doctrinal part of his letter to the Romans (1:18—11:36).

Stage 1   The wrath of God is revealed against those ungodly (1:18–32)

Stage 2   No one will be justified by the works of the law (2:1—3:20).

Stage 3   God's righteousness was shown apart from the law through faith in Christ (3:21–31).

Stage 4   God considered Abraham righteous, for he believed in God's promise (4:1–25).

Paul's ultimate rhetorical goal in the first section (Rom 1:18—11:36) is to argue that everyone, either a Jew or a Gentile, is justified by his or her faith in Jesus Christ, based on the faithfulness of Jesus Christ. Paul's rhetorical goal in Rom 1:18—3:20 is to show that both Jews and Gentiles sinned against God. In Rom 3:20, Paul concludes, "For by works of the law no human being will be justified in his sight, since through the law comes knowledge of sin" (Rom 2:12). Paul has described the total depravity of humanity in Rom 1:18–32. Although there is no explicit mention of Gentiles in Rom 1:18–32, it resonates with a typical Jewish portrait of pagan Gentiles and we can understand it as Paul's accusation of all humanity with his particular reference to pagan Gentiles. While knowing the Creator from the creation, all humanity worshipped the creation rather than the Creator and suppressed his truth. No one has an excuse. Then, Paul discusses God's righteous judgment in Rom 2:1-16. His point here is twofold: (1) God "will render to each one according to his works" (2:6) and (2) God "shows no partiality" (2:11).[17]

Some scholars argue that Paul alludes to Jer 31:33 MT (Jer 38:33 LXX) and refers to Christian Gentiles in Rom 2:14. For instance, Wright points out:

> I find it next to impossible that Paul could have written this phrase, with its overtones of Jeremiah's new covenant promise, simply to refer to pagans who happen by accident to share some of Israel's moral teaching. More likely by a million miles that he is hinting quietly, and proleptically, at what he will say far more fully later on: that Gentile Christians belong within the new covenant. . . In short, if [Rom] 2.25-9 is an anticipation of fuller statements, within the letter, of Paul's belief that Christian Gentiles do indeed fulfill the law even though they do not

---

17. Paul uses the phrase Ἰουδαῖος τε πρῶτον καὶ Ἕλληνος (1:16; 2:9, 10) and its equivalent expressions (3:9, 29; 9:24; 10:12) throughout Romans, to emphasize the humanity's universal need for the gospel of Jesus Christ.

possess it, 2.13–14 looks as though it is a still earlier statement of very nearly the same point.[18]

Robert Jewett similarly states, "The most likely of these views from a rhetorical point of view is that Paul is here describing the status of converted Gentiles." Jewett goes on, "The alleged contradiction between these verses and chapter 3 is removed if one takes the latter as claiming that all unconverted Gentiles and Jews have sinned and fallen short of the glory of God, and that salvation is by grace alone for Jews as well as Gentiles."[19] Paul writes in Rom 3:23, "for all have sinned and fall short of the glory of God." When we look at Rom 2:14 from "a rhetorical point of view," by the word πάντες ("all") here, Paul most likely means "all humanity" at this stage of his argument. As Brendan Byrne observes, "The tension is best resolved when seemingly inconsistent statements across Romans 1–3 are not played off against one another in a systematizing way but seen as individual stages in a total rhetorical construction."[20] Therefore, it is unconvincing that, by "all" (Rom 3:23), Paul only refers to "all unconverted Gentiles and Jews."

Paul does not condemn Gentiles (Rom 1:18–32) and Jews (Rom 2:1—3:8) for the sake of simply condemning them. Paul condemns both Jews and Gentiles to convince them that they all must believe in the atoning work of Jesus Christ, God's righteousness apart from the Torah. If Paul refers to Gentile Christians already in Rom 2:14, he would have confused his attentive readers. They may have thought that they themselves could obtain eternal life from God, solely by their own good works (Rom 2:7, 10). Those who claim that Paul refers to Gentile Christians in Rom 2:14 argue that Paul only shames arrogant and hypocritical Jews, but he is not actually saying here that there are pagan Gentiles who do some aspects of the law. As Hans Lietzmann observes, however, Paul is seeing matters "from a pre-gospel standpoint (*vom vorevangelischen Standpunkt*)" and setting out what would have been the case "if (1) there was no gospel (*das Evangelium nicht da wäre*), and (2) it were possible to fulfill the Law (*die Erfüllung des Gesetzes möglich wäre*)."[21] Michael Bird categorizes this view as "Hypothetical."[22] I

---

18. Wright, "The Law in Romans 2," 147.

19. Jewett, *Romans*, 213.

20. Byrne, *Romans*, 91.

21. Lietzmann, *An die Römer*, 39–40; Longenecker's summary and translation in his commentary on Romans.

22. Bird, *Saving Righteousness of God*, 159–60. Bird lists four arguments against this view: (1) "there are no conditional clauses in the section"; (2) "to play the hypothetical card . . . seriously undermines the integrity of the Pauline gospel in the process"; (3) "similar statements about works are identifiable elsewhere in Paul's letters (1 Cor 3:10–15; 2 Cor 5:10; Rom 14:10)"; (4) "we need to appreciate the full force of Rom 3:20

... where Paul does not merely deny the *reality* of justification by works, but he denies the very *possibility*." I find none of Bird's arguments against the hypothetical view convincing. First, Paul is a creative theologian and a skillful rhetorician, and it is difficult to suppose that Paul can make a hypothetical argument only when he uses a conditional clause. Second, the fact that Paul builds up step by step that all—Jews and Gentiles—must believe in Jesus to be justified does not "seriously undermine the integrity of the Pauline gospel in the process," as Bird claims. Third, we have to keep in mind the flow of Paul's logic in Rom 1:18—3:20, in order to understand what he means by Rom 2:6. Fourth, when saying "He [God] will render to each one according to his works" (Rom 2:6), Paul is concerned with logic rather than possibility (1 Cor 10:23), and there is no real tension between the hypothetical view and Rom 3:20.

Kent Yinger sees no contradiction between Rom 2:6 and Rom 3:19-20, 28, because he follows the New Perspective on Paul and limits the "works of the law" only to Jewish identity markers. Yinger notes, "What Paul rejects as law-works is not some form of merit theology but Judaism's own understanding of the identity of God's people and the conditions for belonging. Though the meaning of ἔργα νόμου is broader than a few selected identity markers, the focus of Paul's usage is on circumcision and food laws because it was precisely this subset of religious activity which both Jews and non-Jews recognized as the distinguishing identifiers of Jewishness and which Paul understood to be relativized through faith in Christ"; Yinger, *Paul, Judaism, and Judgment*, 171. I cannot discuss in details Paul's use of the phrase ἔργα νόμου here. As I argued, however, we must understand what Paul means in Rom 2:6 in the context of the progression of his larger argument for his gospel in Rom 1:18—3:20. Paul is addressing here not only Jews but also Gentiles; "the Jew first and also the Greek" (Rom 2:9-11). Therefore, Paul could not have meant Jewish identity markers only, by "works" in Rom 2:6.

Simon J. Gathercole supports that Paul refers to Gentile Christians in Rom 2:14, with four arguments: "First, the φύσει ('by birth/nature') of 2:14, contra Dunn, can go just as easily (in fact, more easily) with what precedes than what follows. Second, 'the matters of the Law' (τὰ τοῦ νόμου) are not isolated parts of Torah but refer to the Torah in its entirety: 'the matters of . . .' (τὰ τοῦ . . . or τὰ τῆς . . .) phrase in the NT have comprehensive, not partial, reference. Third, as a result of this, those who do Torah in 2:14 bear a strong resemblance to those who do Torah in 2:13b, and who are subsequently justified. Finally . . . the rhetorical point Paul is making to his Jewish interlocutor is that *some* gentiles may even have *defending* thoughts on the Day of Judgment (transformed from the kind of thoughts described in 1:21, 28). Thus, to sum up, 2:14-15 is providing concrete examples of those in 2:13 who are justified on the final day by virtue of their obedience"; Gathercole, *Where Is Boasting?*, 126-27.

I will present briefly counterarguments to these. First, in order to identity what the phrase φύσει modifies, we need to think about the meaning of the clause "they are a law to themselves." If the phrase modifies τὰ μὴ νόμον ἔχοντα ("not having the law"), the adverb would be redundant and does not add any particular meaning, because Gentiles, needless to say, do not have the law. It is more likely that Paul connects it with what it follows: "when Gentiles who do not have the law, do the things of the law by nature, they become a law to themselves." Second, I agree with Gathercole that "'the matters of the Law' (τὰ τοῦ νόμου) refer to the Torah in its entirety," but I do not see how it supports his view that Paul had in mind here Gentile Christians. As I discuss below, there is a difficulty to see Paul's allusion to Jer 38:33 LXX here. Third, Paul's statement "the doers of the law who will be justified" (Rom 2:13) contradicts his later statement "For by works of the law no human being will be justified in his sight" (Rom 3:20), unless

find it very difficult that Paul, a skilled and persuasive writer, could have confused his audience and weakened his own argument by "hinting quietly, and proleptically, at what he will say far more fully later on: that Gentile Christians belong within the new covenant."[23]

Second, the phrase οὗτοι νόμον μὴ ἔχοντες ἑαυτοῖς εἰσιν νόμος (Rom 2:14) does not closely parallel the phrase φησὶν κύριος Διδοὺς δώσω νόμους μου εἰς τὴν διάνοιαν αὐτῶν καὶ ἐπὶ καρδίας αὐτῶν γράψω αὐτούς (Jer 38:33 LXX). As Thomas R. Schreiner notes, it would be "an odd way of describing the law of God that Jeremiah 31:33 says is written on people's hearts under the new covenant."[24] As Ben Witherington III points out, "Jer 31:33 is not in view here, any more than Gentile Christians are."[25] Some scholars connect the dative singular noun φύσει with the preceding phrase ἔθνη τὰ μὴ νόμον ἔχοντα.[26] Longenecker, however, rightly refutes this for two considerations, "For if Paul had meant φύσει to be understood adjectively, he could better have placed it within the participial phrase τὰ μὴ νόμον ἔχοντα . . . Further, it needs to be noted that an adjectival understanding of φύσει here makes a rather odd sentence, since to add that it was 'by birth' that Gentiles do not have the law sets up another redundancy." As Longenecker argues, "φύσει should be understood as an adverb and taken with what follows."[27] If Paul refers to Gentile Christians in Rom 2:14, he would be saying that Gentile Christians are the Torah to themselves, by doing what the Torah requires. It makes no sense and the Old Testament nowhere presents such an idea. It makes a much better sense that Paul refers to "pagan Gentiles who observe some of the moral precepts of the Mosaic law without being acquainted with law itself." The third νόμος in Rom 2:14 refers to "a generalized 'law,'

---

the former is a "hypothetical" (or, unreal) statement. Once again, we need to carefully follow Paul's argument for the universal need for his gospel (Rom 1:18—3:20), in order to discern what he means by Rom 2:14. Finally, Paul's rhetorical point here is not that *some* gentiles will be justified by their good works on the Day of Judgment but that, just as the Torah will judge Jews, the universal moral code that God has imprinted in the hearts of Gentiles in their being created in the image of God will judge them, even though they never received the Jewish Torah, so that no one will be able to make any excuse, or be justified by their own works. For Paul, this is exactly the basis of the universal need for the gospel.

23. See Lee, *Paul, Scribe of Old and New*.

24. Schreiner, "Did Paul Believe in Justification?," 144.

25. Witherington, *Paul's Letter to Romans*, 83.

26. E.g., Jewett, *Romans*, 213–14; Kruse, *Paul's Letter to Romans*, 131; Achtemeier, "Some Things in Them," 255–59; Cranfield, *Epistle to Romans*, 1:156–57.

27. Longenecker, *Epistle to the Romans*, 274–75; Seifrid, "Natural Revelation and Purpose," 115–29.

a moral code," that is, a universal moral code engraved in pagan Gentiles' conscience, having been created in the image of God (Rom 1:18–23).

Third, as Schreiner points out, "if Gentile Christians are meant [in Rom 2:14–16], it is also odd that Paul speaks of their thoughts bringing accusations on the day of judgment."[28] Wright responds to Schreiner, "They are not simply lawless Gentiles; but the Jewish law, which is now in some sense or other written on their hearts, and which in some sense they 'do,' nevertheless has a sufficiently ambiguous relation to them for them still to be concerned that the eventual issue might be in doubt."[29] This confusing statement is loaded with indefiniteness. The point of the Day of the Lord both in the Old and the New Testament is that God (with Christ as his appointed judge) would judge everyone according to his or her works. It never hints at any internal struggle of one's conscience. Paul emphasizes in 1 Cor 4:1–5 that it is the Lord who will judge everyone, not one's own conscience.

Fourth, Paul's reference to Gentile Christians in Rom 2:29 with the characteristic expression περιτομὴ καρδίας ἐν πνεύματι οὐ γράμματι (Rom 7:6; 2 Cor 3:6) does not necessitate that he refers to Gentile Christians as well in Rom 2:14. Bird argues:

> It seems fairly straightforward that reference to the Jewish law is made in 2.12, but some would argue that the idea of a "natural law" that mirrors moral elements of the Mosaic law is introduced in 2.14. But Paul appears to have finished with any reference to "natural law" or natural theology in Rom 1.18–32, and his subsequent legal language must be situated in relation to the Torah. Moreover, natural law in 1.18–32 seems to function exclusively negative, it imparts enough knowledge to condemn but not enough to save or justify . . . This is a description that fits more naturally with Gentile Christians than it does with non-Christian Gentiles who unconsciously fulfill the Jewish law.[30]

As we already have discussed, however, we must consider first the overall flow of Paul's argument in the doctrinal part of Romans (1:18—11:36). To convince his readers that all humanity sinned against God and need to turn to Jesus Christ, God's righteousness apart from the law, Paul at first accuses both Jews and Gentiles of their transgression. As I will come back to this shortly, the creation story—the fall of humanity in Gen 2–3 in particular—provides the most relevant Scriptural context for Paul's condemnation of

28. Schreiner, *Romans*, 140.
29. Wright, "Law in Romans 2," 146.
30. Bird, *Saving Righteousness of God*, 171–72; similarly, Wright, "Letter to Romans," 147.

humanity in Rom 1:18–32. Unlike Bird's suggestion, Paul does not suddenly stop thinking about the universal fall of humanity by the end of chapter 1 and move onto something new in chapter 2, for in Rom 5:12–21 Paul comes back to the fall of Adam and contrasts it with the redemption that Christ brings. While in Rom 2:29 Paul alludes to Gentile Christians, in Rom 2:14, he is still building his core argument that God shows no impartiality and both Jews and Gentiles sinned against God. In Rom 2:14–16, Paul's concern is still God's impartiality and the total depravity of the humanity, and not yet that "the law's righteous requirements so that they [Gentile Christians] are regarded as being effectively Jewish."

I support Kruse's first identification that Rom 2:14 refers to "pagan Gentiles who observe some of the moral precepts of the Mosaic law without being acquainted with law itself," for the following reasons.[31] First, as I already pointed out, it makes the best sense of Paul's logic in the light of the flow of his argument in Rom 1:18—4:25. Second, it most resonates with Rom 1:18–32 and corresponds with Rom 5:12–21. Paul has described the wrath of God revealed from heaven against all humanity in Rom 1:18–32. Paul writes in Rom 2:5, "But because of your hard and impenitent heart you are storing up wrath for yourself on the day of wrath when God's righteous judgment will be revealed." Paul compares and contrasts Adam and Christ in Rom 5:12–21. Adam and Christ are similar to each other, in that (a) Adam represents the old humanity and Christ represents the new humanity—the eschatological people of God, and (b) their life and legacy affected everyone else. Paul's emphasis, however, is the contrast between Adam and Christ in that sin and death came into the world through Adam's disobedience, while justification and life came through Christ's obedience (Rom 5:12–14). In Gen 2:16–17, God warns Adam, "You shall eat for food of every tree that is in the orchard, but of the tree for knowing good and evil, of it you shall not eat; on the day that you eat of it, you shall die by death" (NETS). However, being seduced by the serpent, Adam and Eve fall into their desire to be like gods (ἔσεσθε ὡς θεοί) (Gen 3:5 LXX). While Gen 2:16–17 LXX does not mention the word νόμος, God clearly gave Adam a law long before he gave Israel the Torah through Moses. Adam's conscience was a law—"a generalized 'law,' a moral code"—to himself. Although those who lived between Adam and Moses did not receive a direct warning from God, as Adam did, they also transgressed God's law—"a generalized 'law,' a moral code"—in their conscience, for God clearly had shown to them about himself from his creation (Rom 5:12–14). Put differently, although Gentiles do not have the

---

31. Similarly, Longenecker, *Epistle to Romans*, 260–89; Schreiner, "Did Paul Believe in Justification?," 131–35; Dunn, *Romans 1–8*, 86, 98, 100, 106–7, 122–25; Fitzmyer, *Romans*, 310, 322; Käsemann, *Commentary on Romans*, 59, 65, 73.

Torah, they theoretically can do some aspects of the Torah, whenever they obey their God-given conscience. God originally created Adam in his image and that image of God was tainted, but never totally lost after the fall of Adam—Gen 9:6. Every vice in Rom 1:18–32 is a fruit of humanity's idolatry, not worshipping the Creator but the creation.

Paul most likely has Adam and Eve in mind in Rom 3:23, because Adam and Eve first sinned against God and failed to live out as those who are created in the image of God; 1 Cor 11:7; Gen 1:26–27. Joseph A. Fitzmyer lists some of the prominent Greek, Roman, and Jewish religious philosophers of Paul's day and their statements as the backgrounds of the phrase ἑαυτοῖς εἰσιν νόμος (Rom 2:14)—Plutarch, *De stoicorum repugnantiis* 9.1035C; Cicero, *De legibus* 1.6.18; Philo, *De Abr.* 46.276; *Quod omnis probus liber* 7.46; *De Josepho* 6.29; 1 Enoch 2.1–5.[32] However, the fall of Adam and Eve (Gen 1–3) lays the biblical foundation of Paul's accusation of all humanity under sin, both Jews and Gentiles. As Longenecker notes, "The 'problem passages' of Romans 2 must be understood in the context of the entire argument in 1:18—3:20 . . . he appears not to have had any desire to bring into his presentation the topics of faith and salvation from a Christian perspective, evidently desiring to reserve these discussions until he moves from this section on 'wrath of God revealed' (1:18—3:20) to the following section on 'the righteousness of God revealed' (3:21—4:25)."[33] Rom 2:1–16 makes clear sense, only when we look at the overall flow of Paul's argument concerning the humanity's universal need for Christ, God's righteousness apart from the Torah. While the word νόμος typically refers to the Torah in Rom 1:18—3:20, the third νόμος in Rom 2:14 refers to "a generalized 'law,' a moral code."

God's Righteousness through Faith in Jesus Christ (Rom 3:21—4:25)

Paul uses the word νόμος twelve times in Rom 3:21—4:25 (3:21 [x2], 27 [x2], 28, 31 [x2]; 4:13, 14, 15 [x2], 16). In this section, Paul argues that Abraham was justified by faith, not the works of the law, because "Abraham believed God, and it was counted to him as righteousness" (4:3, citing Gen 15:6) and "received the sign of circumcision as a seal of the righteousness that he had by faith while he was still uncircumcised" (4:11a). Paul continues, "The purpose was to make him the father of all who believe without being circumcised, so that righteousness would be counted to them as well, and

---

32. Fitzmyer, *Romans*, 64.
33. Longenecker, *Epistle to Romans*, 269.

to make him the father of the circumcised who are not merely circumcised but who also walk in the footsteps of the faith that our father Abraham had before he was circumcised" (4:11b–12). In this section, by the word νόμος, Paul consistently refers to the Jewish law, the Torah. However, Rom 3:27 is an exception, where Paul contrasts the law of works and the law of faith. It is interesting, because Paul frequently mentions ἔργα νόμου ("the works of the law"; Rom 3:20, 27, 28; Gal 2:16, 3:2, 5, 10) but nowhere else νόμος ἔργων. Wright comments on Rom 3:27:

> Paul is thus distinguishing, not for the last time in the letter, between the Torah seen in two different ways. On the one hand, there is "the Torah of works"—this is Torah seen at that which defines Israel over against the nations, witnessed by the performance of the works that Torah prescribes—not only Sabbath, food-laws and circumcision, though these are the obvious things that, sociologically speaking, give substance to the theologically based separation. On the other hand, there is the new category Paul is forging here: "the Torah of faith," in a sense yet to be explained (like many things in chapter 3).[34]

While the first νόμος refers to the Torah, the second νόμος cannot refer to the Torah, when we consider the immediate context of Rom 3:27. Paul just have emphatically disclosed Jesus Christ, God's righteousness apart from the Torah (Rom 3:21–26). Paul writes, "For there is no distinction: for all have sinned and fall short of the glory of God, and are justified by his grace as a gift, through the redemption that is in Christ Jesus, whom God put forward as a propitiation by his blood, to be received by faith" (Rom 3:22b–25a). Paul starts to build the antithetical relationship between νόμος and πίστις from Rom 3:27, which continues to the end of his letter to Romans (3:28, 31; 4:13, 14, 16; 10:4; 13:8–10; 14:17–18). As many commentators note, the second νόμος carries the sense of "a generalized principle."[35] While Jewett admits, "The Jewish concept of law is thus rendered ambivalent. . . [Paul] wishes to render 'law' ambivalent and to eliminate all forms of boasting as inconsistent with faith in Christ crucified," he insists that Paul consistently refers to the Torah in Rom 3:27.[36] Paul could not be contrasting here between the Torah of works and the Torah of faith. Paul's concern here is not to explain how Christians should apply the Torah to themselves but

---

34. Wright, "Letter to Romans," 480–81; similarly, Ito, "*Nomos (ton) ergon*," 256; Cranfield, *Epistle to Romans*, 1:220.

35. E.g., Kruse, *Paul's Letter to Romans*, 194–96; Byrne, *Romans*, 136–37; Fitzmyer, *Romans*, 363; Moo, *Epistle to Romans*, 249.

36. Jewett, *Romans*, 297–98.

to underscore the radical newness of the gospel of Jesus Christ, God's righteousness apart from the Torah (Rom 3:21). While the word νόμος typically refers to the Torah in Rom 3:21—4:25, the second νόμος in Rom 3:27 refers to "a generalized principle."

Effects of Justification by Faith (Rom 5:1—8:39)

Paul uses the word νόμος thirty-three times in Rom 5:1—8:39 (5:1 [x2], 20; 6:14, 15; 7:1 [x2], 2 [x2], 3, 4, 5, 6, 7 [x3], 8, 9, 12, 14, 16, 21, 22, 23 [x3], 25 [x2]; 8:2 [x2], 3, 4, 7). While Paul, by the word νόμος, normally refers to the Jewish law, the Torah, Rom 7:23, 25; 8:2 are exceptions. In Rom 7:22-23, Paul writes, "For I delight in the law of God, in my inner being, but I see in my members another law waging war against the law of my mind and making me captive to the law of sin that dwells in my members." Here, Paul mentions (1) "the law of God," (2) "another law (ἕτερος νόμος)," that is, "the law of sin (ὁ νόμος τῆς ἁμαρτίας)," and (3) "the law of my mind (νόμος τοῦ νοός μου)." Dunn and Wright argue that all refer to the Torah—"the law of sin" signifies the law as a "base of operations" for sin and "the law of my mind" is the law that the mind approves.[37] However, as Douglas J. Moo points out, "there are serious objections to this view, both exegetical and theological. The greatest exegetical difficulty is Paul's qualification of the *nomos* in v. 23a as 'another.'"[38] If Paul consistently refers to the Torah here, he would not have used the adjective ἕτερος just to confuse his readers. While "the Torah of God" makes sense, "the Torah of my mind" and "the Torah of sin" make no sense. As Kruse notes, "Paul does use the word 'law' with different shades of meaning in 7:22-23 and that, in particular, when the apostle refers to 'another law' and the 'law of sin,' he is referring to a principle of sin, a power, or a controlling force operating within humanity."[39] As Longenecker suggests, this may have been Paul's typical preaching to "pagan Gentiles in his Gentile mission—and therefore it need not be viewed as strange that Paul used νόμος in that soliloquy not only in the sense of 'the law of God' but also in ways that his Gentile audience would understand as connoting a 'rule,' 'principle,' or 'body of teaching.'"[40] Paul writes in Rom 7:25, "Thanks be to God through Jesus Christ our Lord! So then, I myself serve the law of God with my mind,

---

37. Wright, "Letter to Romans," 569–70; Dunn, *Romans 1–8*, 377, 392, 395.

38. Moo, *Epistle to Romans*, 463.

39. Kruse, *Paul's Letter to Romans*, 310; similarly, Longenecker, *Romans*, 665–66; Witherington, *Romans*, 201; Bryne, *Romans*, 228; Moo, *Romans*, 464; Cranfield, *Romans*, 1:361–62, 364.

40. Longenecker, *Epistle to Romans*, 665–66; 1 Thess 1:9–10; Acts 17:29–31.

but with my flesh I serve the law of sin." As in the case of Rom 7:23, Paul could not possibly mean here, "I serve the Torah of sin." It makes more sense to interpret this as "I serve the principle or rule of sin." As we can see, the second νόμος in Rom 7:25 refers to "a generalized principle."

Paul writes in Rom 8:1–2, "There is therefore now no condemnation for those who are in Christ Jesus. For the law of the Spirit of life has set you free in Christ Jesus from the law of sin and death." Paul mentions here the phrase "the law of the Spirit of life in Christ Jesus" and "the law of sin and death." Dunn argues that Paul consistently refers to the Torah here, "Paul is able to think of the law in two different ways: the law caught in the nexus of sin and death, where it is met only by *sarx* ['flesh'], is the law as *gramma* ['letter'], caught in the old epoch, abused and destructive . . .; but the law rightly understood, and responded to *en pneumati ou grammati* ['by Spirit, not by letter'] is pleasing to God (2:29)."[41] However, in Rom 8:1–17, Paul says nothing about what Christian—genuinely "spiritual"—use of the Torah may look like, but he only elaborates Christians' new life in the Spirit. In other words, Paul's contrast here is between the Torah and the new life in the Spirit, rather than the "fleshly" use of the Torah and the "spiritual" use of the Torah. As Longenecker notes, "Most interpreters have also seen in the two uses of the articular expression ὁ νόμος ('the law') not a 'Jesus code of regulations' in the first sentence or a 'Moses code of regulations' in the second instance, but in both situations a broader reference to 'principles' or 'matters that pertain to' these two contrasting clauses."[42] While the word νόμος typically refers to the Torah in Rom 5:1—8:39, the word νόμος (x3) in Rom 7:23 and the second νόμος in Rom 7:25 and the first νόμος in Rom 8:2 refer to "a generalized principle."

God's Righteousness and Israel (Rom 9:1—11:36)

Paul uses the word νόμος 4 times in Rom 9:1—11:36 (9:31 [x2]; 10:4, 5). Rom 10:4 provides the key to understand the relationship between the Torah and Christ, "For Christ is the end of the law for righteousness to everyone who believes." Paul in this section consistently refers to the Torah by the word νόμος.

---

41. Dunn, *Romans 1–8*, 417; similarly, Wright, "Letter to Romans," 577; Jewett, *Romans*, 481.

42. Longenecker, *Epistle to Romans*, 685; similarly, Kruse, *Paul's Letter to Romans*, 324–25; Witherington, *Paul's Letter to Romans*, 211–12; Fitzmyer, *Romans*, 482–83; Byrne, *Romans*, 235–36; Moo, *Epistle to Romans*, 474–76; Ziesler, *Paul's Letter to Romans*, 202.

God's Righteousness to be Revealed in Christian Life (Rom 12:1—13:14)

Paul uses the word νόμος 2 times in Rom 12:1—13:14 (13:8, 10). Paul writes in Rom 13:8, "Owe no one anything, except to love each other, for the one who loves another has fulfilled the law." Paul in this section consistently refers to the Torah by the word νόμος.

Summary

Paul uses the word νόμος 74 times in Romans. While it typically refers to the Jewish law, the Torah, there are a few important exceptions (Rom 2:14; 3:27; 7:23, 25; 8:2). The third νόμος in Rom 2:14 cannot refer to the Torah. Paul could not be saying that Gentiles are the Torah to themselves here. It refers to "a generalized 'law,' a moral code." When Gentiles do what the Torah requires, they are "a moral code" to themselves; their conscience is their moral compass. This would have been the most natural way in which Gentile believers in Rome may have understood Rom 2:14, for the concept of a universal moral code was common to their world. Some commentators argue that Paul has in mind Gentile Christians in Rom 2:14. However, this is unconvincing for several reasons. First, Paul has not yet discussed God's righteousness apart from the Torah through faith in Jesus Christ. Second, the supposed parallel between Rom 2:14 and Jer 31:33 MT (Jer 38:33 LXX) is not close. It makes no sense biblically that, when someone keeps the Torah, he or she is the Torah to himself or herself. Third, the point of the Day of the Lord is that God judges everyone according to his or her works. It is not one's conscience that judges himself or herself. Fourth, Paul's allusion to Gentile Christians in Rom 2:29 does not necessarily mean that he refers to them in Rom 2:14. Instead, Rom 2:14 means that, when Gentiles do what the Torah requires, they become "a generalized 'law,' a moral code" to themselves; their conscience is their moral compass.

In Rom 3:27, Paul contrasts "the law of works" and "the law of faith." Paul could not be referring to the Torah in the expression "the Torah of faith." The second νόμος in Rom 3:27 refers to "a generalized principle." This would have been the most likely way how Paul's readers may have understood this verse.

In Rom 7:23, Paul mentions (1) "the law of God," (2) "another law," that is, "the law of sin," and (3) "the law of my mind." Because of the adjective ἕτερος, it is impossible to think of "another law" as the Torah. In the expressions "the law of sin" and "the law of my mind," Paul most likely means "a generalized principle," rather than the Torah.

In Rom 7:25, Paul could not have meant, "I serve the Torah of sin." It is better to take the second νόμος in Rom 7:25 as "a generalized principle." Paul is saying here, "I [against my will] serve the principle or rule of sin." This would have been the most sensible way in which the Roman Christians may have understood Rom 7:25.

In Rom 8:2, Paul contrasts "the law of the Spirit of life in Christ Jesus" and "the law of sin and death." Paul is not encouraging his readers to apply the Torah to themselves in spiritual ways, because Jewish people applied the Torah to themselves in sinful and deadly ways. No, Paul is reminding his readers of God's righteousness apart from the Torah, demonstrated in faith in Jesus Christ (Rom 3:21), and showing both Jewish and Gentile believers' new life in the Spirit, who is later called "the Spirit of Christ" (Rom 8:9). This would have been the most appropriate way in which Paul's readers may have understood Rom 8:3, in the light of Paul's argument so far in his letter. The first νόμος in Rom 8:2 refers to "a generalized principle."

While Paul typically refers to the Jewish law, the Torah, by the word νόμος, there are significant exceptions. Therefore, Wright's claim that, by the word νόμος, Paul always refers to the Torah but never "a generalized 'law,' a moral code" or "a generalized principle" is simply wrong. Paul's use of the word νόμος in the sense of reference to "a generalized 'law,' a moral code" (Rom 2:14) and "a generalized principle" (Rom 3:27; 7:23, 25; 8:2) most likely reflects his typical preaching to Gentiles, in the light of 1 Thess 1:9–10 (Acts 17:29–31). If someone told Paul's original readers that the word νόμος always refers to the Jewish law, the Torah, they must have been perplexed, for that is a particular meaning of the word but by no means a general meaning of the word. Before concluding this study, I would like to briefly draw attention to one passage from Philo, in which we can observe a parallel between Paul and Philo, with respect to their use of the word νόμος, typically referring to the Jewish law, the Torah but, at times, the universal law of nature, the Logos, for their rhetorical purposes.

Philo's *On the Creation* 8.1–3

Philo begins his treatise *On the Creation*:

> [1] Of other lawgivers, some have set forth what they considered to be just and reasonable, in a naked and unadorned manner, while others, investing their ideas with an abundance of amplification, have sought to bewilder the people, by burying the truth

> under a heap of fabulous inventions. [2] But Moses, rejecting both of these methods, the one as inconsiderate, careless, and unphilosophical, and the other as mendacious and full of trickery, made the beginning of his *laws* entirely beautiful, and in all respects admirable, neither at once declaring what ought to be done or the contrary, nor (since it was necessary to mould beforehand the dispositions of those who were to use his *laws*) inventing fables himself or adopting those which had been invented by others. [3] And his exordium, as I have already said, is most admirable; embracing the creation of the world, under the idea that the *law* corresponds to the world and the world to the *law*, and that a man who is *obedient to the law*, being, by so doing, a citizen of the world, arranges his actions with reference to the intention of nature, in harmony with which the whole universal world is regulated.[43]

Philo uses the word νόμος twice in *On the Creation* 8.2 and two more times and the adjective νόμιμος ("lawful") in 8.3. Philo refers solely to the Mosaic Law in *On the Creation* 8.2 on both occasions. Philo associates the Mosaic Law with the universal law of nature—the Logos in Stoicism—in *On the Creation* 8.3.[44] Gregory E. Sterling comments, "The statements sound Stoic, but there is an important difference between the Stoic view and Philo's position . . . The Stoics identified the natural law with the Logos, but not with the laws of a state." Sterling continues, "Philo does something in this text that a Stoic would not do: he makes a subtle play between the law of Moses and the law of nature . . . We can summarize by saying that in his thought natural and the law of Moses are not identical but are harmonious."[45] John W. Martens states, "Philo was intent on convincing the Hellenistic world that the law of nature had been uncovered, that the true law could be followed. He extends Judaism to the world in Greek dress. . . And far from being coming a subverter of the faith in his work on the law, he is, indeed, a protector."[46] Comparing Philo and Paul on their use of the word νόμος, Sterling notes, "Paul appears to make the same conflation [in Rom 2:14] . . . The law is both the law of Moses—otherwise the argument about their keeping the law fails—and the law of nature. The point is that the same ambiguity exists in Paul that we find in Philo. . . The

---

43. I am using C. D. Yonge's translation of Philo; my italicization for emphasis.
44. Niehoff, *Philo of Alexandria*, 154–61; McFarland, *God and Grace*, 76–80; Hadas-Lebel, *Philo of Alexandria*, 188–89.
45. Sterling, "'A Law to Themselves,'" 33.
46. Martens, *One God, One Law*, 126–30.

two are supposed to be separate. The attempt to associate them inevitably produced ambiguities."⁴⁷ Sterling concludes:

> Philo had a view of limited universalism in the sense that non-Jews could and did have a valid understanding of God; in this sense he was universal in his outlook. At the same time, he did not believe that all non-Jews had such an understanding; in this sense his universalism was limited. . . Paul went much further than Philo by denying the validity of the law. . . At the same time, for Paul the Christ event changed how one might approach God. He knew the universalizing arguments that Jewish intellectuals like Philo used and employed them, but with a very different end in view.⁴⁸

There is no evidence that Paul knew about Philo's writings. However, we can say that both Paul and Philo seek to engage in a meaningful dialogue with the dominant Greco-Roman worldview of their day. Both Paul and Philo typically use the word νόμος to refer to the Jewish law, the Torah; however, they also at times refer to the universal law of nature for their rhetorical purposes.

Conclusion

N. T. Wright in *Paul and His Recent Interpreters* (2015) claims, "When Paul speaks of 'the law,' he is talking of the Jewish law, the Torah. We cannot, without ruining his arguments, make *nomos* into something universal . . . I suspect that the negative reaction to Dunn's proposal [that the law serves as the Jewish boundary marker] has to do with a deep-seated western protestant reading of the whole question." This study carefully investigates Wright's claim in the 118 cases in which Paul attests the word νόμος in his seven "undisputed" letters. While Paul typically uses the word νόμος to refer to the Jewish law, the Torah, however, there are six significant exceptions (Gal 6:2; Rom 2:14; 3:27; 7:23, 25; 8:2). In these passages, contrary to Wright's claim, Paul refers to "a generalized 'law,' a moral code" or "a generalized principle." This should not surprise anyone, because that is the most typical sense of the word in Greek. If someone informed Paul's original readers that the word νόμος always means "the Jewish law, the Torah," but never "a general principle," they must have been confused, because the latter is a general sense of the word and the former is a particular sense of the word.

47. Sterling, "'A Law to Themselves,'" 44.
48. Sterling, "'A Law to Themselves,'" 46–47.

Philo, Paul's contemporary Jewish writer, also uses the word νόμος typically to refer to the Torah; however, at times, Philo refers to the universal law of nature, in order to explain his limited universalism that some Gentiles—philosophers—could have understood some aspects of God the Creator. Both Paul and Philo demonstrate limited universalism in their efforts to engage in a meaningful dialogue with the dominant Greco-Roman worldview of their day. These findings indicate that Wright's claim that Paul always uses the word νόμος to refer to the Jewish law, the Torah, and any other interpretation of it inevitably ruins Paul's argument is simply wrong. Paul's use of the word νόμος in reference to "a generalized 'law,' a moral code" or "a generalized principle" in Gal 6:2; Rom 2:14; 3:27; 7:23, 25; 8:2 is not due to "a deep-seated western Protestant reading" but based on a careful exegesis of the Pauline texts in their literary contexts.

Bibliography

Achtemeier, Paul J. "Some Things in Them Hard to Understand." *Interpretation* 38 (1984) 255–59.

Barclay, John M. B. *Obeying the Truth: Paul's Ethics in Galatians*. Edinburgh: T. & T. Clark, 1988.

Baumert, Norbert. *Der Weg des Trauens: Übersetzung und Auslegung des Briefes an die Galater und des Briefes an die Philipper*. PNG. Würzburg: Echter, 2009.

Betz, Hans Dieter. *Galatians*. Hermeneia. Philadelphia: Fortress, 1979.

Bird, Michael. *The Saving Righteousness of God: Studies on Paul, Justification, and the New Perspective*. PBM. Eugene, OR: Wipf & Stock, 2007.

Bruce. F. F. "The Curse of the Law." In *Paul and Paulinism: Essays in Honour of C. K. Barrett*, edited by Morna G. Hooker and S. G. Wilson, 27–36. London: SPCK, 1982.

Byrne, Brendan. *Romans*. SP 6. Collegeville, MN: Liturgical, 1996.

Chester, Andrew. *Messiah and Exaltation: Jewish Messianic and Visionary Traditions and New Testament Christology*. WUNT 207. Tübingen: Mohr/Siebeck, 2007.

Cranfield, C. E. B. *The Epistle to the Romans*. Vol. 1, *Romans I–VIII*. ICC. Edinburgh: T. & T. Clark, 1975.

Davies, Glen N. *Faith and Obedience in Romans: A Study in Romans 1–4*. JSNTSup 39. Sheffield: JSOT Press, 1990.

Davies, W. D. *Paul and Rabbinic Judaism: Some Rabbinic Elements in Pauline Theology*. London: SPCK, 1948.

De Boer, Martinus C. *Galatians: A Commentary*. NTL. Louisville: Westminster John Knox, 2011.

Deidun, T. J. *New Covenant Morality in Paul*. Analecta Biblica 89. Rome: Pontifical Biblical Institute, 1981.

Dodd, C. H. *More New Testament Studies*. Manchester: Manchester University Press, 1968.

Dülmen, Richard von. *Die Theologie des Gesetzes bei Paulus*. SBM 5. Stuttgart: Katholisches Bibelwerk, 1968.

Dunn, James D. G. *The Epistle to the Galatians*. BNTC. Peabody, MA: Hendrickson, 1993.
———. *The New Perspective on Paul*. Rev. ed. Grand Rapids: Eerdmans, 2008.
———. *Romans 1–8*. WBC 38A. Dallas: Word, 1988.
Fee, Gordon D. *God's Empowering Presence: The Holy Spirit in the Letters of Paul*. Peabody, MA: Hendrickson, 1994.
Fitzmyer, Joseph A. *Romans*. AB 33. New York: Doubleday, 1993.
Fung, Ronald Y. K. *The Epistle to the Galatians*. NICNT. Grand Rapids: Eerdmans, 1988.
Furnish, Victor Paul. *Theology and Ethics in Paul*. Nashville: Abingdon, 1968.
Garlington, Don B. *An Exposition of Galatians: A New Perspective/Reformational Reading*. Eugene, OR: Wipf & Stock, 2003.
Gathercole, Simon J. *Where Is Boasting? Early Jewish Soteriology and Paul's Response in Romans 1–5*. Grand Rapids: Eerdmans, 2002.
Hadas-Lebel, Mireille. *Philo of Alexandria: A Thinker in the Jewish Disapora*. Translated by Robyn Fréchet. SPA 7. Leiden: Brill, 2012.
Hays, Richard B. "Christology and Ethics in Galatians: The Law of Christ." *CBQ* 49 (1987) 268–90.
Hong, In-Gyu. *The Law in Galatians*. JSNTSup 81. Sheffield: JSOT Press, 1993.
Horrell, David G. *Solidarity and Difference: A Contemporary Reading of Paul's Ethics*. London: T. & T. Clark, 2005.
Ito, Akio. "*Nomos (ton) ergon* and *nomos pisteos*: The Pauline Rhetoric and Theology of *Nomos*." *NovT* 45 (2003) 237–59.
Jewett, Robert. *Romans: A Commentary*. Hermeneia. Minneapolis: Fortress, 2006.
Käsemann, Ernst. *Commentary on Romans*. Translated by G. W. Bromiley. Grand Rapids: Eerdmans, 1980.
Kertelge, Klaus. "Gesetz und Freiheit im Galaterbrief." *NTS* 30 (1984) 382–94.
Kruse, Colin G. *Paul's Letter to the Romans*. PNTC. Grand Rapids: Eerdmans, 2012.
Lee, Yongbom. *Paul, Scribe of Old and New: Intertextual Insights for the Jesus-Paul Debate*. LNTS 512. London: T. & T. Clark, 2015.
Lietzmann, Hans. *An die Römer: Einführung in die Textgeschichte der Paulusbriefe*. HNT 8. Mohr/Siebeck: Tübingen, 1919.
Longenecker, Richard N. *The Epistle to the Romans*. NIGTC. Grand Rapids: Eerdmans, 2016.
———. *Galatians*. WBC 41. Dallas: Word, 1990.
Martens, John W. *One God, One Law: Philo of Alexandria on the Mosaic and Greco-Roman Law*. Studies in Philo of Alexandria and Mediterranean Antiquity 2. Boston: Brill Academic, 2003.
Martyn. J. Louis. *Galatians*. AB 33A. New York: Doubleday, 1997.
Matera, Frank J. *Galatians*. SP 9. Collegeville, MN: Liturgical, 1992.
McFarland, Orrey. *God and Grace in Philo and Paul*. NovTSup 164. Leiden: Brill, 2016.
Moo, Douglas J. *The Epistle to the Romans*. NICNT. Grand Rapids: Eerdmans, 1996.
———. *Galatians*. BECNT. Grand Rapids: Baker, 2013.
Morris, Leon. *The Epistle to the Romans*. Grand Rapids: Eerdmans, 1988.
Mussner, Franz. *Der Galaterbrief*. 5th ed. HTKNT 9. Freiburg: Herder, 1988.
Niehoff, Maren R. *Philo of Alexandria: An Intellectual Biography*. AYBRL. New Haven: Yale University Press, 2018.
Philo. *The Works of Philo*. Translated by C. D. Yonge. Peabody, MA: Hendrickson, 1993.
Räisänen, Heikki. *Paul and the Law*. WUNT 29. Tübingen: Mohr/Siebeck, 1983.

Ridderbos, Herman. *Paul: An Outline of His Theology*. Translated by John Richard DeWitt. Grand Rapids: Eerdmans, 1975.
Sanders, E. P. *Paul, the Law, and the Jewish People*. Minneapolis: Fortress, 1983.
Schrage, Wolfgang. "Probleme paulinischer Ethik anhand von Gal 5,25—6,10." In *La foi agissant par l'amour (Galates 4,12-6,16)*, edited by A. Vanhoye, 155–94. Rome: Abbaye de S. Paul, 1996.
Schreiner, Thomas R. "Did Paul Believe in Justification by Works? Another Look at Romans 2." *BBR* 3 (1993) 131–58.
———. *The Law and Its Fulfillment: A Pauline Theology of Law*. Grand Rapids: Baker, 1993.
———. *Romans*. BECNT. Grand Rapids: Baker, 1998.
Schürmann, Heinz. "'Das Gesetz des Christus' (Gal 6,2): Jesu Verhalten und Wort als Letztgültige sittliche Norm nach Paulus." In *Neues Testament und Kirche*, edited by J. Gnilka, 282–300. Frieburg: Herder, 1974.
Seifrid, Mark A. "Natural Revelation and the Purpose of the Law in Romans." *TynBul* 49 (1998) 115–29.
Smiles, Vincent M. *The Gospel and the Law in Galatia: Paul's Response to Jewish-Christian Separatism and the Threat of Galatian Apostasy*. Collegeville, MN: Liturgical, 1998.
Stanton, Graham N. "The Law of Moses and the Law of Christ: Galatians 3:1—6:2." In *Paul and the Mosaic Law*, edited by James D. G. Dunn, 99–116. WUNT 89. Tübingen: Mohr/Siebeck, 1996.
Sterling, George E. "'A Law to Themselves: Limited Universalism in Philo and Paul." *ZNW* 107 (2016) 30–47.
Stuhlmacher, Peter. *Paul's Letter to the Romans: A Commentary*. Translated by Scott J. Hafemann. Edinburgh: T. & T. Clark, 1994.
Thielman, Frank. *Paul and the Law: A Contextual Approach*. Downers Grove, IL: InterVarsity, 1994.
Thompson, James W. *Moral Formation according to Paul: The Context and Coherence of Pauline Ethics*. Grand Rapids: Baker, 2011.
Thurén, Lauri. *Derhetorizing Paul: A Dynamic Perspective on Pauline Theology and the Law*. WUNT 124. Tübingen: Mohr/Siebeck, 2000.
Vouga, Francois. *An die Galater*. HNT. Tübingen: Mohr/Siebeck, 1998.
Wilson, Todd A. *The Curse of the Law and the Crisis in Galatia: Reassessing the Purpose of Galatians*. WUNT 225. Tübingen: Mohr/Siebeck, 2007.
Winger, Michael. "The Law of Christ." *NTS* 46 (2000) 537–46.
Witherington, Ben III. *Grace in Galatia: A Commentary on St Paul's Letter to the Galatians*. London: T. & T. Clark, 1998.
———. *Paul's Letter to the Romans: A Socio-Rhetorical Commentary*. Grand Rapids: Eerdmans, 2004.
Wright, N. T. "The Law in Romans 2." In *Paul and the Mosaic Law*, edited by James D. G. Dunn, 131–50. WUNT 89. Tübingen: Mohr/Siebeck, 1996.
———. "The Letter to the Romans: Introduction, Commentary, and Reflections." In *The New Interpreter's Bible*, edited by Leander E. Keck, 9:393–770. Nashville: Abingdon, 2002.
———. *Paul and His Recent Interpreters*. London: SPCK, 2015.
Yinger, Kent. *Paul, Judaism, and Judgment According to Deeds*. SNTSMS 105. Cambridge: Cambridge University Press, 1999.
Ziesler, John. *Paul's Letter to the Romans*. London: SCM, 1989.

Part 2

Historical Theology and Philosophy

6

Theonomous, Autonomous, and *Heteronomous* Conscience

Conscience in Luther and Kant, and Indonesian Moral Perception

FITZERALD KENNEDY SITORUS

Introduction

JAKARTA'S NOTORIOUS TRAFFIC CAN be described in one word: *chaos*. When foreigners visit Jakarta and experience its traffic for the first time, many of them are shocked. There are literally hundreds of motorcycles and automobiles, all mingled up without lanes, slowly moving together like bees, in limited road space with poor infrastructure that is in dire need of improvement. Two things surprise these visitors. First, Indonesian drivers do not obey traffic lights strictly. A red light does not necessarily mean stop. It is simply a suggestion. Second, while all these cars and motorcycles do not keep traffic lights strictly, they still move in such chaotic harmony that is almost like Jazz. Everyone plays "by ear," so to speak. Indonesian drivers seem to have some kind of unspoken and unlegislated ways of driving, knowing when to be aggressive and when to yield the right of the way to others. Relatively speaking, the number of accidents is low, considering this complete chaos. Generally speaking, Indonesians have relaxed attitude towards laws and regulations, possibly, due to their particular historical, socio-political, and cultural backgrounds. This phenomenon may have to do with Indonesia's 350 years of colonialism under the Netherlands and the Japanese occupation during the World War II (1942–1945), and its pluralstic society with many ethnic groups with different languages and cultures. As I will discuss later, generally speaking, Indonesians are not conscious of breaking laws and regulations, as long as they are not the only ones who do that. Their conscience is group-oriented rather than individually oriented, as reflected in Jakarta traffic.

I am a native Indonesian male in his 40s, who received a doctorate degree in Philosophy from a German university, specializing in Immanuel Kant, and came back to Indonesia to teach philosophy in a Christian university, Universitas Pelita Harapan. The topic of "conscience" grabbed my attention as I prepared for a paper for *Sola Scriptura in Asia* conference in May 2017 at UPH. Thomas Aquinas, in his *Summa Theologiae* (1–2, q. 19, aa. 5–6), considers conscience as an application of general moral consciousness (*synderesis*) to a concrete situation. Based on Thomas Aquinas' *Disputed Questions on Truth*, 16–17, Potts explains:

> *Synderesis*, according to Aquinas, is a natural disposition of the human mind by which we apprehend the basic principles of behaviour, parallel to that by which we apprehend the basic principles of theoretical disciplines, and in both cases these principles are apprehended without inquiry . . . The disposition in question, he concludes, is a disposition of the potentiality of reason, but *synderesis* can be used either to mean this disposition, which is comparable to that by which theoretical principles are apprehended, or to mean the potentiality of reason as endowed with this disposition. *Conscientia*, by contrast, Aquinas holds to be an actualisation, the application of deontic first principles known by *synderesis*. He distinguishes two kinds of application: the case in which a person asks himself the question, before acting, "What ought I to do?" from that in which, afterwards, he asks himself "Did I do the right thing?" Since Aquinas hold that basic deontic propositions are known to us without inquiry, we should expect him to say that *synderesis* cannot do wrong . . . Aquinas does allow, of course, that *conscientia* can be mistaken, and illustrates two ways in which this can happen: first, through invalid reasoning; second, by combining a deontic first principle with a false premise, when valid reasoning will not be enough to guarantee a true conclusion.[1]

In this study, I will discuss the concept of conscience in Martin Luther and Immanuel Kant, followed by an introduction to the Indonesian moral perception in dialogue with Luther and Kant. As reflected in the title of this chapter, I describe Luther's view of conscience as *theonomous* ("God-rule"),

---

1. Potts, "Conscience," 700–701.

Kant's view of conscience as *autonomous* ("self-rule"), Indonesian moral conception as *heteronomous* ("others-rule"). As we will see shortly, Luther found the importance of one's conscience in his personal experience and theology of justification by faith and believers' freedom in Christ. Kant developed Luther's insight of one's own conscience into one's categorical imperative and internal tribunal. In contrast to Luther's and Kant's view, Indonesians, like Asians in general, demonstrate strong group identity and effort to keep their social harmony, even to the point of repressing an individual's conscience in support of his or her group conscience. My discussion of Luther and Kant will be based on my reading of some key texts, while my discussion of the role of conscience in Indonesian moral perception will be based on my own personal experience and reflection on that topic, as I could not find any relevant academic writing on the topic of the role of conscience in Indonesian moral perception either in Indonesian or in English.

Martin Luther's *Theonomous* Conscience

Luther's Personal Experiences

Luther emphasizes the role of his conscience before God, as he recalls his past experience, when he rediscovered the Pauline gospel—justification by faith—and he defended himself against the indictment of the Roman Catholic Church. In the *Preface to the Complete Edition of Luther's Latin Writing* (1545), Luther reflects on his own experience:

> Though I lived as a monk without reproach, I felt that I was a sinner before God with an extremely disturbed conscience. I could not believe that he was placated by my satisfaction. I did not love, yet, I hated the righteous God who punishes sinners, and secretly, if not blasphemously, certainly murmuring greatly, I was angry with God, and said, "As if, indeed, it is not enough, that miserable sinners, eternally lost through original sin, are crushed by every kind of calamity by the law of the decalogue, without having God add pain to pain by the gospel and also by the gospel threatening us with his righteousness and wrath!" Thus I raged with a fierce and troubled conscience . . . At last, by the mercy of God, meditating day and night, I gave heed to the context of the words, namely, "In it the righteousness of God is revealed, as it is written, 'He who through faith is righteous shall live.'" There I began to understand that the righteousness of God is that by which the righteous lives by a gift of God, namely by faith. And this is the meaning:

> the righteousness of God is revealed by the gospel, namely, the passive righteousness with which merciful God justifies us by faith, as it is written, "He who through faith is righteous shall live." Here I felt that I was altogether born again and had entered paradise itself through open gates.[2]

Luther shares his rediscovery of the doctrine of justification by faith from his fresh reading of Rom 1:17, as he was giving his lectures on Romans in 1515–1517. As Luther embraced the gospel truth of justification by faith and believers' identity as *simul iustus et peccator* ("simultaneously righteous and a sinner"), he experienced the full assurance of his salvation on the basis of the redemptive work of Christ through faith in Christ, and his "fierce and troubled consciences" was relieved.

Luther also emphasizes the role of his conscience before God in his famous apologetic speech before the Diet of Worms on April 18, 1521, in which he was given one last opportunity to recant his writings against the Roman Catholic Church. Luther defended himself and responded to the Holy Roman Emperor Charles V:

> Since then your serene majesty and your lordships seek a simple answer, I will give it in this manner, neither horned nor toothed: Unless I am convinced by the testimony of the Scriptures or by clear reason (for I do not trust either in the pope or in councils alone, since it is well known that they have often erred and contradicted themselves), I am bound by the Scriptures I have quoted and my conscience is captive to the Word of God. I cannot and I will not retract anything, since it is neither safe nor right to go against conscience. I cannot do otherwise, here I stand, may God help me, Amen.[3]

Luther here defies the authority of the Roman Catholic Church of his day, and refuses to withdraw his critiques of its doctrinal errors and unbiblical practices, based on the authority of the Scriptures and his inability to contradict his own God-given conscience. Karl Holl describes Luther's religion as "a religion of conscience" (*Gewissensreligion*), referring to a religion in which one can approach God no other way than through one's conscience.[4]

---

2. *LW* 34:336–37.
3. *LW* 32:112–13.
4. Holl, *Gesammelte Aufsätze zur Kirchengeschichte*, 35.

Simul Iustus et Peccator

Conscience takes a crucial role in Luther's understanding of justification by faith and the idea of a believer as *simul iustus et peccator*. To begin with, Luther's view of conscience is rooted in his anthropology, which he bases on the biblical story of the Fall of humanity. According to Luther, this original sin (Gen 2:16—3:24) led human beings to the condition of total depravity, having corrupted the original image of God in them and affected their ability to freely choose. In relation to this, Luther makes the following comments:

> "Man is by nature unable to want God to be God. Indeed, he himself wants to be God, and does not want God to be God."[5]

> "Original sin itself, therefore, leaves free choice with no capacity to do anything but sin and be damned."[6]

> "It is false to state that man's inclination is free to choose between either of two opposites. Indeed, the inclination is not free, but captive. This is said in opposition to common opinion."[7]

> "All men are ungodly and wicked, and in their wickedness they suppress the truth, hence they are all deserving of wrath."[8]

Luther's pessimistic view of human beings' ability to know God contrasts with more positive assessments of human beings by many medieval scholastic theologians such as Peter Abelard and Thomas Aquinas, who considered human beings as autonomous beings with reason.[9] Paul writes in Rom 3:20–22, "For by works of the law no human being will be justified in his sight, since through the law comes knowledge of sin. But now the righteousness of God has been manifested apart from the law, although the Law and the Prophets bear witness to it—the righteousness of God through faith in Jesus Christ for all who believe." Luther highlights every person's desperate need for the righteousness of God through faith in Jesus Christ by faith,

---

5. *LW* 31:10.
6. *LW* 33:272.
7. *LW* 31:9.
8. *LW* 33:248.

9. Heinzmann generally describes the philosophy of the medieval scholasticism, "All autonomy, self-worth, and self-efficacy of the world themselves are concentrated, so to speak, in human beings, in the autonomy of reason"; my translation of "Alle Eigenständigkeit, Eigenwertigkeit und Eigenwirksamkeit der Welt konzentriert sich gewissermaßen im Menschen, in der Autonomie der Vernunft"; Heinzmann, *Philosophie des Mittelalters*, 204.

apart from works of the law. Luther, in his *Preface to the New Testament* (1522, revised 1546) writes:

> For the Gospel does not expressly demand works of our own by which we become righteous and are saved; indeed it condemns such works. Rather the Gospel demands faith in Christ: that He has overcome for us sin, death, and hell, and thus gives us righteousness, life, and salvation not through our works, but through his own works, death, and suffering, in order that we may avail ourselves of his death and victory as though we had done it ourselves.[10]

Luther notes, "Then, when a man becomes aware of the disease of sin, he is troubled, distressed, even in despair. The law is no help, much less can he help himself. There is need of another light to reveal the remedy. This is the voice of the gospel, revealing Christ as the deliverer from all these things."[11] Luther also writes, "It is certain that man must utterly despair of his own ability before he is prepared to receive the grace of Christ."[12]

Luther differentiates sanctification from justification by faith. Although believers have been justified by God's grace alone (*sola gratia*) and by their faith in Christ alone (*sola fide*), it does not mean that they already have been made perfect. Luther sees a believer in Christ as simultaneously righteous and a sinner (*simul iustus et peccator*) before God. In his *Lectures on Romans* (1515–16), Luther writes:

> Since the saints are always conscious of their sin, and seek righteousness from God in accordance with his mercy, they are always reckoned as righteous by God. Thus in their own eyes, and as a matter of fact, they are unrighteous. But God reckons them as righteous on account of their confession of their sin. In fact, they are sinners; however, they are righteous by the reckoning of a merciful God. Without knowing it, they are righteous; knowing it, they are unrighteous. They are sinners in fact, but righteous in hope.[13]

Luther makes it clear that his understanding of justification by faith does not in any shape or form promotes antinomianism or immorality. Luther clarifies, "We do not become righteous by doing righteous deeds but, having been made righteous, we do righteous deeds. This is opposition to the

---

10. *LW* 35:360.
11. *LW* 33:262.
12. *LW* 31:40.
13. *WA* 56.343.16–19; McGrath's translation in McGrath, *Iustitia Dei*, 226.

philosophers."[14] Luther once again brings up the impact of justification by faith upon a believer's conscience, "Therefore we define a Christian as follows: A Christian is not someone who has no sin or feels no sin; he is someone to whom, because of his faith in Christ, God does not impute his sin. This doctrine brings firm consolation to a troubled conscience amid genuine terrors."[15]

Luther perceives multiple dimensions of the freedom of one's conscience through faith in Christ. He makes a testimonial comment in his *Letter of Spiritual Counsel* 9: "My conscience has been freed, and that is the most complete liberation. Therefore, I am still a monk and yet not a monk. I am new creature, not of the pope, but of Christ."[16] In this comment, we see three dimensions of the freedom of one's conscience through faith in Christ.

First, the freedom of one's conscience through faith in Christ refers to a believer's freedom from the works of law. In *The Freedom of a Christian* he writes, "A Christian has no need of any work or law in order to be saved since through faith he is free from every law and does everything out of pure liberty and freely. He seeks neither benefit nor salvation since he already abounds in all things and is saved through the grace of God because in his faith he now seeks only to please God."[17]

Second, the freedom of one's conscience through faith in Christ refers to a believer's freedom from any internal accusation—one's holistic internal peace, because one has received the forgiveness of sins by the grace of God through one's faith in Christ. Luther in *De votis manasticis* 1521 writes, "Thus a good conscience is freed from all works, not only those that ought to be done, but from those that accuse us as well as those that shield us from condemnation."[18] In *The Freedom of a Christian* he states, "Our faith in Christ does not free us from works but from false opinion concerning works, that is, from the foolish presumption that justification is acquired by works. Faith redeems, corrects, and preserves our conscience so that we know that righteousness does not consist in works."[19]

Third, the freedom of one's conscience through faith in Christ involves one's political freedom. It is a kind of political freedom where a person is free from all worldly powers, even king or pope. A person has dignity, because his or her conscience is captured by God and God is in him or her. Luther in *The*

---

14. *LW* 31:12.
15. *LW* 26:133.
16. Luther, *Letters of Spiritual Counsel*, 262.
17. *LW* 31:361–62.
18. *LW* 44:301.
19. *LW* 31:372–73.

Freedom of a Christian writes, "I shall set down the following two propositions concerning the freedom and the bondage of the Spirit: A Christian is a perfectly free lord of all, subject to none. A Christian is a perfectly dutiful servant of all, subject to all."[20] However, Luther does not suppose that one's conscience makes him or her independent of God. I call Luther's position "*theonomous* conscience," because Luther faithfully exegetes the Scriptures and understands the gospel truth that, when a believer trusts in Jesus Christ and becomes captured by the Word of God, the believer experiences the complete freedom of conscience from condemnation and "the law of sin and death" (Rom 8:1–2) and submits himself or herself to God as his servants (Rom 6:1–14) and offers himself or herself to God as living sacrifices (Rom 12:1). In contrast, as we will see shortly, while developing Luther's insight of one's own conscience, Kant overlooks Luther's emphasis on Christian discipleship, using God-given freedom to serve God and others. Luther writes, "We conclude, therefore, that a Christian lives not in himself, but in Christ and in his neighbor. Otherwise he is not a Christian. He lives in Christ through faith, in his neighbor through love. By faith he is caught up beyond himself into God. By love he descends beneath himself into his neighbor. Yet he always remains in God and in his love."[21]

Luther's Legacy

Michael Allen Gillespie identifies Luther as "one of the founders of the modernity."[22] As is well known, Luther's reformation was not limited to the Protestant Christianity but affected the whole of European society. Ernst-Wolfgang Böckenförde, a judge of German Federal Constitutional Court and an expert in constitutional law, argues, "Luther's thought has not just influenced theological conception of the relationship of God with world, the position and the role of a person in the world, the order of the world and a person's position in it, the more important thing is Luther's deep influence on the modern philosophy of rights, on the philosophy of state and on the relationship between individuals and the state authority."[23] Luther's rediscovery of Paul's gospel of justification by faith and a believer's

20. *LW* 31:344.
21. *LW* 31:371.
22. Gillespie, *Theological Origins of Modernity*, 101.
23. "So hat Luthers Auffasung über das Verhältnis Gottes zur Welt, über Stellung und Aufgabe des menschen in der Welt, über die Ordnungen dieser Welt und die Einfügung der Menschen in sie das Denken und den religiösmentalen Habitus der Glaubens- und Bekenntnisgemeinschaft der Lutheraner nachhaltig geprägt"; Böckenförde, *Geschichte der Rechts*, 429.

status as *simul iustus et peccator* and the freedom of conscience from condemnation through faith in Christ laid the foundation for the concept of modern subjectivity and freedom, not only in politics but also in existentialism.[24] Böckenförde notes, "the freedom of conscience is rightly seen as the principle of the right of freedom of the individual in the modern era; it is the principle of modern freedom."[25] Luther's theological breakthrough led to great attention to individuals and their dignity. G. W. F. Hegel, in his *Lecture of the Philosophy of History*, writes, "Luther's simple doctrine is that the *concrete individual*, infinite subjectivity, that is, true spirituality, Christ—is in no way present and actual in outward manner, but, being essentially spiritual, is obtained only in being reconciled to God—*in faith and enjoyment*."[26] Hegel also notes, "Thus subjective spirit becomes free in the truth, denies its particularity and comes to itself in its truth. Thus has Christian freedom become real. . . This is the essential content of the Reformation: man sets himself to be free."[27] As in the case of Kant, Hegel highlights Luther's discovery of one's own conscience but misrepresents Luther's teaching of Christian freedom, by caricaturing it as "man sets himself to be free," as if Luther ever promoted antinomianism—everyone can and should do whatever he or she wants to do.

Immanuel Kant's *Autonomous* Conscience

Immanuel Kant was educated since his childhood in the spirit of Protestant Pietism, an influential religious movement motivated by Luther's theology. While Kant did not follow Luther's theology in particular, he received his inspiration of the autonomy of a person's conscience from Luther's understanding of the freedom and wholeness of a believer's conscience in Christ. Friedrich Paulsen calls Kant "the exponent of the spirit of the modern era and the Reformation."[28] Gutberlet Constantin writes, "Kant had given the philosophical basis for the subjectivism of Protestantism and he can be named as the philosopher of Protestantism."[29]

24. I follow Kant's definition of a person in *The Metaphysics of Morals* [6:223], "A person is a subject whose actions can be imputed to him. Moral personality is therefore nothing other than the freedom of a rational being under moral laws"; Kant, *Practical Philosophy*, 378.

25. Böckenförde, *Staat, Verfassung, Demokratie*, 203.

26. Hegel, *Lectures on Philosophy*, 374.

27. Hegel, *Lectures on Philosophy*, 375–76.

28. Paulsen, *Kant*, 26.

29. "Kant den Subjektivismus des *Protestantismus* philosophisch begründet hat, und der Philosoph des Protestatnismus genannt werden kann"; cited in Raffelt, "Kant

While Luther sees conscience as a theological-existential phenomenon, as we will see shortly, Kant sees it as an anthropological-moral phenomenon. Reading his lectures on ethics (*Ethik-Vorlesungen*), we find that Kant started to develop his ideas about conscience early in his career as a philosopher.[30] In this section, I will make two observations with respect to Kant's understanding of conscience.

First, Kant perceives conscience intrinsic to every human being and a natural part of him or her, associated with what he calls the "categorical imperative" (*kategorischer Imperativ*). Kant in *The Metaphysics of Morals* [6:399] notes, "Since any consciousness of obligation depends upon moral feeling to make us aware of the constraint present in the thought of duty, there can be no duty to have moral feeling or to acquire it; instead every human being (as a moral being) has it in him originally."[31] Kant in *The Metaphysics of Morals* [6:401] notes, "Every human being, as a moral being, *has* a conscience within him originally. . . Conscience is not something that can be acquired, and we have no duty to provide ourselves with one . . . The duty here is only to cultivate one's conscience, to sharpen the attentiveness to the voice of the inner judge and to use every means to obtain a hearing for it (hence the duty is only indirect)."[32]

Second, Kant uses the imagery of a tribunal to illustrate how one's conscience works in a person. In the *Metaphysics of Morals* [6:438–440], he portrays conscience as a tribunal process with a judge, an accused, and a prosecutor:

> Every concept of duty involves objective constraint through a law (a moral imperative limiting our freedom) and belongs to practical understanding, which provides a rule. . . All of this takes place before a *tribunal* (*coram iudicio*), which, as a moral person giving effect to the law, is called a *court* (*forum*). Consciousness of an *internal court* in the human being ("before which his thoughts accuse or excuse one another") is conscience. . . Now, this original intellectual and (since it is the thought of duty) moral predisposition called *conscience* is peculiar in that, although its business is a business of a human being with himself, one constrained by his reason sees himself constrained to carry it on as at the bidding *of another person*. For the affair here is that of trying *a case* (*causa*) before a court.

---

als Philosoph," 140.

30. Thomas Sören Hoffman provides an excellent analysis of Kant's early philosophy of conscience. Hoffman "Gewissen als praktische Apperzeption," 424–43.

31. Kant, *Practical Philosophy*, 528.

32. Kant, *Practical Philosophy*, 529–30.

> But to think of a human being who is *accused* by his conscience as *one and the same person* as the judge is an absurd way of representing a court, since then the prosecutor would always lose. For all duties a human being's conscience will, accordingly, have to think of *someone other* than himself (i.e., other than the human being as such) as the judge of his actions, if conscience is not to be in contradiction with itself. This other may be an actual person or a merely ideal person that reason creates for itself. Such an ideal person (the authorized judge of conscience) must be a scrutinizer of hearts, since the court is set up *within* the human being. But he must also *impose all obligation,* that is, he must be, or be thought as, a person in relation to whom all duties whatsoever are to be regarded as also his commands; for conscience is the inner judge of all free actions.[33]

The whole process in the moral tribunal then brings some interesting questions, especially because this process takes place within an individual human being. How is it possible that there are different agents within a person, as Kant describes? Could we say that all parties which partake in the tribunal, namely the prosecutor, the accused, and the judge, are the one and the same person? If the prosecutor always loses the case, then, it means that the accused always wins. This may be certainly the case for a sociopath or psychopath. To avoid any self-contradiction within oneself, one may consider that the accused and prosecutor are not the same person within oneself. Kant may be hinting at this idea, when he writes, "This other may be an actual person or a merely ideal person that reason creates for itself."

Kant provides an indirect proof of the existence of God, based on practical and subjective reason. Kant states:

> Now since such a moral being must also have all power (in heaven and on earth) in order to give effect to his laws (as is necessarily required for the office of judge), and since such an omnipotent moral being is called God, conscience must be thought of as the subjective principle of being accountable to God for all one's deeds. In fact the latter concept is always contained (even if only in an obscure way) in the moral self-awareness of conscience. This is not to say that a human being is entitled, through the idea to which his conscience unavoidably guides him, to *assume* that such a supreme being *actually exists* outside himself—still less that he is *bound* by his conscience to do so. For the idea is not given to him *objectively,* by theoretical reason, but only *subjectively,* by practical reason, putting itself

---

33. Kant, *Practical Philosophy,* 559–61.

> under obligation to act in keeping with this idea; and through using practical reason, but *only in following out the analogy* with a lawgiver for all rational beings in the world, human beings are merely pointed in the direction of thinking of conscientiousness (which is also called *religio*) as accountability to a holy being (morally lawgiving reason) distinct from us yet present in our inmost being, and of submitting to the will of this being, as the rule of justice. The concept of religion is here for us only "a principle of estimating all our duties as divine commands."[34]

As above, Kant argues that, based on the phenomenon of conscience and the moral tribunal, the question of an ideal person leads our reason to presuppose God's existence in us in our moral faculty.

While Kant's description of each person in the moral tribunal is helpful, it is not completely clear. Kant explains in detail the role of each person in the tribunal under a footnote:

> A human being who accuses and judges himself in conscience must think of a dual personality in himself, a double self which, on the one hand, has to stand trembling at the bar of a court that is yet entrusted to him, but which, on the other hand, itself administers the office of judge that it holds by innate authority. This requires clarification, if reason is not to fall into self-contradiction—I, the prosecutor and yet the accused as well, am the same *human being* (*numero idem*). . . The verdict of conscience upon the human being, *acquitting* or *condemning* him with rightful force, which concludes the case. It should be noted that when conscience acquits him it can never decide on a *reward* (*praemium*), something gained that was not his before, but can bring with it only *rejoicing* at having escaped the danger of being found punishable. Hence the blessedness found in the comforting encouragement of one's conscience is not *positive* (*joy*) but merely *negative* (relief from preceding anxiety); and this alone is what can be ascribed to virtue, as a struggle against the influence of the evil principle in a human being.[35]

---

34. Kant, *Practical Philosophy*, 559–61.

35. Kant, *Practical Philosophy*, 559–62; as we can see, Kant argues that conscience belongs to human beings' practical reasoning. He differentiates practical reasoning from theoretical reasoning: human beings use theoretical reasoning to know empirical reality, while they use practical reasoning to determine their will and action, which has to do with ethics. Kant in *Critique of Pure Reason* [A634/B662] comments, "Here I content myself with defining theoretical cognition as that through which I cognize what exists, and practical cognition as that through which I represent what ought to exist. According to this, the theoretical use of reason is that through which I cognize *a priori* (as necessary) that something is; but the practical use is that through which it is

While I think that Kant effectively explains the activity of conscience with his analogy of a tribunal, I propose that it is better to perceive four agents in the internal tribunal in one's conscience: (1) the accused; (2) the prosecutor; (3) the advocate; and (4) the judge. All the four agents all are authentic parts of oneself, or one's conscience. What Kant describes as the prosecutor plays an independent role of bringing the awareness of the categorical imperative into one's conscience, unaffected by the other parties. However, the final verdict of such tribunal is made not by the prosecutor but by the judge who either accepts the accusation of the prosecutor (categorical imperative) or rejects it. Once the judge makes the final verdict, he or she has to deal with any feelings from either accepting his or her conscience (the prosecutor) or repressing it. The judge has an independent choice in making his or her final verdict. Regardless of this technical description of how one's conscience works in internal tribunal, I call Kant's understanding of conscience *autonomous*, because Kant emphasizes that each individual has a conscience and responds to categorical imperative independently from what the others think or do, which lays the philosophical foundation of strong individualism in the Western societies.

Indonesians' *Heteronomous* Conscience

In Indonesian, there are two expressions closely related to the phenomenon of conscience, which many people use interchangeably: *hati nurani* and *suara hati*. The word *hati* means, "heart," and *nurani* means, "light," which makes *hati nurani* mean, "the light of heart." The word *suara* means, "voice," which makes *suara hati* mean, "the voice of heart." *Hati* can be understood as the center of one's personality, the most private instance in a person. I see a parallel between these Indonesian expressions and the medieval theological terms related to conscience. *Hati nurani* can be understood as a moral consciousness in general—*synderesis*—while *suara hati* means moral judgment in a concrete situation—*conscientia*. While Indonesians frequently use the two expressions in everyday life, only a few Indonesian moral philosophers have touched upon the phenomenon of conscience. For instance, Franz Magnis-Suseno, an Indonesian philosopher, only briefly discusses the phenomenon of conscience in his influential book *Etika Dasar*, defining *suara hati* as "moral consciousness in a concrete situation."[36] Magnis-Suseno does not differentiate between *suara hati* and *hati nurani* and it seems that

---

cognized, *a priori* what ought to happen"; Kant, *Critique of Pure Reason*, 585.

36. Magnis-Suseno, *Etika Dasar*, 53, 63; all English translations of Magnis-Suseno are mine and, due to limited space, I am not including the original text in Indonesian.

he assumes that the two words basically have the same meaning in Indonesian. It is worth noting that, when discussing the philosophy of Thomas Aquinas, he differentiates rightly between *hati nurani* and *suara hati*, as he writes, "*Synderesis* is intuitive knowledge about moral principles, while *conscientia* is the application of those principles to a concrete case. *Hati nurani* comes directly from God and it is infallible."[37] Kees Bertens, another Indonesian philosopher, defines conscience as "understanding of good or bad concerning our concrete attitude. Conscience orders or prohibits us to do something here and now."[38] Bertens, who does not mention *suara hati* (*conscientia*) in his book, divides conscience in two forms: retrospective and prospective conscience. Retrospective conscience is the conscience that gives evaluation and criticism of what has been done in the past, while prospective conscience is the conscience which warns us not to do a certain action in the future.[39] This division is similar to Kant's distinction between warning conscience and judging conscience.

In the context of a very limited discussion of the phenomenon of conscience in Indonesian moral philosophy, I want to make a preliminary attempt to reflect on it in the Indonesian context, in the light of my earlier discussion of Luther and Kant. Of course, it is methodologically challenging to speak about Indonesians' understanding of conscience, considering its extraordinary ethnic, linguistic, religious, and cultural diversity. Of course, it goes beyond my expertise and the scope of this chapter to delve in different understandings of conscience in different groups in Indonesia with more than 261.1 million people (2016). However, it seems reasonable to presuppose that there are some cultural values among Indonesians, which shape their basic understanding of conscience.[40] One of the cultural values is Indonesians' strong sense of their group identity, which I call here "collectivism." Collectivism is the perspective in which the members of a society places their group identity before their individual identity. Collectivism holds that the social collectivity is the highest standard of moral value to which the individuals refer for their moral decision.[41] Emil Durkheim calls this "social determinism" and comments, "Society penetrates the consciousness and the individual and fashions it in its image and resemblance."[42] In contrast to Kant who contends that a person is intrinsically aware of the categorical

---

37. Magnis-Suseno, *13 Tokoh Etika Sejak Zaman Yunani sampai Abad ke-19*, 91.
38. Bertens, *Etika*, 51.
39. Bertens, *Etika*, 54.
40. De Bary, *Asian Values and Human Rights*.
41. Westen, *Self and Society*.
42. Durkheim, *On Morality and Society*, 149.

imperative (moral duty), because of his or her conscience, Durkheim argues that morality originates from a society and its members embrace its social imperative through socialization, as he notes, "Society is something more than a material power; it is a moral power. It surpasses us physically, materially and morally. Civilization is the result of the co-operation of men in association through successive generations; it is essentially a social product. Society made it, preserves it and transmits it to individuals."[43]

Durkheim's observation of social determinism in moral affairs finds a parallel in Indonesian society today and in the past. Like many Asian societies, collectivism is also a main value of cultures in Indonesia. Indonesians prioritize collectivism, togetherness, rather than individualism. To be individually different from the society or to take a moral action that it is not in accordance with the public expectation is not welcomed by many Indonesians. The definition of good is often determined by what the other members of the society perceive as good, rather than one's own conscience in accordance with the categorial imperative (moral law). M. Djojodiguno writes: "We are a socio- and tradition-bound people, every one of us has to act and to behave as all others do, one has to be common, *biasa* (Javanese: *lumrah*). Being different from others is being strange, astonishing, wicked, condemnable. In short, what is normal gets a normative trait."[44]

Accordingly, moral education in Indonesia focuses on conformism and social harmony, rather than one' conscience. Students are encouraged to find their personal identity in their family, community, and the nation of Indonesia but an opportunity to explore their own unique personal identity is largely ignored. Students from early on are not encouraged to think critically for themselves and act upon their own personal convictions based on their moral conscience but they are simply asked to conform to the rules and regulations of the society. Sometimes, a right moral action that somehow disturbs social harmony is negatively portrayed. In other words, maintaining harmony is more important than being right, which is sometimes described as "saving face." Stephanus Ozias Fernandez notes, "[In Indonesia] an individual is considered to have a value if he is involved actively in keeping a harmonious social life. A man is to be a true man if he is not separating himself from society, if he lives and thinks socially and collectively. Therefore, a man must always attempt to keep a good relationship with the society and its members."[45]

---

43. Durkheim, *On Morality and Society*, 27.
44. Cited in Subagya, *Agama dan Alam Kerohanian Asli di Indonesia*, 173.
45. Fernandez, *Citra Manusia*, 31.

In contrast to Luther's "*theonomous* conscience" and Kant's "*autonomous* conscience," I want to call Indonesians' collective conscience "*heteronomous* conscience," for the Greek adjective *heteros* means, "other." Luther focuses on the liberation of a Christian believer's conscience before God, by the grace of God and through his or her faith in Christ, on the basis of the redemptive work of Jesus Christ on the cross. Having been inspired by Luther's rediscovery of this result of a believer's justification by faith, Kant observes in the tribunal in one's conscience the total independence of the *conscience* (the prosecutor)—discerning the situation from the categorical imperative (universal moral law) and that of the judge (the accused) in deciding whether or not to accept the verdict of the conscience (the prosecutor). In this way, I call Kant's understanding of conscience "autonomous." Collectivism is one of the values that many Indonesians hold in making a moral judgment. Therefore, Indonesians' moral perception depends on how the others think about their action; therefore, it is an other-centered—*heteronomous*—conscience.

In such a collective society as Indonesia, a person is more identified as a member of the society than as an individual. A person is more affected by others' moral judgment than the Western societies in which individualism dominates. Fernandez states, "The Indonesian always thinks socially. The Indonesian thinking is determined by societal interest as the essence of a social relationship. He lives as a unity, which has social and symbolic status. His dimension of life is individual identity, which is social."[46] This observation makes us question how conscience functions among Indonesians. In our discussion of Luther and Kant, we observed that an individual has freedom to take a moral action, based on his or her own conscience. In contrast, Indonesians consider *hati nurani* or *suara hati* as the social norms that they must follow. They do not perceive conscience as something individual but something collective and societal. In such a society, the society rather than what Kant calls "categorical imperative" determines what is right and what is wrong; therefore, I will call this "social imperative." As I mentioned earlier, this is why I describe Indonesians' understanding of conscience as *heteronomous*, in contrast to Luther's *theonomous* understanding of conscience and Kant's *autonomous* understanding of conscience. In such a collective society as Indonesia, members understand freedom not as liberation from external factors but as their ability to support the moral values of the society. Indonesia could be identified with what some scholars call a "communitarian" society.[47]

---

46. Fernandez, *Citra Manusia*, 107.
47. Honneth, *Kommunitarismus*.

I do not mean that there is no sense of the individual in Indonesia. I am just pointing out that, in Indonesia, an individual's conscience plays a much less significant role in moral perception than that in liberal societies in the West. As history proves time and time again, a society can have skewed moral perceptions that lead to self-destruction. A society is vulnerable to injustice and deception as much as each individual. The total depravity of humanity is demonstrated throughout the Scriptures. There can be a situation in which an individual makes a poor choice, deviating from the wisdom of his or her community. However, there can be a situation in which an individual has to stand up for what is right and just, in opposition to social injustice and oppression. In recent years, there have been many serious socio-political problems in Indonesia, such as the rise of radical Islam, the violation of basic human rights, and the marginalization of ethnic and religious minorities. While respecting various traditions and social norms, Indonesians today must think about what Luther said before the Diet of Worms 500 years ago, "I cannot do otherwise, here I stand, may God help me, Amen," in their fight against social injustice.

Conclusion

In this chapter, I have explored (1) Martin Luther's emphasis on one's own conscience in his rediscovery of Paul's gospel—justification by faith and a believer's freedom in Christ, (2) Immanuel Kant's development of Luther's insight of one's own conscience into his categorical imperative and the role of conscience in one's internal tribunal in his or her moral judgment, and (3) the role of conscience in Indonesians' moral perception.

In the *Preface to the Complete Edition of Luther's Latin Writing* (1545), Luther highlights the significance of his own conscience, when he shares his testimony of rediscovering the gospel truth of justification by faith, based on his fresh reading of Rom 1:17. Luther also argues that he cannot contradict his own conscience in his defense before the Diet of Worms on April 18th, 1521, when he was commanded to recant all his writings against the Roman Catholic Church. Luther explains in detail how God justifies sinners by his grace alone (*sola gratia*) through their faith in Christ alone (*sola fide*), and a believer's status as *simul iustus et peccator*, in which a believer's conscience is often the focus of his discussion. Luther understands a believer's conscience always in relation to God, the Law, and the Gospel. Believers' freedom in Christ is their freedom from the influence of sin and death, and their freedom to serve God and others with the power of the Holy Spirit who dwells in them. Luther never means that believers can do whatever they want, simply because they have conscience. In this aspect, I call Luther's understanding of conscience *theonomous* ("God-rule").

Kant, inspired by Luther's discovery of one's own conscience, further develops it into what he calls the "categorical imperative" and identifies three parties in the internal moral tribunal in one's conscience—the accused, the prosecutor, and the judge. Regardless of how these three parties work together in one's conscience, I call Kant's understanding of conscience *autonomous*, because Kant uniquely emphasizes each individual's conscience that corresponds with categorical imperative, completely independent from others, which is the basis of Western individualism.

In contrast to Luther and Kant, Indonesians heavily focus on what the other members of their society think, when it comes down to making a moral judgment. Indonesians see themselves as members of their society more than as unique individuals. Indonesia could be called a "communitarian" society. I call Indonesians' understanding of conscience *heteronomous* ("others-rule"), because they depend heavily on the moral judgment of their society, valuing societal imperative more than one's own categorical imperative. Indonesians today must think about these differences and move forward as a society with such awareness. While respecting various cultural traditions and the wisdom of the society, Indonesians today must stand against social injustice, standing instead for what is right and just, based on one's own conscience, as they face many socio-political problems.

Bibliography

Bertens, Kees. *Etika*. Jakarta: Gramedia, 1994.
Böckenförde, Ernst-Wolfgang. *Staat, Verfassung, Demokratie. Studien zur Verfassungstheorie und zum Verfassungsrecht*. STW 953. Frankfurt: Suhrkamp, 1991.
Böckenförde, Ernst-Wolfgang. *Geschichte der Rechts- und Staatsphilosophie: Antike und Mittelalter*. 2nd ed. Tübingen: Mohr/Siebeck, 2006.
De Bary, Wm. Theodore. *Asian Values and Human Rights: A Confucian Communitarian Perspective*. Cambridge: Harvard University Press, 2000.
Durkheim, Emile. *On Morality and Society: Selected Writings*. Edited by Robert N. Bellah. Chicago: University of Chicago Press, 1973.
Fernandez, Stephanus Ozias. *Citra Manusia: Budaya Timur dan Barat*. Ende: Nusa Indah, 1990.
Gillespie, Michael Allen. *The Theological Origins of Modernity*. Chicago: University of Chicago Press, 2008.
Hegel, G. W. F. *Lectures on the Philosophy of History*. Translated by Ruben Alvarado. Aalten, Netherlands: WordBridge, 2011.
Heinzmann, Richard. *Philosophie des Mittelalters*. GP 7. Berlin: Kohlhammer, 1992.
Hoffman, Thomas Sören. "Gewissen als praktische Apperzeption: Zur Lehre vom Gewissen in Kants Ethik-Vorlesungen." *Kant-Studien* 93 (2002) 424–43.

Holl, Karl. *Gesammelte Aufsätze zur Kirchengeschichte: Luther*, vol. 1. Tübingen: Mohr/Siebeck, 1932.
Honneth, Axel, ed. *Kommunitarismus: Eine Debatte über die moralischen Grundlagen moderner Gesellschaften*. Frankfurt: Campus, 1993.
Kant, Immanuel. *Critique of Pure Reason*. Translated and edited by Paul Guyer and Allen W. Wood. Cambridge Edition of the Works of Immanuel Kant. Cambridge: Cambridge University Press, 1998.
———. *Practical Philosophy*. Translated and edited by Mary J. Gregor. Cambridge Edition of the Works of Immanuel Kant. Cambridge: Cambridge University Press, 1996.
Luther, Martin. *Letters of Spiritual Counsel*. LCC 18. Philadelphia: Westminster, 1955.
Magnis-Suseno, Franz. *Etika Dasar: Masalah-Masalah Pokok Filsafat Moral*. Yogyakarta: Kanisius, 1987.
———. *13 Tokoh Etika Sejak Zaman Yunani sampai Abad ke-19*. Yogyakarta: Kanisius, 1997.
McGrath, Alister E. *Iustitia Dei: A History of the Christian Doctrine of Justification*. 2 vols. 3rd ed. Cambridge: Cambridge University Press, 2005.
Paulsen, Friedrich. *Kant: Der Philosoph des Protestantismus*. Berlin: Reuther & Reichard, 1899.
Potts, Timothy C. "Conscience." In *The Cambridge History of Later Medieval Philosophy: From the Rediscovery of Aristotle to the Disintegration of Scholasticism 1100–1600*, edited by Norman Kretzmann, Anthony Kenny, and Jan Pinborg, 687–704. Cambridge: Cambridge University Press, 1982.
Raffelt, Albert. "Kant als Philosoph des Protestantismus—oder des Katholizismus." In *Kant und der Katholizismus: Stationen einer wechselhaften Geschichte*, edited by Norbert Fischer, 139–59. FEG 8. Freiburg: Herder, 2005.
Subagya, Rachmat. *Agama dan Alam Kerohanian Asli di Indonesia*. Jakarta: Yayasan Cipta Loka Caraka, 1979.
Westen, Drew. *Self and Society: Narcissism, Collectivism, and the Development of Morals*. Cambridge: Cambridge University Press, 1985.

7

Theologia Crucis in China

Andrew R. Talbert

Introduction

Well into 2014, red crosses punctuated the skyline of Wenzhou in the Zhejiang province of China, but a sudden disruption saw these crosses vanish, frequently with the churches they adorned. Their disappearance was due not to the decline of Christianity in the city. In fact, it seems impossible to stem the tide of church-growth in this communist nation. Instead, a government program of intimidation, and often violence and deconstruction, saw every single crucifix removed and, with the churches that still stood, placed inside their respective church buildings. From the outset, this struggle generated in local Christians not only a greater commitment to their faith, but also a theo-political defense that crystallized in the cross. As this volume examines the impact of Reformational thought and ideals in Asia, it is worth visiting these two major and current developments in the spirit (especially Lutheran) of the Reformation: the rapid growth of the Protestant Chinese House Church movement (henceforth CHC) and the contextually unique *theologia crucis* (theology of the cross) of the Wenzhou CHC. We proceed from here by briefly detailing the growth of the CHC, particularly in the Zhejiang Province to which Wenzhou belongs. This leads to a few theological considerations, namely, Martin Luther's *theologia crucis* put into dialogue with the foundational theology of the CHC and the place of the cross in their particular theological and political matrix.

The Growth of the CHC

The Communist Revolution saw the purging of Christian missionaries from the mainland in 1949, and resulted in the formation of essentially four main groups of Christians (excluding heterodox and indigenous groups): Protestants and Catholics who accepted the oversight of the government, resulting in the creation of the Three-Self Patriotic Movement (TSPM) and the Chinese Patriotic Catholic Church; and Protestant and Catholic underground churches who refused to accept such oversight. For an explicitly atheist nation, as distinct from a functionally (and metaphysically) atheist nation like the United States, China has witnessed an explosion of Christian growth over the last several decades at a rate of approximately ten percent annually since 1979.[1] Current, moderate polls and estimates place the number of Christians in China at around 70 million, with outliers and considerations that many CHC Christians choose not to identify.[2] At a current 3–5 percent of the population, with continual growth, China is set to have the largest world population of Christians in the next few decades. This is a stark contrast to the doom pronounced by Chairman Mao's wife decades ago: "Christianity in China has been confined to the history section of the museum. It is dead and buried."[3] That final sentence has always had a ring of irony to the persecuted church.[4]

The Zhejiang province contributes a significant number of Christians to the current tally, and one of its largest cities, Wenzhou, boasts a population of over one million (in excess of 10 percent) Christians, thereby garnering it the title "Jerusalem of the East."[5] A Christian presence flourished in Wenzhou after the Revolution thanks to indigenous Christian communities, whose ongoing presence then contributed to the rapid growth of the church, paralleling the economic growth of Wenzhou following the privatization of the economy in 1978.[6]

But the numbers are not the only things that make Wenzhou an exceptional locale of the church. Partnered with the economic growth was the rise of what are known as the "boss-Christians" of the Wenzhou churches. These "bosses" are quite literally owners of successful businesses in Wenzhou, who

1. Albert, "Christianity in China."
2. The Pew Forum on Religion and Public Life, "Global Christianity," 97. Even extremely conservative, state-sponsored polls of the PRC observed a 50 percent increase in Chinese Christians from 1997–2006 (14 million to 21 million).
3. Fu and French, *God's Double Agent*, 5.
4. 1 Cor 15:3–4.
5. Cao, *Constructing China's Jerusalem*, 232; Conkling, *Mobilized Merchants*, 172.
6. Cao, *Constructing China's Jerusalem*, 16.

led the development of local churches, contribute financially to their congregations, serve as church leaders, and have even at times allowed Christian groups to hold proselytizing studies in their factories with their employees.[7] Their financial capabilities have also resulted in a relatively unique, and ironic, experience to Wenzhou Christians: constructing independent church buildings for the CHC. This development began in the 1980s, with over 500 churches built in that decade.[8] It is not, however, as though a church is built overnight to the surprise of Wenzhou government officials. Instead, the church leaders of Wenzhou, who are often boss-Christians, have developed a strategy of minimally complying with federal laws regarding religion without compromising their beliefs that is termed "cooperative resistance."[9]

Cooperative resistance entails registering with the provincial government as a religious body. Unregistered religious groups (i.e., most of the CHC) are regarded as "cults" under PRC legal code and are not allowed to worship, proselytize, gather, or have financial assets. Registration brings these churches under the Religious Affairs body of the Zhejiang government and leads shortly to permission for constructing a church. Yet, a gathering of mainland CHC leaders in Hong Kong (2015) recently revealed deep divisions among the broader CHC over this practice, with some regarding it as a partnership with "Babylon," and being essentially the same as the state-controlled TSPM. Wenzhou, however, has repeatedly proved itself as a place of confrontation with "Babylon," rather than compromise.

The Wenzhou churches do not have government-approved pastors, nor could the government reasonably supply one at the current rate of church growth. In what amounted to a showdown with the local government over Sunday school, the Wenzhou CHC united and repeatedly challenged government officials for violating their constitutional rights of freedom of religion (as registered churches) for forbidding them to hold Sunday school classes for their children. Despite threats of complete closure, extortion, and physical violence, the CHC leaders continued to defend their rights collectively and, importantly, in writing throughout this season of persecution in 2001–2002.[10]

This brings us to the most significant confrontation of the Wenzhou CHC with the provincial and local governments in recent years. During an interview with an elder recently released from house-arrest, the foundations of a campaign of persecution in Wenzhou came to light. According

---

7. Cao, *Constructing China's Jerusalem*, 74
8. Cao, *Constructing China's Jerusalem*, 33; Ng, "Chinese Christianity," 160.
9. Conkling, *Mobilized Merchants*, 25–37.
10. Yang, *Religion in China*, 98; Conkling, *Mobilized Merchants*, 9–24.

to this church leader, the PRC Secretary, Xi Jinping, visited the city in 2013 and was struck by the number of churches present in Wenzhou, signaled by their red crosses, and asked, "Is this China or heaven?"[11]

Since the nineteenth century missions under Hudson Taylor, red crosses began to feature prominently on churches in China. Wenzhou is no exception to this phenomenon, and with its large churches appeared proportionally large red crosses on their apexes. For several years, these crosses went up unhindered until the aforementioned watershed visit in 2013.

In April 2014, a campaign of threats and demolitions began in Wenzhou, starting with the largest church built in the city: the Sanjiang Church. Though approved for construction by the provincial government six years prior and costing local Christians several million dollars, government officials had the church demolished within four months of opening. The building exceeded its approved size by nearly four times, but church leaders struck a deal with officials to reduce its structure to a more compliant dimension. In good faith, church members and leaders left the building unprotected long enough for government demolition crews to arrive, seal off access, and dismantle the church. Oddly enough, the Sanjiang Church was listed as a TSPM congregation (though the line between TSPM and CHC is often blurred by the cooperative resistance approach of the CHC).[12] Following this event, the government campaign spread to all the CHC churches in Wenzhou, and in 2015, would extend to over 1,500 congregations throughout the Zhejiang Province.[13]

Yet, different from the ostensible reason for destruction of the Sanjiang Church, this campaign focused exclusively on a single feature of the churches: the red crosses. From interviews with church leaders in 2015, we found a common interaction between church leaders of good-standing in the community and government officials. These officials always approached the church leaders in person or via telephone—never in writing. In their first line of argument, they sought to convince the church leaders they needed to remove the cross for legal reasons (i.e., they were not zoned for a "statue," which accounts for the modified religion law of 2017[14]), which was quickly supplemented with the argument that churches should reflect their Eastern roots and not the Western influence of American Christianity.[15] Refusals were met with threats to find "zoning problems" with

11. See also Gan, "What next for China's Heavy-Handed Cross Toppler?"
12. Tracy, "Walls Came Tumbling Down."
13. Catholic News Service, "Number of Churches Demolished."
14. See Conclusion below.
15. The great irony here that seems lost on communist officials, though, is that the

churches, audits of boss-Christians' businesses, forceful removal of crosses, arrests, torture, murder, and, in the case of at least one church, rendering it completely inaccessible to traffic by walling in the street and turning the parking area into a municipal dump. The reaction of the Wenzhou CHC to this antagonism and persecution brings us to their theology of the cross in the lineage of the great Reformer, Martin Luther.

Luther and the Wenzhou *Theologia Crucis*

Though not a major feature of his voluminous works, Luther has been historically associated with a "theology of the cross" that characterized the Heidelberg Disputations. The longevity of this expression and association is due to the fact that he articulates the Reformers' theology precisely as a *theologia crucis* over against the *theologia gloriae* (theology of glory) of the Catholic Church—that somehow *theologia crucis* is *the* foundational concept of Protestant theology.[16]

To clarify, Luther's *theologia crucis* "does not refer to a bound set of theological statements but rather a methodological stance in which epistemological fidelity to the modes in which God chooses to reveal himself—in suffering, death, and contradiction to expectation—marks the whole of the theologian's orientation to knowledge of God and the world."[17] That is to say, Luther perceives his opponents as theologians of a semi-Thomist rationalism, who proceed from metaphysical foundations regarded as "ancillary partners of theology (*ancilliae theologiae*)"[18] including ontological and epistemological precursors to "revealed theology" that then order the theological enterprise (e.g., knowledge of first principles). He prefaces *The Heidelberg Disputation* by quoting, "Do not rely on your own insight" (Prov 3:5), a clarion call to where his arguments will lead.[19] Luther perceived in his antagonists' theology an attempt to claim the purity of knowledge of God as "naturally" evident in creation (Rom 1:19–20) that Paul castigates

---

cross is decidedly Eastern (Assyrian) in origin, while communism is most certainly a Western development.

16. *Crux sola est nostra theologia* ("the cross alone is our theology"); Luther, *Orationes in Psalmos* (WA 5.176,32–33); Westhelle, "Luther's Theologia Crucis," 156.

17. Saler, "Cross and Theologia Crucis."

18. Westhelle, "Luther's Theologia Crucis," 156. In fact, the general expression used in the Middle Ages following St. Peter Damiani was *philosophia ancilla theologiae* ("philosophy [is] the handmaiden of theology"), and Luther's attack is directed specifically at the philosophical-theological tradition of the Sorbonne; Maritain, *Christian Philosophy*, 35.

19. In this study, I use the ESV as my primary English translation of the Scriptures.

as futile and corrupted by the humanity of Adam (Rom 1:21–32).[20] It is a *theologia gloriae* because it "exchanged the *glory* of the immortal God for images resembling mortal man and birds and animals and creeping things" (Rom 1:22), and is therefore an ironic use of the term "glory." Luther characterizes the *theologia gloriae* as arrogant, ignorant of the bondage of the will, worldly-wise, wisdom detached from the cross, an attempt to return to works-righteousness, and devoid of faith.[21]

In Scotist and nominalist fashion, Luther advances instead knowledge of God purely through his personal revelation in Jesus Christ, but particularly his death and resurrection—Christ *pro nobis*. Luther's Pauline litany harmonizes the "Adamic" wisdom of Romans 1 with the castigated "wise" in 1 Corinthians, proffering instead the true Wisdom of God: "Jesus Christ and him crucified" (1 Cor 2:2). Luther is here characterized as Scotist and nominalist because this reading squares with Duns Scotus' ontological shift from the Thomist *analogia entis* (analogy of being) to the univocity of being, which—in its emphasis on "being" as the property shared by all beings (including God), God as an infinite being, and (in Ockhamist nominalism)[22] the absolute freedom of the Divine will—severed the rationality of the cosmos from the Divine Logos, because God was freed with regard to being and no longer its ordering, rational Cause.[23] That is to say, in Luther's perspective, any attempt to know God apart from the way in which God has revealed himself in Christ and the witness of Scripture knows only an idol in arrogance, because God does not reveal himself in the terms of worldly wisdom, but in opposition to worldly wisdom as decisively indicated in the cross (1 Cor 1:23).[24]

---

20. This should call to mind Thomas Aquinas' famous five *viae*, by which he demonstrates the existence of God through natural (deductive) reason.

21. Luther, *The Heidelberg Disputation*; LW 31:39–58.

22. Hägglund, *History of Theology*, 197–200; Cunningham, *Genealogy of Nihilism*, 17–20.

23. For an introduction to Luther's affinity for Scotus and Ockham in their rejection of the *analogia entis*, see Muller, *Post-Reformation Reformed Dogmatics*, 223–24. Tyson offers an excellent and brief summary of Aquinas' tripartite ontology, which Scotus rejected, and the ensuing (modern) problems we endure because of Scotism; Tyson, *De-Fragmenting Modernity*, 24–30. Milbank provides an unrelenting assessment of the Scotus influence on Luther and the other Reformers; Milbank, "Reformation 500." Though concentrating on nominalism and Ockham, Hart notes the Scotist contribution to Western nihilism via the Reformation in its severing "the perceptible world from the analogical index of divine transcendence"; Hart, *Beauty of Infinite*, 133–34. Placher shows how Luther strives toward the same goal in his *theologia crucis* as Aquinas; Placher, *Domestication*, 37–51.

24. For a detailed study of Luther's *theologia crucis*, see McGrath, *Luther's Theology of the Cross*.

The Wenzhou *theologia crucis* certainly intersects with Luther at the centrality of the impact of the cross. For Luther, the debate is epistemological, foregrounding the cross as the locus of knowing God and the world, and a rejection of Thomist metaphysics. For the Wenzhou CHC, however, the physical cross *represents* an alternative epistemology only insofar as *what knowledge matters*—in this case, knowing the crucified Christ and the demands he places on the Christian community. Both the Christians and the communist government officials operate under essentially similar realist metaphysics and modes of knowing, "faith" perhaps excepted.[25] More significantly, though, the cross has a different Pauline melody in this community from Luther: the Divine *politeia* and political rights.

As noted previously, the Wenzhou CHC discovered in their need to have church buildings to host their ever-growing congregations that they could comply with the government's demands to register as a church in order to attain building permits. Nothing in this requirement, for the CHC, violated their collective conscience. The theology behind this is grounded in the complexity of Revelation's "Babylon" against the kingdom of the Lamb and his saints and their refusal to compromise in their faithful witness, and in the simplicity of Jesus' statement "render to Caesar the things that are Caesar's, and to God the things that are God's" (Matt 20:21). Registration of a church building does not compromise the church in terms of governance and instruction—elements that these churches retain exclusively. These Christians submit themselves to the Divine *politeia* as it has to do with worship and the Christian community. Yet, they do not understand their position as adversarial to the communist government. It is not the Divine *politeia* vs. the Politburo, because these are unequal powers (the former greater than the latter), and the Wenzhou CHC has no desire whatsoever to overthrow the government or rule the nation. They are proudly Chinese and affirm the promises, provisions, and laws of the communist government insofar as these are proportionally enforced and enacted in a realm belonging to such a government. Carrying forward another Lutheran theme, this perspective is akin to the "two governments" approach to the ordering of the world. God rules all things pertaining to the spiritual, while the civil government has the responsibility to rightly rule all things external and material.[26] They are in full agreement and practice with Paul's call to the Roman Christians to "be subject to the governing authorities" (Rom 13:1). As long as the governing

---

25. At the same time, our very acceptance of the "real world" necessitates a foundational trust in the givenness of things. "Faith" or "belief" is essential to all knowing; Tyson, *De-Fragmenting Modernity*, 109–111.

26. Kolb and Wengert, *Book of Concord* 9.vi. For a recent assessment of Luther's "two kingdoms" and its interpretation, see Wright, *God's Two Kingdoms*.

does not impinge on their faith in Christ, Chinese patriotism and Chinese Christianity are, for the Wenzhou CHC, not mutually exclusive.

Yet the cross creates a difficulty for the church, because it is a physical item theoretically under the jurisdiction of political rulers. Therefore, the CHC marshals two arguments in defense of their installation of crosses. Firstly, it is an evangelistic tool (not a tool for Western propaganda), signaling to their broader community that this is where Christians gather. In this way, they have inverted Paul's message regarding the cross by erecting a symbol of the "word of the cross" (1 Cor 1:18) and literalized it as a means of "preaching" within the community.

The second argument brings us to our further Pauline emphasis partnered with the Divine *politeia*, namely, political rights. With their crosses, the churches of 2014–2016 had at their disposal two legal protections to which they collectively appealed against the local government. Firstly, the PRC constitution enshrines the right to freedom of religion (unofficially exempting party members). Secondly, their building permits allow them to construct buildings of worship within certain parameters. Provincial government officials then declared statues were not permitted outside of the building walls. Church leaders protested officially in writing, appealing to their rights as Chinese citizens much as Paul did as a Roman citizen (Acts 22:22–29) in the hopes that the government would operate with the rule *of* law rather than rule *by* law. Paul's case turned out positively, if only temporarily. For the Wenzhou CHC, however, rule by law won the day. These churches faced the options of having their places of worship destroyed or submitting to the illegal pressure to remove their crosses and have their worship continue uninterrupted. Many chose the latter.

Conclusion

Luther's *theologia crucis* was forged in the fires of debate with an antagonistic power over the interpretation of a shared foundational text, metaphysical posture, and orientation to the Triune God. His was a rejection of a comprehensive, albeit caricatured, theological position regarding all of reality and the positioning of his own, which centered, rightly in many ways, on the Christ event. The Wenzhou *theologia crucis*, alternatively, encounters a comprehensively secular entity with an entirely different foundational text and theological posture. Yet, they have taken up a position where the lines of authority blur, calling on the PRC government to faithfully uphold their own foundational text, while also recognizing the dispute to allow their churches to "bear" their physical crosses (Matt 10:38) is a means of obedience to the Great

Commission (Matt 28:16–20). In 2017, the Chinese government modified its constitution regarding religion, targeting the cross-conflict of Wenzhou specifically when it problematizes the construction of "large outdoor religious statues" without the express approval of the provincial government and the Religious Affairs Department.[27] These regulations went into effect in early 2018. Surprisingly, in defiance of these new laws and three years after their removal, three Wenzhou CHC churches reinstalled their crosses overnight on December 23, 2017, citing the evangelistic opportunities of Christmas and the architectural oddity of a church without a cross. The church leaders organized twenty-four-hour guards of worshipping Christians in a strategy of peaceful resistance to prevent the removal of their crosses that lasted into the new year. If confronted by the government, however, the leaders admit they will comply and remove the crosses again.[28] With the constitutional amendments in place, the churches have entered a new and awkward frontier legally: crosses installed before the new regulations became effective.

The future of the Wenzhou CHC does not appear to be one of decline, but of continual expansion as pastors and elders carefully reflect on the knowledge that matters—Jesus Christ, crucified and raised—and how this knowledge impacts their interactions with an intrusive and controlling government that lacks the same way of knowing. It would seem a way forward could be through the common ground of law and constitutional government, but not until both parties are willing to adhere to these and recognize their respective places of governance. To the PRC belongs the State, not the soul; the constitution, not the gospel; the wisdom of Mao, not the foolishness of the cross.

Bibliography

Albert, Eleanor. "Christianity in China." *Council on Foreign Relations* (blog), *Cfr.org*, Accessed March 2018, https://www.cfr.org/backgrounder/christianity-china.

Cao, Nanlai. *Constructing China's Jerusalem: Christians, Power, and Place in Contemporary Wenzhou*. Palo Alto, CA: Stanford University Press, 2010.

Catholic News Service. "Number of Churches Demolished in Just One Chinese Province Has Reached 1,500." *Catholic Herald* (blog), *CatholicHerald.co.uk*, December 30, 2015, http://www.catholicherald.co.uk/news/2015/12/30/number-of-churches-demolished-in-just-one-chinese-province-has-reached-1500/.

Cheng, June, and Robert Katz. "Cross Current." *World Magazine* (blog), World.wng.org, January 29, 2018, https://world.wng.org/2018/01/cross_current.

China Law Translate. "Religious Affairs Regulations 2017." *News Ticker* (blog), *Chinalawtranslate.com*, September 7, 2017, https://www.cfr.org/backgrounder/christianity-china.

27. China Law Translate, "Religious Affairs Regulations 2017."
28. Cheng and Katz, "Cross Current."

Conkling, Timothy Garner. *Mobilized Merchants-Patriotic Martyrs: China's House-Church Protestants and the Politics of Cooperative Resistance.* CreateSpace, 2014.

Cunningham, Conor. *Genealogy of Nihilism.* London: Routledge, 2005.

Fu, Bob, and Nancy French. *God's Double Agent: The True Story of a Chinese Christian's Fight for Freedom.* Grand Rapids: Baker, 2013.

Gan, Nectar. "What Next for China's Heavy-Handed Cross Toppler?" *South China Morning Post* (blog), *Scmp.com*, April 26, 2017, https://www.scmp.com/news/china/policies-politics/article/2090931/what-next-heavy-handed-cross-toppler-close-xi-jinping.

Hägglund, Bengt. *History of Theology.* Translated by Gene J. Lund. St. Louis: Concordia, 2007.

Hart, David Bentley. *The Beauty of the Infinite: The Aesthetics of Christian Truth.* Grand Rapids: Eerdmans, 2004.

Kolb, Robert, and Timothy Wengert, eds. *The Book of Concord: The Confessions of the Evangelical Lutheran Church.* Minneapolis: Fortress, 2000.

Maritain, Jacques. *An Essay on Christian Philosophy.* New York: Philosophical Library, 1955.

McGrath, Alister E. *Luther's Theology of the Cross: Martin Luther's Theological Breakthrough.* 2nd ed. Oxford: Wiley-Blackwell, 2011.

Milbank, John. "Reformation 500: Any Cause for Celebration?" *Radical Orthodoxy: Theology, Philosophy, Politics* 4 (Dec. 2017) 172–205.

Muller, Richard A. *Post-Reformation Reformed Dogmatics: The Rise and Development of Reformed Orthodoxy.* Vol. 1. Grand Rapids: Baker, 2003.

Ng, Tze Ming Peter. "Chinese Christianity: A 'Global-Local' Perspective." In *Handbook of Global Contemporary Christianity: Themes and Developments in Culture, Politics, and Society*, edited by Stephen Hunt, 152–66. Brill Handbooks on Contemporary Religion 12. Leiden: Brill, 2015.

Pew Research Center. "Global Christianity: A Report on the Size and Distribution of the World's Christian Population." *Religion* (blog), *Pewforum.org*, December 19, 2011, http://www.pewforum.org/2011/12/19/global-christianity-exec/.

Placher, William C. *The Domestication of Transcendence: How Modern Thinking about God Went Wrong.* Louisville: Westminster John Knox, 1996.

Saler, Robert C. "Cross, The, and the Theologia Crucis." In *Oxford Encyclopedia of Martin Luther.* Edited by Derek R. Nelson and Paul R. Hinlicky. 3 vols. New York: Oxford University Press, 2017.

Tracy, Kate. "And the Walls Came Tumbling Down in China's 'Jerusalem.'" *Christianity Today* (blog), *Christianitytoday.com*, May 2, 2014. https://www.christianitytoday.com/news/2014/may/walls-came-tumbling-down-china-jerusalem-wenzhou-sanjiang.html.

Tyson, Paul. *De-Fragmenting Modernity: Reintegrating Knowledge with Wisdom, Belief with Truth, and Reality with Being.* Eugene, OR: Cascade Books, 2017.

Westhelle, Vítor. "Luther's Theologia Crucis." In *The Oxford Handbook of Martin Luther's Theology*, edited by Robert Kolb et al., 156–67. Oxford Handbooks. Oxford: Oxford University Press, 2014.

Wright, William J. *Martin Luther's Understanding of God's Two Kingdoms: A Response to the Challenge of Skepticism.* Grand Rapids: Baker, 2010.

Yang, Fenggang. *Religion in China: Survival and Revival Under Communist Rule.* Oxford: Oxford University Press, 2011.

8

Calvin's Doctrine of God's Providence in Asian Context

Responses to Recent Critics

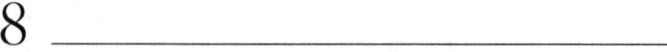 JESSICA NOVIA LAYANTARA

Introduction

JOHN CALVIN IS UNDOUBTEDLY one of the most influential theologians with respect to the doctrine of God's providence. Terrance Tiessen writes, "Among the Protestant Reformers who perpetuated an appreciation for the general approach to God's providence that had been established in the work of Augustine, perhaps none has been more influential than John Calvin."[1] While the topic of God's providence is attested throughout his works, Calvin focuses on it in *Institutes of the Christian Religion* 1.16–18 (the 1559 edition), which influenced Protestant Christianity in his days and beyond.[2] Oliver D. Crisp notes, "For some modern theologians, the doctrines of creation and providence found in the work of a classical theologian like John Calvin either need significant adjustment, or must be done away with altogether in favour of a very different understanding of God's relation

---

1. Tiessen, *Providence and Prayer*, 233; similarly, Schreiner, *Theater of His Glory*, 35.
2. For the thoroughgoing influence of Calvin, for example, on the Puritans, McKim writes, "The view of history appropriately by the Puritans is that of the Calvin/Augustinian tradition. It stresses the transcendence of God and His imminence within the historical process"; McKim, "The Puritan View of History," 215–37; similarly, Schreiner, "Creation and Providence," 267–74.

to his creation."[3] In this study, I will respond to several recent critiques of Calvin's doctrine of God's providence in the context of Asia.

Calvin's Doctrine of God's Providence

Calvin defines God's providence as God's government over his creation (*Inst.* 1.16.2). Calvin elaborates, "At the outset, then, let my readers grasp that providence means not that by which God idly observes from heaven what takes place on earth, but that by which, as keeper of the keys, he governs all events" (*Inst.* 1.16.4).[4] On the one hand, Calvin writes, "Therefore Satan is clearly under God's power, and is so ruled by his bidding as to be compelled to render him service" (*Inst.* 1.14.17). On the other hand, Calvin also emphasizes that humans are responsible for their own choices because they make decisions voluntarily. When a person chooses to commit a crime, even though it has been predetermined by God, he is responsible for his behavior. Calvin notes in *Inst.* 2.3.5:

> The chief point of this distinction, then, must be that man, as he was corrupted by the Fall, sinned willingly, not unwillingly or by compulsion; by the most eager inclination of his heart, not by forced compulsion; by the prompting of his own lust, not by compulsion from without. Yet so depraved is his nature that he can be moved or impelled only to evil.

Calvin does not deny that sometimes God uses mediators to accomplish his purposes. They are often considered secondary causes, used by God to fulfill his government in this world—e.g., the moon, the stars, animals, plants, and even human beings. However, God rules absolutely over every event by his direct intervention or secondary causes (*Inst.* 1.17.1). Even the laws of nature are subject to God's will. Calvin notes, "Also, I say that particular [natural] events are generally testimonies of the character of God's singular providence" (*Inst.* 1.16.7).

Recent Critiques of Calvin's Doctrine of God's Providence

In this section, I will respond to recent critiques of Calvin's doctrine of God's providence under four headings: (1) "Determinism"; (2) "The Problem of the Evil"; (3) "Secondary Causes"; and (4) "Trinity and Christology."

3. Crisp, *Retrieving Doctrine*, 3; similarly, Wood, "Providence," 93.

4. I am using Battles' translation of Calvin's *Institutes of the Christian Religion* in this study.

Determinism

Jack W. Cottrell argues:

> Calvinistic discussions of this problem [the problem of sovereignty and free will] are laced with words like *paradox, antinomy, contradiction,* and *mystery*... My contention is that consistent Calvinism is a genuine determinism... To say that God has an eternal plan that includes "whatsoever comes to pass" is not in itself objectionable. What makes the concept of the decree distinctively Calvinistic and deterministic is the addition of two other qualifiers, namely, that it is both efficacious and unconditional. To say that the decree is efficacious means that whatever happens happens by virtue of the fact that it was included in the decree... The other deterministic element in the decree is its unconditionality. This means that nothing in the decree has been conditioned by anything outside of God; God did not include anything in the decree as a response to or reaction to something.[5]

Jerry Walls and Joseph R. Dongell also regard Calvinism as determinism and argue, "How minutely and particularly has God chosen to control things? It is not essential to biblical faith that God controls things as meticulously as Calvinists claim. What is essential is that he chooses as he will to accomplish his purposes and that he will certainly succeed in doing so."[6] Clark Pinnock also comments, "It would be irrational to worry about anything in the Calvinist's universe. Just submit to the deterministic will of God! If God wants to save you, he will certainly do so, and without you lifting a finger to help Him. If he wants you poor, you might as well get used to it, because there is no changing it."[7]

It seems true that Calvin's view cannot escape determinism. We need to ask ourselves, however, what kind of "determinism" does Calvin hold. I argue that Calvin's view is not fatalism, as these critics claim. Fatalism teaches that nothing can happen other than that which has been destined, and all the efforts of the object are in vain. In fatalism, God is portrayed as a tyrannical and arbitrary dictator. This is contrary to Calvin's concept of God's sovereignty over all of his creation. In *Inst.* 1.17.4, for instance, Calvin never writes that any human effort would be in vain because God already has determined everything. Instead, Calvin emphasizes that Christians should be active in praying and preaching the gospel. Many people misunderstand Calvin's view and think that Calvin rejected the importance

---

5. Cottrell, "Nature of Divine Sovereignty," 98–99.
6. Walls and Dongell, *Why I Am Not a Calvinist*, 152.
7. Pinnock, "Clark Pinnock's Response," 59–60.

of human responsibility for every action.[8] Some of Calvin's writings show a positive outlook on human capabilities. Calvin writes in *Inst.* 1.17.4:

> For he who has set the limits to our life has at the same time entrusted to us its care; he has provided means and helps to preserve it; he has also made us able to foresee dangers; that they may not overwhelm us unaware, he has offered precautions and remedies. Now it is very clear what our duty is: thus, it the Lord has committed to us the protection of our life, our duty is to protect it; if he offers helps, to use them; if he forewarns us of dangers, not to plunge headlong; if he makes remedies available, not to neglect them.

Calvin's approval of human effort differs from Arminians' concept of freedom, which emphasizes that a human can choose the opposite of what God has determined. Calvin understands freedom as a voluntary and non-coercive act. As long as the action is voluntary and non-coercive, the action can still be called "free," even though the action has been predetermined by God. By applying this concept of freedom, Calvin reconciles God's sovereignty and human freedom. This kind of determinism is often called "soft determinism" or "compatibilism."[9]

According to John S. Feinberg, "Calvinists as determinists must either reject freedom altogether or accept compatibilism."[10] Not all Calvinists accept compatibilism. For example, J. I. Packer follows Arminians' definition of free will—a person can choose something freely, even if it is not compatible with God's decree.[11] Nonetheless, many Calvinists follow compatibilism with respect to God's providence.[12]

---

8. Muller, "Grace Election and Contingent Choice," 269.

9. See Feinberg, *No One Like Him*, 640.

10. Feinberg, "God, Freedom, and Evil," 465.

11. Packer writes, "God's sovereignty and man's responsibility are taught to us side by side in the same Bible; sometimes, indeed, in the same text. Both are thus guaranteed to us by the same divine authority; both, therefore, are true. It follows that they must be hold together, and not played off against each other. Man is a responsible moral agent, though he is also divinely controlled; man is divinely controlled, though he is also a responsible moral agent. God's sovereignty is a reality too. This is the revealed antinomy in terms of which we have to do our thinking about evangelism"; Packer, *Evangelism and Sovereignty of God*, 27–28. Packer's definition of free will here contrasts with Calvin's and compatibilists' definition, who suppose that human beings cannot do anything other than God's decree. In Calvin's and compatibilists' view, a human being is still considered as free, because he or she does it voluntarily and without coercion. Hodge takes a similar position to Packer's, whom Carson describes as "a doubtful Calvinist"; Carson, *Divine Sovereignty and Human Responsibility*, 207. In my opinion, the compatibilist view most faithfully explains Calvin's position on God's sovereignty and human free will.

12. E.g., Hunt and White, *Debating Calvinism*, 320; Ware, "Divine Election to Salvation," 1–58; Feinberg, *No One Like Him*, 290–91; Helm, *Calvin at the Centre*, 259.

Arminians also criticize Calvin's teaching about God's government, which entails every minute detail of life. However, Jesus says in Matt 10:29–30, "Are not two sparrows sold for a penny? And not one of them will fall to the ground apart from your Father. But even the hairs of your head are all numbered," which supports Calvin's doctrine of God's providence.[13] Craig Keener comments on Matt 10:29–30:

> Yet as worthless as sparrows were to people, God watched over them. Even some Jewish teachers who followed the traditional insistence that one should not pray for something as insignificant as bird's nest or even think that God's laws really concerned animals could recognize that God was sovereign over each bird's fate, how much more, then, may disciples be assured that nothing happens to them when God is not looking.[14]

Jerry Bridges notes, "God does not exercise his sovereignty in only a broad way, leaving the smaller details of our lives to 'chance' or 'luck.' God, our Father, who exercises his sovereignty in such minute details as to control the destiny of a little bird, will certainly exercise his sovereignty to control even the most insignificant details of our life."[15] The assurance that God rules even in the smallest parts of human life should make Christians feel secure. It enables Christians to trust God fully and obey Jesus' command not to worry about anything, because God is sovereign over everything. Therefore, the Arminian position that God's sovereignty excludes human free will is simply wrong. For compatibilists, as long as one's decision is not compelled by a factor outside himself or herself, it is a free decision.[16] While God is sovereign over everything and has predestined everything, God calls his people to choose to worship him and live holy and righteous lives out of their free will, because they are his chosen people. Everyone will be held responsible for his or her actions in God's last judgment (Rom 2:6; 1 Cor 3:8; 4:5; 2 Cor 5:10).

The Problem of the Evil

Calvin underscores that God has ordained everything, including the evil. To some, this statement makes God's goodness questionable. Kalbryn A.

13. In this study, I use the ESV as the primary English translation of the Scriptures.
14. Keener, *A Commentary on Gospel*, 327
15. Bridges, "Does Divine Sovereignty?," 299.
16. Higton notes, "And that is, of course, what I mean by saying that the decision was mine: it emerged from my thoughts, impressions, feelings, and preferences at the particular moment when I took it"; Higton, *Christian Doctrine*, 196.

McLean writes, "God, as author of all things, even plans evil in its specificity and uses it to serve the divine purpose. When confronted with existential malice and tragedy, we humans may find this a baffling portrait of the God whom we worship and from whom we seek comfort."[17] Calvin writes in *Inst.* 1.16.9, "Therefore I shall put it this way: however all things may be ordained by God's plan, according to a sure dispensation, for us they are fortuitous." Calvin continues, "Not always does a like reason appear, but we ought undoubtedly to hold that whatever changes are discerned in the world are produced from the secret stirring of God's hand. But what God has determined must necessarily so take place, even though it is neither unconditionally, nor of its own peculiar nature, necessary." Calvin writes in his *Treatises on the Eternal Predestination of God*, "So mighty, therefore, are the works of God, so gloriously and exquisitely perfect in every instance of His will, that by a marvelous and ineffable plan of operation peculiar to Himself, as the 'all-wise God,' that cannot be done, *without* His will, which is even *contrary* to His will; because it could not be done without His permitting it to be done, which permission is evidently not *contrary* to His will, but *according* to, His will."[18] Cottrell comments, "It is no wonder, then, that Calvinists give God's permissive decree a connotation that sounds much more like determination than true permission."[19]

Calvin never considers God as the creator of evil, which is not something that comes naturally from this creation (*ex natura*), but is only a consequence of the fallen nature of the creation (*ex naturae corruptione*) (*Inst.* 1.14.3, 16). Evil is a possibility that accompanies human beings as free and rational beings. From the beginning, God did not want to create human beings as mindless, follow-the-rule-puppets, or robots that always obey him mechanically. God created human beings as creatures able to choose between good and evil. Millard J. Erickson notes, "The possibility of evil was a necessary accompaniment of God's good plan to make people fully human."[20]

Furthermore, Calvin believes that God can use evil to fulfill his plan. As noted above, Calvin refutes the use of the phrase, "God's permission," which suggests that God passively permits evil. The phrase, "God's permission," also indicates that God cannot do things differently from what happens. For that reason, Calvin does not use the term, "God's permission," even when he discusses the problem of evil. God rules over the evil actively;

17. McLean, "Calvin and Personal Politics," 109.
18. Calvin, *Calvin's Calvinism*, 26.
19. Cottrell, "Nature of Divine Sovereignty," 106.
20. Erickson, *Christian Theology*, 395.

if he so desired, he could have prevented evil from happening. If God does not prevent evil but allows evil to happen, he does so in order to fulfill his mysterious and higher purpose, the greater good. Bruce Ware argues:

> One can possess both *the will and the ability to save certain people*, and this will can be genuine and the ability real. Yet one can also possess, at the same time, a *will not to save those same persons whom one could have saved*. Why would one not save those whom one both could and wants to save? Answer: One would not to save only if there are greater values and higher purposes that could only be accomplished in choosing not to save those whom one could save, those whom one would otherwise want to save. Scripture does give us some indication that this is the case with God.[21]

God is good and God brings every good thing. Calvin believes that God has revealed some aspects of his will but hidden other aspects of his will. Paul Helm states, "A central part of Calvin's account of reprobation lies in his doctrine of God's two wills, between the secret and the revealed will of God."[22] The revealed will of God is what God desires things to be, while the secret will of God speaks of what God has determined to actually happen. Calvin mentions biblical examples in which God's revealed will and his hidden will overlap each other: God allows Absalom's incest to happen as the punishment for David's adultery, even though God hates incest (2 Sam 16:22–23). God allows the sons of Eli to be killed, even though he hates murder (1 Sam 2:34). Calvin comments, "Out of the impious nation he raised up executioners for the son of Eli because he willed to kill them."[23] This does not mean that God has two different wills or contradictions within himself. God has one will but has different ways of fulfilling his plan. Calvin admits that human beings in their limitations cannot understand the hidden will of God. Calvin argues, "However skillful your questions may appear to you, 'If there is any secret will of God, how was it made available to me?' I have no difficulty in responding to it, so long as you permit me to follow my master, the Holy Spirit. . . In the book of Job there are many splendid eulogies that celebrate the wisdom of God so that mere mortals may learn not to measure God's wisdom by their own understanding."[24]

---

21. Ware, "Divine Election to Salvation," 34–35.

22. Calvin, *Secret Providence of God*, 25; Carson, *Divine Sovereignty and Human's Responsibility*, 214; Grudem, *Systematic Theology*, 214–15.

23. Calvin, *Secret Providence of God*, 95.

24. Calvin, *Secret Providence of God*, 96.

Arminian theologians also criticize Calvin's account of "the greater good." Calvin believes that God allows the evil to bring the greater good and writes, "Now you hear that man does have a will to hand by nature, but one which is evil and cannot be good of itself or aspire to the good, and it is not annulled by the grace of God, so as not to exist but it is corrected and turned from being evil, so as to be good."[25] This raises the question why God needs evil to bring the greater good. If God has to use evil to bring forth the greater good, then, there are two possibilities. The first possibility is that evil is a necessity for God—God needs evil to fulfill his plan. The second possibility is that God loves evil. God specifically plans evil and uses it to fulfill his purpose. McLean comments, "God, as author of all things, even plans evil in its specificity and uses it to serve the divine purpose."[26] Surely, this is not a biblical picture of God. Also, Calvin's view of the greater good can lead to confusion in defining good and evil. Gregory Boyd questions:

> It is not even clear what the word "good" means if it is used to describe the "design" that orchestrates such things as killer diseases, mudslides that bury children alive or typhoons that drown thousands. If such things are in any sense good, what does evil look like? If such things are the work of a loving and all-good God, what would the work of hateful devil look like?[27]

Alister McGrath argues that Calvin's view of the greater good is somewhat influenced by a Scholastic concept called "voluntarism,"[28] and he defines this term as "the doctrine that the ultimate grounds of merit lie in the will of God, not in the intrinsic goodness of an action."[29] This view makes God appear to be a selfish God, who justifies everything he does for his own glory, regardless of the intrinsic value of the act. Austin Fischer comments, "God's desire to glorify himself had not only subsumed but consumed all his other desires, so that the only thing I understood about God was that he would glorify himself. Love, justice, and goodness had been warped beyond recognition as they were sucked into the black hole of glory."[30] This view also obscures the definition of good and evil; it is not clear what is good and what is evil. Walls and Dongell state, "It's our judgment, however, that the Calvinist account poses particularly severe difficulties, especially with

25. Calvin, *Bondage and Liberation of Will*, 122.
26. McLean, "Calvin and Personal Politics," 109.
27. Boyd, *Satan and the Problem*, 249–50.
28. McGrath, *Intellectual Origins*, 99.
29. McGrath, *Reformation Thought*, 72.
30. Fischer, *Young, Restless*, 35.

respect to the problem of evil, and this is one preliminary but significant reason not to be a Calvinist."[31]

Helm rightly refutes the accusation that Calvin obscures the definition of kindness, "After all, the fact that certain evils are logical preconditions for certain goods does not, by itself, provide a justification for permitting evils. All it says is that it is impossible to have the goods without the evils; not that the goods justify the evils. One must not confuse logical justification with ethical justification."[32] Logically, the understanding that there is the greater good behind evil makes evil a natural thing. However, what is evil is evil, even if it leads to the greater good. Ware echoes this, "Christian should never be led to think that, if they were really spiritual, they should 'feel good' about suffering and evil. Absolutely not. But notice: it is quite a different thing, as we shall see, to feel good about God in the midst of suffering. . . Suffering is not good; God does not think so, nor should we."[33] Calvin highlights great consolation to believers amidst the problem of evil (*Inst.* 1.17.1).

Secondary Causes

Cottrell considers the term "secondary cause" as unsuitable for Calvin to describe God's instrument for fulfilling his will.[34] The use of the word "cause" means the secondary cause works with the primary cause to do one thing together. Therefore, if anyone demands accountability for an act, the primary cause and the secondary cause are equally responsible, working together with his or her own free will. However, Cottrell argues that the secondary cause that Calvin describes only acts as an instrument. If someone used a shovel to dig the ground, the shovel cannot be considered the primary cause. It is only the secondary cause, because it cannot move itself. The shovel cannot be held accountable, because that is the active act of the primary cause. Thus, according to this logic, Calvin also cannot impose responsibility on man as an instrument that God uses to accomplish his purpose. A human being is like a shovel and God is like a man using the shovel to dig the ground. A human being cannot do anything other than what is ordained by God, because he or she is only an instrument. The critics argue that, if God is the primary cause of everything, God should be responsible for everything that happens, including evil.

---

31. Walls and Dongell, *Why I Am Not a Calvinist*, 152.
32. Helm, *Providence of God*, 203.
33. Ware, *God's Greater Glory*, 166.
34. Cottrell, "Nature of Divine Sovereignty," 104.

Two considerations must be made here. First, we must distinguish God's decree from actual human action. For example, someone may accuse God of killing six million innocent Jews during the holocaust. While God allowed it to happen, Hitler and the Nazis are responsible for the genocide. We cannot say that, for, since God let it happen, God is responsible, and Hitler and the Nazis are not. Second, in the sense of compatibilism, human beings can be held accountable for their actions, because they do it freely, in the sense that God does not force them to do so. Louis Berkhof argues, "Moreover, it should be borne in mind that God has not decreed *to effectuate by His own direct action* whatsoever must come to pass. The divine decree only brings certainty into the events but does not imply that God will actively effectuate them, so that the question really resolves itself into this, whether previous certainty is consistent with free agency."[35] These two causes are in two different dimensions and at different levels. When an event occurs, God as the primary cause ensures that the event occurs from the divine perspective, while a human being as the secondary cause makes sure that the event takes place from the human perspective. It is like two sides of a coin. The difference in the degree and dimension of the primary cause and secondary cause leads Calvin to distinguish between God's purpose and a human's purpose in the same event, as seen in the example of Joseph's story in Genesis and that of Judas' betrayal of Jesus in the Gospels.[36]

Yet, we must admit that Calvin's account of the secondary cause is still inadequate in explaining the role of the primary cause and the secondary cause in the same event. If the secondary cause also confirms something happening (from a human point of view), then, how important is the role of the primary cause? If the secondary cause were capable of achieving what it wants, then, God's role as the primary cause would be only an additional requirement for something to happen and not a necessary condition. As Helm points out, "In summary, it is hard to see that there can be two separate sets of necessary and sufficient conditions for the same action, even if one of these sets is a set of primary conditions, and the other a set of secondary conditions."[37] However, the question of how important the role of primary and secondary cause does not make this teaching useless. Cottrell's criticism that, according to Calvin, God is the cause of evil and must be held responsible for evil does not consider every dimension of Calvin's view of secondary causes, nor can Calvin's view of secondary causes be identified with determinism.

35. Berkhof, *Systematic Theology*, 106.
36. Helm, *Providence of God*, 179.
37. Helm, *Providence of God*, 182.

Trinity and Christology

Crisp notes, "Some contemporary theologians think that the classical picture of God with which Calvin, like so many others, was enamoured, is simply hopeless because it is not sufficiently Christological in character."[38] Ron Highfield suggests further, "I think that the Reformed view of divine providence is insufficiently Christocentric and Trinitarian, a characteristic it shares with much Western theology written since the Middle Ages."[39] Some argue that Calvin's doctrine of God's providence focuses on the doctrine of creation (i.e., the work of God the Father), whereas all Christian doctrine should be faithful to the New Testament teaching that all God's work is the work of the Triune God.[40] Charles M. Wood comments, "In systematic theology, on the whole, providence has been 'appropriated' to the Father, and its treatment is largely uninformed by Christological or pneumatological considerations. It is typically lodged within or appended to the doctrine of creation, where its chief function is to state that the same God who created the world sustains and cares for it."[41]

I argue that Calvin's doctrine of creation and providence is based on an understanding of the Triune God. In Calvin's teaching, the Triune God is not only active in creation but also actively cares for the world, for the world of creation is itself a reflection of the existence of the Triune God. As Kurt Anders Richardson notes, "When Calvin moves on to the life of the Spirit within the Trinitarian life of the Godhead he, as always, resorts to a classic set of scriptures (for example, Ps. 33:6; Mt. 28:19) and sees in them constant reference to creation as the evidence of Trinitarian reality."[42] Therefore, Calvin's teaching of God's providence is inseparable from his teaching on creation, and both of them are centered on the Triune God. Crisp highlights that Calvin always refers to the Triune God when he discusses all the external works of God, including when he discusses God's providence, and states, "I assume in what follows, as Calvin and all orthodox theologians would, that all external works of God are triune works, even if some of these works terminate on a particular divine person."[43]

---

38. Crisp, *Retrieving Doctrine*, 23.

39. Highfield, "Response to Paul Kjoss Helseth," 67.

40. E.g., Wood, *Question of Providence*, 83; Highfield, "Response to Paul Kjoss Helseth," 67; Coppedge, *The God Who is Triune*, 320; McCormack, "The Actuality of God," 242.

41. Wood, *Question of Providence*, 66–67.

42. Richardson, "Calvin on the Trinity," 37.

43. Crisp, *Retrieving Doctrine*, 7.

While the *Institutes* seldom discuss the Trinity with regard to the doctrine of creation and providence, this is not the case with his other writings. Calvin often attributes the Trinity to the doctrine of creation in his commentaries. In his comments on John 1:4, Calvin affirms the role of Christ in creation: "In a word, what Paul ascribes to God, that *in him we are, and move, and live,* (Acts 17:28,) John declares to be accomplished by the gracious agency of *the Speech;* so that it is God who gives us *life*, but it is by the eternal *Speech*."[44] In his comments on Col 1:15, Calvin states, "God in himself, that is, in his naked majesty, is *invisible*, and that not to the eyes of the body merely, but also to the understandings of men, and that he is revealed to us in Christ alone, that we may behold him as in a mirror."[45] Moreover, in his comments on 1 Pet 1:20–21, Calvin writes, "It is hence evident that we cannot believe in God except through Christ, in whom God in a manner makes himself little, that he might accommodate himself to our comprehension; and it is Christ alone who can tranquillize consciences, so that we may dare to come in confidence to God."[46] Looking at these comments, it is clear that Calvin holds the doctrine of the Trinity and Christology together with his doctrine of creation and providence. The recent criticism that Calvin's doctrine of providence is not Trinitarian and Christocentric is unwarranted. Cornelis van der Kooi puts it this way,

> At the exact point where theology in the twentieth century often posed an opposition, Calvin did not see this opposition because he operated with a trinitarian perspective on revelation within which the Spirit plays a dominant role. Precisely in the school of Christ can creation, providence, and the hidden work of the Spirit be called upon. In fact, the school of Christ includes classes and grades where we initially receive a faint notion of God, then a more powerful impression of his majesty and judgement, and finally Christ appears as the image of the loving Father—as the centre and goal of the knowledge of God.[47]

---

44. Calvin, *John 1–10*, 10–11.
45. Calvin, *Galatians*, 308.
46. Calvin, *Hebrews and 1 & 2 Peter*, 250.
47. Van der Kooi, "Calvin's Theology of Creation," 64.

Relevance of Calvin's Doctrine of God's Providence in Asia

Calvin's doctrine of God's providence is close to many deterministic traditional Asian worldviews. The concept of fate and destiny is embraced in three major religions in Asia: Islam, Hinduism, and Buddhism. Chinese philosophies influential in the mindset of many Asian societies also contain a similar concept. I suggest that Calvin's teaching on God's providence is a relevant starting point for Christians to engage in a dialogue with non-Christians in Asia. As we will see, however, despite some similarities, Calvin's doctrine of God's providence is unique from the concept of fate and destiny in Asian religions and philosophies. In the following, I will briefly highlight the uniqueness and relevance of Calvin's doctrine of God's providence in Asian context.

Islam

Islam is the largest religion in Asia and approximately the twenty-five percent of the Asian population identify themselves as Muslims. It is well-known that Islam emphasizes the concept of God's providence. In Indonesia and Malaysia, this concept is called *takdir* ("fate")—*Qada/Qadar* in Arabic. Similar to Calvin's teaching, God's providence in Islam has been established by God without the knowledge of human beings for the highest purpose. Nor Ba'ayah Abdul Kadir and Kamsiah Ali note, "*Takdir* means events that happen in human life which are determined by God and its beneficial aspects (hikmah) that may occur from it without an individual's concern or knowledge."[48] In contrast to the karmic concepts in Hinduism and Buddhism, the concept of *takdir* in Islam is not associated with an individual's past experience, previous life, or punishment of the past sin.[49]

Takdir in Islam is divided into *Qada* and *Qadar*. *Qada* is the provisions created by *Allah* based on his will, while *Qadar* is the manifestation of the will and provisions of *Allah* over everything. The concepts of *Qada* and *Qadar* are similar to the concept of God's "hidden will" and "revealed will," respectively, in Calvin's teaching. Similar to Calvin's teaching, Islam's doctrine of providence does not neglect human effort. Although *Allah* has established everything, he also encourages the efforts of people, and the teaching of fate keeps them humble. Kadir notes:

---

48. Kadir and Ali, "Women's Voices in Relation to Fate," 108.
49. Kadir and Ali, "Women's Voices in Relation to Fate," 108.

On the other hand, the concept of effort (or *usaha* in Malay term) emerged to persuade people to be more positive in order to enhance their life satisfaction and well-being. In this connection, Moslems believe that God helps those people who put an effort to improve their life. In addition to that, fate helps them to be more humble and sensitive of the needs and welfare of others. Thus, fate does reflect active participation and action of human in seeking culturally appropriate attainments in a contemporary society.[50]

Looking at the similarities that exist between Calvin's doctrine of God's providence and the concept of *takdir* in Islam, this could be a starting point of a dialogue between Asian Christians Asian Muslims.

Hinduism and Buddhism

In Hinduism and Buddhism, the term *karma* describes the deterministic patterns of causality. Simply put, *karma* can be defined as "fate." However, this concept is different from the understanding of *takdir* in Islam. *Karma* in Hinduism and Buddhism is not determined by a personal God, but rather by an impersonal force (*braman*). As Kevin O'Donnel points out, *Karma* is the result of one's own deeds in one's present and previous lives. O'Donnel writes, "Karma is rather the power of your actions over a lifetime or several lifetime."[51]

Karma, which is the outcome of one's past actions, cannot be changed. Hindu society in India is familiar with the Tamil saying, "*talaiyeḻuttu iruntāl atai yār mārra muṭiyum?*" ("If it is in the head writing who can change it?"). According to Eliza F. Kent, Hindus in India believe that after a baby is born, there is a god who writes destiny alive on his or her forehead. When a particular destiny has been written, no one can change it. Kent notes, "Similar in some ways to the well-known Indian concept of karma, the motif of head writing expresses in a highly condensed fashion that one must bear one's fate, whatever it is, since no amount of effort can alter it."[52] Buddha follows this tradition (*Dhammapada* 9.126–27), "Some are born in a womb, wrongdoers, in hell. Those of good course go to heaven, to Nibbāna those without influxes. That spot in the world is not found, neither in the sky nor

---

50. Kadir and Ali, "Women's Voices in Relation to Fate," 109.
51. O'Donnel, *Inside World Religions*, 28.
52. Kent, "What's Written on the Forehead," 2.

in the ocean's depths, nor having entered into a cleft in mountains, where abiding, one would be released from the bad deed."[53]

Despite some similarities with respect to determinism, Calvin's doctrine of God's providence substantially differs from the concept of destiny in Hinduism and Buddhism. Instead of an impersonal force of destiny (*braman*) that determines each person's life, the Christian Scriptures point out to a personal creator God who allows each individual freedom to choose. Calvin writes in *Inst.* 1.16.8:

> We do not, with the Stoics, contrive a necessity out of the perpetual connection and intimately related series of causes, which is contained in nature; but we make God the ruler and governor of all things, who in accordance with his wisdom has from the farthest limit of eternity decreed what he was going to do, and now by his might carries out what he has decreed. From this we declare that not only heaven and earth and the inanimate creatures, but also the plans and intentions of men, are so governed by his providence that they are borne by it straight to their appointed end.

Calvin criticizes here the Stoic teaching, which resonates with the concept of *karma* in Hinduism and Buddhism. Again, Calvin's doctrine of God's providence, both in terms of its similarities and differences, opens up discussion about providence, but also the very nature of God with Hindus and Buddhists in Asia.

Traditional Chinese Philosophies

Traditional Chinese philosophies such as Confucianism and Taoism are more comprehensive than western philosophies, and they have incorporated various religious beliefs and practices into their systems. Traditional Chinese philosophies frequently discuss the concept of fate and destiny. Confucius writes in *Analects* 20.3, "One who does not understand fate lacks the means to become a gentleman [*junzi*]."[54] Lao Tzu identifies fate with the concept of *Tao* (path) in the teachings of Taoism (*Tao Te Ching* 16). Though Mencius alludes to the concept, he does not explain it clearly, saying, for example, "There is, for everything, a destiny, but one should follow and accept only what is proper for oneself."[55] The concept of fate and destiny

---

53. Carter and Palihawadana, *The Dhammapada*, 34.
54. Confucius, *Essential Analects*, 56.
55. Mencius, *Mencius*, 144.

taught in Chinese philosophies generally resemble the concept of *karma* in Hinduism and Buddhism. The difference is that Chinese philosophies in general suppose that a person is also responsible for his or her destiny. While *karma* is deeply fatalistic, Chinese philosophies generally maintain that one's destiny has been established from the beginning, but one's effort is also needed. Xunwu Chen argues, "Correspondingly, an individual person is both an embodiment of fate as given and a spinner of fate in making. The duality of fate as both 'made' and 'in making' further conceives the openness of fate, which in turn leads to the idea of human responsibility."[56] Traditional Chinese philosophies seem to affirm both the concept of destiny and that of human responsibility, which is similar to Calvin's doctrine of God's providence—especially, what has been called "compatibilism," which refers to the view that God has established everything but does not neglect the secondary cause. Despite this similarity, there is a fundamental difference between the two. Traditional Chinese philosophies do not believe in the existence of God as a person. The concept of divinity in traditional Chinese philosophies is not systematic as in the cases of many Asian religions. For example, Lao Tzu understands god as *Tao* ("way") and emphasizes that it cannot be defined (*Tao Te Ching* 1). Confucianism and Taoism have here a fundamental point of contact with Calvinism.

Conclusion

I have introduced a few recent critiques of Calvin's doctrine of God's providence and responded to their arguments. Despite recent criticisms, Calvin's doctrine of God's providence has been influential among Christian churches in Asia for several reasons. First, Calvin's doctrine of God's providence is thoroughly based on the Scriptures. Calvin does not attempt to come up with a creative solution to resolve all of the theological paradoxes in the Scriptures for himself. Calvin allows the Scriptures to speak for themselves and only attempts to faithfully articulate what they say about God's providence. This is why Calvin simultaneously affirms both God's sovereignty and human responsibility—compatibilism—based on his interpretation of the Scriptures, while admitting human limitation in understanding God's providence 100 percent. Second, Calvin's doctrine of God's providence does not contradict God's attributes such as his infinity, immutability, and sovereignty. Third, Calvin's doctrine of God's providence comforts and encourages Christian believers that, no matter what happens, they can trust in God's goodness and God's sovereignty—Rom 8:28.

56. Chen, "Fate and Humanity," 67.

Finally, Calvin's doctrine of God's providence provides Asian Christians with a unique point of engagement with their Muslim, Hindu, Buddhist, Confucian, and Taoist neighbors.

Bibliography

Berkhof, Louis. *Systematic Theology*. New ed. with a preface by Richard A. Muller. Grand Rapids: Eerdmans, 1996.

Boyd, Gregory. *Satan and the Problem of Evil: Constructing a Trinitarian Warfare Theodicy*. Downers Grove, IL: InterVarsity, 2001.

Bridges, Jerry. "Does Divine Sovereignty Make a Difference in Everyday Life." In *Still Sovereign: Contemporary Perspectives on Election, Foreknowledge and Grace*, edited by Thomas R. Schreiner and Bruce A. Ware, 295–306. Grand Rapids: Baker, 1995.

Calvin, John. *The Bondage and Liberation of the Will: A Defence of the Orthodox Doctrine of Human Choice Against Pighius*. Edited by A. N. S. Lane. Translated by G. I. Davis. Grand Rapids: Baker, 2012.

———. *Calvin's Calvinism: Treatises on the Eternal Predestination of God and the Secret Providence of God*. Translated by Henry Cole. Grand Rapids: Reformed Free Publishing Association, 2006.

———. *Galatians, Ephesians, Philippians, and Colossians*, edited by David W. Torrance and Thomas W. Torrance. Translated by T. H. L. Parker. CNTC 11. Grand Rapids: Eerdmans, 1965.

———. *John 1–10*. Edited by David W. Torrance and Thomas W. Torrance. Translated by T. H. L. Parker. CNTC 4. Grand Rapids: Eerdmans, 1961.

———. *Hebrews and 1 & 2 Peter*. Edited by David W. Torrance and Thomas W. Torrance. Translated by William B. Johnson. CNTC 12. Grand Rapids: Eerdmans, 1963.

———. *Institutes of the Christian Religion*. Edited by John T. McNeill. Translated by Ford Lewis Battle. LCC 20. Louisville: Westminster John Knox, 1960.

———. *The Secret Providence of God*, edited by Paul Helm. Wheaton, IL: Crossway, 2010.

Carson, D. A. *Divine Sovereignty and Human's Responsibility: Biblical Perspective in Tension*. 1994. Reprint, Eugene, OR: Wipf and Stock, 2002.

Carter, John Ross and Mahinda Palihawadana, eds. *The Dhammapada*. Oxford World's Classics. Oxford: Oxford University Press, 2000.

Chen, Xunwu. "Fate and Humanity." *Asian Philosophy* 20 (2010) 67–77.

Confucius. *The Essential Analects: Selected Passages with Traditional Commentary*. Translated by Edward Slingerland. Cambridge, MA: Hackett, 2006.

Coppedge, Allan. *The God Who is Triune: Revisioning the Christian Doctrine of God*. Downers Grove, IL: InterVarsity, 2007.

Cottrell, Jack W. "The Nature of the Divine Sovereignty." In *The Grace of God, the Will of Man: A Case for Arminianism*, edited by Clark H. Pinnock, 97–120. Grand Rapids: Zondervan, 1995.

Crisp, Oliver D. *Retrieving Doctrine: Essays in Reformed Theology*. Downers Grove, IL: InterVarsity, 2010.

Erickson, Millard J. *Christian Theology*. 3rd ed. Grand Rapids: Baker, 2013.

Feinberg, John S. "God, Freedom, and Evil in Calvinist Thinking." In *The Grace of God and the Bondage of the Will*, edited by Thomas R. Schreiner and Bruce A. Ware, 459–84. Grand Rapids: Baker, 1995.

———. *No One Like Him: The Doctrine of God*. Wheaton, IL: Crossway, 2001.

Fischer, Austin. *Young, Restless, No Longer Reformed: Black Holes, Love, and a Journey In and Out of Calvinism*. Eugene, OR: Cascade Books, 2014

Grudem, Wayne. *Systematic Theology: An Introduction to Biblical Doctrine*. Grand Rapids: Zondervan, 1994.

Helm, Paul. *Calvin at the Centre*. Oxford: Oxford University Press, 2010.

———. *Providence of God: Contours of Christian Theology*. Downers Grove, IL: InterVarsity, 1993.

Highfield, Ron. "Response to Paul Kjoss Helseth: God Causes All Things." In *Four Views on Divine Providence*, edited by Dennis W. Jowers, 141–64. Grand Rapids: Zondervan, 2011.

Higton, Mike. *Christian Doctrine*. London: SCM, 1998.

Hodge, A. A. *Evangelical Theology*. London: Nelson, 1890.

Hunt, Dave and James White, *Debating Calvinism: Five Points, Two Views*. Colorado Springs: Multnomah, 2004.

Kadir, Nor Ba'ayah Abdul, and Kamsiah Ali. "Women's Voices in Relation to Fate, Cultural Practices and Life Satisfaction: A Case Study of Sarawakian Single Mothers in Samarahan, Sarawak." *JSSH* 7 (2012) 107–18.

Keener, Craig S. *A Commentary on the Gospel of Matthew*. Grand Rapids: Eerdmans, 1999.

Kent, Eliza F. "What's Written on the Forehead Will Never Fail: Karma, Fate, and Headwriting in Indian Folktales." *Asian Ethnology* 68 (2009) 1–26.

McCormack, Bruce. "The Actuality of God: Karl Barth in Conversation with Open Theism." In *Engaging the Doctrine of God: Contemporary Protestant Perspectives*, edited by Bruce McCormack, 185–244. Grand Rapids: Baker, 2008.

McGrath, Alister E. *Reformation Thought: An Introduction*. 4th ed. Chichester, UK: Wiley, 2012.

———. *The Intellectual Origins of European Reformation*. 2nd ed. Oxford: Blackwell, 2004.

McKim, Donald K. "The Puritan View of History: Providence Without and Within." *EvQ* 52 (1980) 215–37.

McLean, Kalbryn A. "Calvin and the Personal Politics of Providence." In *Feminist and Womanist Essays in Reformed Dogmatics*, edited by Amy Plantinga Pauw and Serene Jones, 107–24. CSRT. Louisville: Westminster John Knox, 2006.

Mencius. *Mencius*. Edited by Philip J. Ivanhoe. Translated by Irene Bloom. Translations from the Asian Classics. New York: Columbia University Press, 2009.

Muller, Richard A. "Grace, Election and Contingent Choice: Arminius's Gambit and the Reformed Response." In *The Grace of God, the Bondage of the Will*, vol. 2, *Historical and Theological Perspectives on Calvinism*, edited by Thomas Schreiner and Bruce Ware, 251–78. Grand Rapids: Baker, 1995.

O'Donnel, Kevin. *Inside World Religions: A Vivid Portrait of Faith around the World*. Oxford: Lion Hudson, 2006.

Packer, J. I. *Evangelism and the Sovereignty of God*. Downers Grove, IL: InterVarsity, 1961.

Pinnock, Clark. "Clark Pinnock's Response to John Feinberg: God Ordains All Things." In *Predestination and Free Will: Four Views of Divine Sovereignty and Free Will*, edited by David Basinger and Randall Basinger, 141–62. Downers Grove, IL: InterVarsity, 1986.

Richardson, Kurt Anders. "Calvin on the Trinity." In *John Calvin and Evangelical Theology: Legacy & Prospect*, edited by Sung Wook Chung, 32–42. Louisville: Westminster John Knox, 2009.

Schreiner, Susan E. "Creation and Providence," In *The Calvin Handbook*, edited by Herman J. Selderhius, 267–74. Translated by Henry J. Baron, Judith J. Guder, and Randi H. Lundell. Grand Rapids: Eerdmans, 2009.

———. *The Theater of His Glory: Nature and the Natural Order in the Thought of John Calvin*. Grand Rapids: Baker, 1991.

Tiessen, Terrance. *Providence and Prayer: How Does God Work in the World?* Downers Grove, IL: InterVarsity, 2000.

Van der Kooi, Cornelius. "Calvin's Theology of Creation and Providence: God's Care and Human Fragility." *IJST* 18 (2016) 47–65.

Walls, Jerry, and Joseph R. Dongell. *Why I Am not a Calvinist*. Downers Grove, IL: InterVarsity, 2004.

Ware, Bruce A. "Divine Election to Salvation: Unconditional, Individual, and Infralapsarian." In *Perspectives on Election*, edited by Chad Owen Brand, 59–69. Nashville: Broadman & Holman, 2006.

———. *God's Greater Glory: The Exalted God of Scripture and the Christian Faith*. Wheaton, IL: Crossway, 2004.

Wood, Charles M. "Providence." In *The Oxford Handbook of Systematic Theology*, edited by John Webster, Kathryn Tanner, and Ian Torrance, 91–104. Oxford: Oxford University Press, 2007.

———. *The Question of Providence*. Louisville: Westminster John Knox, 2008.

Part 3

Christian Worldview

9

Human Rights in Islam and Christianity

Implications for the Pluralistic Society in Indonesia Today

───── Yonathan Wijaya Lo and Yongbom Lee

Introduction

On May 9, 2017, a Jakarta court sentenced the former Jakarta deputy governor Basuki "Ahok" Purnama, a Chinese Indonesian Christian, to a two-year prison sentence at Cipinang Penitentiary in Jakarta, with the charge of blasphemy against Islam. Prior to that, during Jakarta's gubernatorial election in April 2017, radical Islamic groups accused Ahok of blasphemy against Islam and persuaded many Muslim voters not to support Ahok, a popular deputy governor of Jakarta at that time, because the Qur'an does not allow any non-Muslim to rule over Muslims. Ahok was defeated by his Muslim competitor Anies Baswedan in the second round run-off election. This surprising turn of political events showed the rise of radical Islam in Indonesian politics, which made moderate Indonesians feel insecure about democracy and the freedom of speech, guaranteed in the *Pancasila* in the Constitution of Indonesia (*Undang-Undang Dasar Republik Indonesia* 1945).[1] In this study,

---

1. The *Pancasila* refers to the five founding principles of the Republic of Indonesia in its 1945 Constitution, which includes (1) Belief in the One and Only God; (2) Just and Civilized Humanity; (3) the Unity of Indonesia; (4) Democracy Guided by the Inner Wisdom of the Unanimity Arising out of Deliberations amongst Representatives; (5) Social Justice for the Whole of the People of Indonesia.

we will reflect on Islamic and Christian understandings of human rights—religious rights and women's rights in particular—and consider their implications in the pluralistic society in Indonesia today.

Islamic Understanding of Human Rights

The Qur'an and the Sunnah are the primary sources of divine laws in Islam. For Muslims, the Qur'an is the very word of Allah himself. Ibn Warraq notes that the Sunnah—"a path or way or manner of life"—expresses the custom or manner of life of Muslims, based on the deeds and words of the Prophet Mohammad.[2] The Sunnah complements and clarifies the Qur'an. Divine laws (the Qur'an and the Sunnah) and their interpretations (Shari'a) are closely related to each other, though Shari'a should not be identified with divine laws themselves.

Islam understands human rights on the basis of Allah's sovereignty. The Qur'an states that Allah created every human being to serve him. Qur'an 6:101-102 writes, "To Him is due the primal origin of the heavens and the earth: How can He have a son when He hath no consort? He created all things, and He hath full knowledge of all things. That is Allah, your Lord! there is no god but He, the Creator of all things: then worship ye Him: and He hath power to dispose of all affairs."[3] According to the Qur'an, Allah has granted human beings freedom (91:8) and this freedom provides the ground for human rights. To deny or violate this freedom is to deny or violate what makes someone a human being. The Qur'an is deeply concerned about liberating human freedom from every kind of bondage. The Qur'an rejects any kind of slavery and promotes liberation. For instance, while the Qur'an condemns the other religions, it also makes it clear that it is only Allah who will judge them (Qur'an 42:21). Allah alone is the one to worship and the one who commands (Qur'an 12:40). Unlike Christianity, Islam does not recognize the consequence of Adam and Eve's original sin. Everyone is completely responsible for his or her actions based on his or her free will.

The Qur'an allows religious freedom for monotheistic non-Muslims who live among Muslims. Qur'an 2:256 writes, "Let there be no compulsion in religion"; Qur'an 109:1-6. Riffat Hassan notes:

> The Qur'an also makes clear that God will judge human beings not on the basis of what they profess but on the basis of their belief and religious conduct, as indicated by Surah 2: Al-baqarah:

2. Warraq, *Why I Am Not A Muslim*, 165.

3. In this study, I am using Abdulla Yusuf Ali's English translation of the Qur'an, except for its English translations included in secondary sources.

62 which states: "Those who believe (in the Qur'an) and those who follow the Jewish (scriptures), and the Christians and the Sabians, any who believe in God and the Last Day, and work righteousness, shall have their reward saith the Lord; on them shall be nor fear, nor shall they grieve." The Qur'an recognizes the right to religious freedom not only in the case of other believers in God, but also in the case of non-believers in God (if they are not aggressive toward Muslims). For instance, Surah 6: *Al-An'am*: 108 states: "Revile not ye those whom they call upon besides God, lest they out of spite revile God in their ignorance. Thus have We made alluring to each people its own doings. In the end they return to their Lord, and We shall then tell them the truth of all that they did."[4]

However, the Qur'an strictly prohibits any Muslim—including anybody from a Muslim family—from converting to any other religion and condemns it as an act of apostasy, as indicated in the following Qur'an passages:

But those who reject Faith after they accepted it, and then go on adding to their defiance of Faith—never will their repentance be accepted; for they are those who have (of set purpose) gone astray (3:90). How (can there be such a league), seeing that if they get an advantage over you, they respect not in you the ties either of kinship or of covenant? With (fair words from) their mouths they entice you, but their hearts are averse from you; and most of them are rebellious and wicked. The Signs of Allah have they sold for a miserable price, and (many) have they hindered from His way: evil indeed are the deeds they have done. In a Believer they respect not the ties either of kinship or of covenant! It is they who have transgressed all bounds. But (even so), if they repent, establish regular prayers, and practice regular charity—they are your brethren in Faith: (thus) do We explain the Signs in detail, for those who understand. But if they violate their oaths after their covenant, and taunt you for your Faith—fight ye the chiefs of Unfaith: for their oaths are nothing to them: that thus they may be restrained. Will ye not fight people who violated their oaths, plotted to expel the Messenger, and took the aggressive by being the first (to assault) you? Do ye fear them? Nay, it is Allah Whom ye should more justly fear, if ye believe! Fight them, and Allah will punish them by your hands, cover them with shame, help you (to victory) over them, heal the breasts of Believers, And still the indignation of their

---

4. Hassan, "Rights of Women," 376.

> hearts. For Allah will turn (in mercy) to whom He will; and Allah is All-Knowing, All-Wise (9:8–15).
>
> Make ye no excuses: ye have rejected Faith after ye had accepted it. If We pardon some of you, We will punish others amongst you, for that they are in sin (9:66).
>
> Anyone who, after accepting faith in Allah, utters Unbelief—except under compulsion, his heart remaining firm in Faith—but such as open their breast to Unbelief, on them is Wrath from Allah, and theirs will be a dreadful Penalty (16:106).

While the Qur'an allows religious rights for monotheistic non-Muslims, it forbids a Muslim's conversion to any other religion. Abdurahman Wahid, the former Chairman of Nahdlatul Ulama (NU), observes:

> The writings have shown that Islam supports human rights and Islam is a democratic religion, but in fact, that claim is not in accord with practical life. For we see, in most countries, Islamic communities have greatly violated human rights, including in Indonesia. If we don't recognize that fact, then we only affirm Islam as an idealistic perspective, where its teaching has no relation to human rights. If this is the case, Islam's claims for human rights are only empty profession without any purchase on real life.[5]

The violation of human rights has been a critical social issue in many Islamic societies. As Wahid points out, this calls Muslims to think about the Qur'an's tolerance towards non-Muslims who live among Muslims, and how they can respect their non-Muslim neighbors' religious rights today.

Regarding women's rights, Islam presents a number of challenges. Hassan differentiates the Qur'an from Gen 3 in the Hebrew Bible and makes three observations:

> First, the myth that Eve was created from the rib of Adam has no basis whatever in the Qur'an which, in the context of human creation, speaks always in completely egalitarian terms . . . Second, in the context of the story of the "Fall," it needs to be pointed out that the Qur'an provides no basis whatever for asserting, suggesting, or implying that "*Hawwa*" (Eve) was tempted by "*ash-Shaitan*" (the Satan), in turn tempted and deceived Adam, and led to his expulsion from "*al-jannah*" (the Garden) . . . Third, the Qur'an, which does not discriminate against women in the context of creation or the "Fall" story, does not support

---

5. Wahid, *My Islam, Your Islam, and Our Islam*, 121; this book is written in Indonesian and this is my English translation.

the view—held by many Muslims, Christians, and Jews—that woman was created not only *from* man, but also *for* man.⁶

In the following page, Hassan continues to emphasize the Qur'an's teaching of gender equality:

> According to the Qur'an, service to God cannot be separated from service to humankind, or, in Islamic terms, believers in God must honor both "*Haquq Allah*" (rights of God) and "*Haquq al-ibad*" (rights of creatures). Fulfillment of one's duties to God and humanity constitutes the essence of righteousness. That men and women are equally called upon by God to be righteous and will be equally rewarded for their righteousness is stated unambiguously in a number of Qur'anic verses [Qur'an 3:195; 4:124; 9:71–72; 16:97; 23:35]. Not only does the Qur'an make it clear that man and woman stand absolutely equal in the sight of God, but also they are "members" and "protectors" of each other. In other words, the Qur'an does not create a hierarchy in which men are placed above women (as they are by many formulators by the Christian tradition), nor does it pit men against women in an adversary relationship. They are created as equal creatures of a universal, just and merciful God whose pleasure it is that they live—in harmony and righteousness—together.⁷

However, Hassan also recognizes the discrepancy between the Qur'an's teaching of gender equality and the gender inequality in Islamic societies, "In spite of the Qur'anic affirmation of the quality of man and woman, Muslim societies in general have never regarded men and women as equal, particularly in the context of marriage."⁸ Hassan argues that, while the Qur'an teaches gender equality, in practice, there has been serious gender inequality in Muslim societies.

---

6. Wahid, *My Islam, Your Islam, and Our Islam*, 384.

7. Wahid, *My Islam, Your Islam, and Our Islam*, 385.

8. Hassan, "Rights of Women within Islamic Community," 385; Hassan cites a passage from Mernissi, which he believes, generally describes Muslim culture: "One of the distinctive characteristics of Muslim sexuality is its territoriality, which reflects a specific division of labor and a specific conception of society and of power. The territoriality of Muslim sexuality sets ranks, tasks and authority patterns. Spatially confined the woman was taken care of materially by the man who possessed her, in return for her total obedience and her sexual and reproductive services. The whole system was organized so that the Muslim 'ummah' was actually a society of male citizens who possessed among other things the female half of the population . . . Muslim men have always had more rights and privileges than Muslim women, including even the right to kill their women . . . The man imposed on the woman an artificially narrow existence, both physically and spiritually," Mernissi, *Beyond the Veil*, 103.

In contrast to Hassan, Warraq argues that the Qur'an itself undermines gender equality. Warraq highlights, "women are inferior under Islamic law; their testimony in the court of law is worth half that of a man; their movement is strictly restricted; they cannot marry non-Muslims."[9] Warraq also comments, "Slavery is recognized in the Koran. Muslims are allowed to cohabit with any of their female slaves (sura 4.3); they are allowed to take position of married women if they are slaves (sura 4.28). The helpless position of the slave in regard to his or her master illustrates the helpless position of the false gods of Arabia in the presence of their Creator (sura 16.77)."[10] It goes beyond our expertise and the scope of this chapter to discuss whether or not the Qur'an itself promotes gender inequality. Regardless of that, however, historically speaking, gender inequality has been a serious social concern in many Islamic societies.

Christian Understanding of Human Rights

We can summarize a Christian worldview's unique understanding of human rights with one of the most important theological expressions—*Imago Dei* ("the image of God"). Gen 1:26–28 writes:

> Then God said, "Let us make man in our image, after our likeness. And let them have dominion over the fish of the sea and over the birds of the heavens and over the livestock and over all the earth and over every creeping thing that creeps on the earth." So God created man in his own image, in the image of God he created him; male and female he created them. And God blessed them. And God said to them, "Be fruitful and multiply and fill the earth and subdue it, and have dominion over the fish of the sea and over the birds of the heavens and over every living thing that moves on the earth."[11]

Ps 8:3–6 reflects on God's amazing grace in his creation of human beings and their special role in the world that he created. We will highlight Christian understanding of human rights in this section in four parts. First, we will discuss the biblical backgrounds of *Imago Dei*. Second, we will explore the implications for *Imago Dei* in response to the four acts of the biblical drama. Third, we will introduce John Calvin's understanding of *Imago Dei*

---

9. Warraq, *Why I Am Not a Muslim*, 173.
10. Warraq, *Why I Am Not a Muslim*, 173.
11. In this study, I am using the ESV translation unless otherwise noted.

in his *Institutes of Christian Religion*. Fourth, we will highlight the implications of *Imago Dei* for religious rights and women's rights.

Biblical Backgrounds of *Imago Dei*

In the context of Gen 1–3, *Imago Dei* refers to five distinctive roles of human beings in relation to God and his creation: (1) rulers; (2) jars of clay; (3) stewards; (4) free moral agents; and (5) male and female. First, God has appointed human beings as his image-bearers as the rulers of all of his creation. The word *ha Adam* ("[the] Adam") not only refers to the first man in Gen 1:27 but the whole of humanity, represented by the first man, because the text itself clarifies, "male [*zakar*] and female [*nekēbah*] he [God] created them." God calls both Adam and Eve to rule over his creation on behalf of him, as his vassals. In the Ancient Near East, only kings were considered to be the images of their gods and goddesses, and called to rule everyone else on behalf of them. J. Richard Middleton in *The Liberating Image* explains in detail how revolutionary the Scripture's claim that every human being is created in the image of God and is called to rule on behalf of him must have been in its socio-political and cultural context.[12] The emphasis that God created both male and female in his image is important for us keep in mind.

Second, God created human beings out of dust, by breathing the breath of life into them. Gen 2:7 writes, "Then the LORD God formed the man of dust from the ground and breathed into his nostrils the breath of life, and the man became a living creature." Paul reflects on this earthly fragile nature of human body in contrast to invaluable faith in Christ, "But we have this treasure in jars of clay, to show that the surpassing power belongs to God and not to us" (2 Cor 4:7). The human body is made up of the same chemical elements as those of any other creation. What is special about human beings is the fact that only they are God's image-bearers, and God created each person unique in the entire history of the universe.

Third, God called human beings to serve as the stewards of his creation. Gen 2:15 writes, "The LORD God took the man and put him in the Garden of Eden to work [*ebed*] it and keep [*shamar*] it." In the Torah, these two words are often used in reference to the Levitical priests' activities in the tabernacle.[13] This suggests that the Garden of Eden was the sanctuary of God and Adam, the first human being and the representative of humanity, was created to cultivate the Garden and serve and worship God as a priest through his cultivating work in the tabernacle or temple of

12. Middleton, *The Liberating Image*, 185–234.
13. Wenham, *Genesis 1–15*, 68; Middleton, *Liberating Image*, 82–88.

God. This is related to the cultural mandate that God gave human beings. They are called to make things grow and make things better, using their God-given creativity and authority. This stewardship (Gen 2:15) clarifies the rule (Gen 1:26–28). Human beings do not own this world. God does. God in his sovereign grace entrusted human beings as his stewards to take good care of his creation.

Fourth, God created human beings as free moral agents. In Gen 2:16–17, God warns Adam, "You may surely eat of every tree of the garden, but of the tree of the knowledge of good and evil you shall not eat, for in the day that you eat of it you shall surely die." Some people wonder why God put such a temptation for Adam and Eve in the Garden of Eden, in the first place. This signifies that God did not create human beings as machines. Instead, God created persons in his image, who are free moral agents, reflecting his own personhood. God wanted human beings to freely choose to worship and obey him. This was so important for God that he even risked the possibility of evil in his creation.

Fifth, God created both male and female in his image (Gen 1:26–28). Some people argue that women are inferior to men, because God created Eve as Adam's helper (Gen 2:20) and out of Adam's rib (Gen 2:22). The Hebrew word ʿēzer ("helper") in Gen 2:20 by no means suggests gender inequality, when we consider the fact that God is called to be ʿēzer ("helper") throughout the Hebrew Bible (Deut 33:7; Hos 13:9; Ps 70:5; 121:1, 2; 124:8; 146:5). The fact that God is Israel's helper does not mean that God is inferior to Israel. God created both Adam and Eve in his image. God gave Adam and Eve as a husband and a wife different roles; however, that has nothing to do with gender inequality.

Imago Dei in the Four Acts of the Biblical Drama

In the biblical metanarrative, there are four distinctive acts or chapters: (1) Creation; (2) Fall; (3) Redemption; and (4) Consummation. God created everything good (Gen 1:1—2:3) and God created human beings in his image as the stewards of his good creation (Gen 1:26–28). However, Adam and Eve, seduced by the serpent, transgressed against God's command not to eat the fruit of the Tree of Knowledge of Good and Evil (Gen 2:16–17). This brought sin and death to this world (Rom 5:12–21), which affected not only Adam and Eve but also the whole creation (Rom 8:19–20). Jesus Christ, the incarnate Son of God, came to this world and completed his work of atonement on the cross to redeem lost humanity (John 1:14; 3:16–17). Second

Corinthians 5:17 states, "Therefore, if anyone is in Christ, he is a new creation. The old has passed away; behold, the new has come." However, there is an eschatological tension of "already, but not yet." The kingdom of God came through the person and work of Jesus Christ; however, it will be consummated only when Jesus Christ comes back to judge the world (Matt 19:28; John 5:24–27; Acts 17:31–32; 2 Cor 5:10) and there will be a new heaven and a new earth (Rev 21:1–4). The following table captures the biblical understanding of *Imago Dei* in each of the four biblical drama:

Creation	Fall	Redemption	Consummation
Original Image of God	Corrupted Image of God; Yet with Common Grace	Restored and Renewed Image of God in Christ	Image of God Completely Restored

God created Adam and Eve in his image (Gen 1:26–28). Adam and Eve sinned against God and fell short of God's glory (Gen 3; Rom 3:23), and the image of God was corrupted but not completely destroyed. God shows his common grace to all people (Matt 5:43–45). The redemptive work of Christ, who is the exact image of God, and one's faith in the gospel of Christ (2 Cor 4:6) restores and renews the image of God (2 Cor 5:17). Although Adam was already created in the image of God, he sought to be like God (Gen 3:5) and, through his transgression, sin and death came to this world (Rom 5:12–21). In contrast, "though he [Christ] was in the form of God, did not count equality with God a thing to be grasped, but emptied himself, by taking the form of a servant, being born in the likeness of men. And being found in human form, he humbled himself by becoming obedient to the point of death, even death on a cross" (Phil 2:6–8). Therefore, the life of Christ illustrates what it means to be a true human being, which Adam failed to be. God predestined believers to "be conformed to the image of his Son, in order that he might be the firstborn among many brothers" (Rom 8:29). However, the restored and renewed image of God in believers is not yet complete until the End, as Paul writes, "For now we see in a mirror dimly, but then face to face. Now I know in part; then I shall know fully, even as I have been fully known" (1 Cor 13:12). When Jesus returns to judge the world, the restoration of the image of God in believers will be completed in the new heaven and a new earth, and paradise will be restored, in which God's servants worship him and see his face (Rev 21:1–5; 22:1–5).

Calvin's Understanding of *Imago Dei*

John Calvin covers various topics of anthropology in his *Institutes of Christian Religion* (1559). *Institutes* 1.15 includes discussion of human nature as created beings, faculties of the human soul, the image of God, free will, and the original integrity of human nature. We will highlight a few of Calvin's points related to his understanding of *Imago Dei* in this section. To begin with, Calvin supposes that God created human beings in his image and, before their fall, they had "originally upright nature" (*Inst.* 1.15.1).[14] Calvin writes, "God's image was visible in the light of the mind, in the uprightness of the heart, and in the soundness of all the parts" (*Inst.* 1.15.4). Calvin discusses the constitutional nature of a human being, "Now I understand by the term 'soul' an immortal yet created essence, which is his nobler part. Sometimes it is called 'spirit'... Surely the conscience, which, discerning between good and evil, responds to God's judgment, is an undoubted sign of the immortal spirit... Therefore the spirit must be the seat of this intelligence" (*Inst.* 1.15.2). Calvin recognizes that Adam had genuine free will as a part of being created in the image of God, when he decided to disobey God's commandment not to eat the fruit of the tree of knowledge of good and evil (Gen 2:16–17) (*Inst.* 1.15.8).[15]

Calvin discusses in detail the human condition after the Fall. Calvin writes, "There is no doubt that Adam, when he fell from his state, was by this defection alienated from God. Therefore, even though we grant that God's image was not totally annihilated and destroyed in him, yet it was so corrupted that whatever remains is frightful deformity" (*Inst.* 1.15.4). However, despite the devastating consequences of the Fall, God's image in Adam was not completely destroyed. Calvin notes, "Even though in man's corruption this last point [human souls' intrinsic desire to honor God] is not clearly perceived, yet some vestige remains imprinted in his very vices" (*Inst.* 1.15.6). Later in *Inst.* 2.2, Calvin further explains this deformity of the image of God in human beings in three ways.

First, Calvin differentiates the natural and the supernatural gifts of humanity, associated with having been created in the image of God. Calvin writes:

> And, indeed, that common opinion which they have taken from Augustine [*On Nature and Grace*] pleases me: that the natural

---

14. I am using Battles' translation of the *Institutes* in this study.

15. Calvin comments, "Here it would be out of place to raise the question of God's secret predestination because our present subject is not what can happen or not, but what man's nature was like."

gifts were corrupted in man through sin, but that his supernatural gifts were stripped from him. For by the latter clause they understand the light of faith as well as righteousness, which would be sufficient to attain heavenly life and eternal bliss. Therefore, withdrawing from the Kingdom of God, he is at the same time deprived of spiritual gifts, with which he had been furnished for the hope of eternal salvation. From this it follows that he is so banished from the Kingdom of God that all qualities belonging to the blessed life of the soul have been extinguished in him, until he recovers them through the grace of regeneration. Among these are faith, love of God, charity toward neighbor, zeal for holiness and for righteousness (*Inst.* 2.2.12).

Calvin's distinction between the corrupted natural gifts and the stripped supernatural gifts presupposes that there was a time in which human beings possessed both uncorrupted natural gifts and supernatural gifts, before Adam and Eve fell into sin.

Second, Calvin supposes that, while the natural gifts of human beings were "partly weakened and partly corrupted" due to the Fall, they still differentiate humans from beasts. Calvin notes: "In these words [John 1:5] both facts are clearly expressed. First, in man's perverted and degenerate nature some sparks still gleam. These show him to be a rational being, differing from brute beasts, because he is endowed with understanding. Yet, secondly, they show this light choked with dense ignorance, so that it cannot come forth effectively" (*Inst.* 2.2.12). Human beings' ability to reason stands out from the other creatures, and provides the evidence for Calvin that the natural gifts of human beings are corrupted but have not completely vanished.

Third, Calvin argues that human beings' desire for justice and civil society reflects their corrupted and faint, but yet remaining image of God in them. Calvin writes, "Hence no man is to be found who does not understand that every sort of human organization must be regulated by laws, and who does not comprehend the principles of those laws. Hence arises that unvarying consent of all nations and of individual mortals with regard to laws. For their seed have, without teacher or lawgiver, been implanted in all men. . . . And this is ample proof that in the arrangement of this life no man is without the light of reason" (*Inst.* 2.2.13). In *Inst.* 2.7.6–9, Calvin surveys three functions of what he calls "the 'moral law'"—(1) "while it shows God's righteousness alone acceptable to God, it warns, informs, convicts, and lastly condemns, every man of his own unrighteousness" (*Inst.* 2.7.6); (2) "at least by fear of punishment to restrain certain men who are untouched by any care for what is just and right unless compelled by hearing the dire threats in the law" (*Inst.* 2.7.10); (3) "The third and principal use, which pertains more closely to the proper purpose of the law, finds its place among believers in whose hearts the Spirit of God already lives and reigns" (*Inst.* 2.7.12). Calvin's discussion of the moral law for both the elect and the reprobate is rooted in his understanding of the post-fall state of human beings. Human beings are not deprived of their natural gifts consisting in their faculties of the soul that comprise mind and understanding (e.g., knowledge concerning earthly things). The seed of the moral law and political order are implanted in human beings' mind. Although humans are unrighteous, they are still aware of their moral transgression and feel guilty in their own conscience. In Calvin's mind, such a fact indicates the partly weakened and partly corrupted image of God that still faintly remains in the human soul. In Calvin's thought, one's conscience is one's witness before God in his judgment, which does not allow anyone to hide his or her sins before God. No one can suppress one's God-given conscience, which Calvin describes as "this awareness which hales man before God's judgment is a sort of guardian appointed for man to note and spy out all his secrets that nothing may remain buried in darkness" (*Inst.* 3.19.15). The moral law can convict human beings of their sins, because of their God-given conscience.

While Calvin recognizes that the damage of the Fall on human beings was real and the original image of God in human beings was corrupted, Calvin also states that the image of God in human beings is not totally lost, because even ungodly human beings still desire justice and civil society and they are convicted of their sins by their God-given conscience. Calvin refers to God's common grace given to all humanity throughout *Institutes* (1.5.3; 1.8.1; 2.2.1; 2.2.17; 2.3.3; 2.3.4; 3.2.11; 3.2.12; 3.24.15). As Louis Berkhof notes, "[Common grace] curbs the destructive power of sin, maintains in a measure the moral order of the universe, thus making an orderly life possible, distributes in varying degrees gifts and talents among men, promotes the development of science and art, and showers untold blessings upon the children of men."[16]

Religious Rights and Women's Rights

Christian Scriptures uniquely present the concept of *Imago Dei*. Jesus commissions his disciples: "All authority in heaven and on earth has been given to me. Go therefore and make disciples of all nations, baptizing them in the name of the Father and of the Son and of the Holy Spirit, teaching them to observe all that I have commanded you" (Matt 28:18–20a). However, there

16. Berkhof, *Systematic Theology*, 434.

is no evidence in the four canonical Gospels that Jesus forced anyone to follow him. Jesus only invited the others to his message of the kingdom of God (e.g., Matt 6:33; Mark 1:15; 10:14–15; Luke 4:43; 9:2, 11, 60; 10:9; 18:16–17). In Matt 5:13–16, Jesus instructs his disciples:

> You are the salt of the earth, but if salt has lost its taste, how shall its saltiness be restored? It is no longer good for anything except to be thrown out and trampled under people's feet. "You are the light of the world. A city set on a hill cannot be hidden. Nor do people light a lamp and put it under a basket, but on a stand, and it gives light to all in the house. In the same way, let your light shine before others, so that they may see your good works and give glory to your Father who is in heaven.

In its beginning, Christianity was a persecuted religious minority in the Roman Empire and Christian Scriptures encourage believers to persevere in their persecution (1 Cor 4:1–21; 15:29–34; Phil 2:17; 2 Tim 3:10—4:8; Heb 12:1–6; 1 Pet 1:3–12). Emperor Theodosius' installation of Christianity as the state religion of Rome (380 AD), the Roman Catholic Church's subsequent political hegemony in medieval Europe, the conflicts between Roman Catholics and Protestants after the Protestant Reformation, native people's forced conversion to Christianity during Europe's colonization of Africa, Asia, and Americas are cases of the violation of religious rights by European Christians. However, it is important to note that the New Testament itself recognizes God's common grace for all human beings and supports religious rights.

In parallel with Christian Scriptures' emphasis on the dignity of every human being who is created in the image of God, they underscore gender equality, when we consider their particular socio-cultural contexts. In the previous section, we cited a passage from Hassan, in which he implicit claims that the Qur'an teaches gender equality, while the Hebrew Bible does not. Hassan makes three arguments: (1) the Qur'an never mentions that "Eve was created from the rib of Adam"; (2) "the Qur'an provides no basis whatever for asserting, suggesting, or implying that '*Hawwa*' (Eve) was tempted by '*ash-Shaitan*'"; and (3) the Qur'an does not teach that "woman was created not only from man, but also for man."[17] While recognizing that the Qur'an presents a different version of Gen 2:4—3:24, we disagree with Hassan's implicit claim that the Hebrew Bible presents gender inequality for three reasons. First, as we mentioned earlier, the fact that God took one of Adam's ribs to create Eve (Gen 2:21) by no means suggests Eve's inferiority to Adam in its literary context. Second, according to Gen 3:1–5, Satan

17. Hassan, "Rights of Women," 384.

tempted only Eve who later tempted Adam. It is worth noting that, when God forbade Adam eating the fruit of the Tree of Knowledge of Good and Evil (Gen 2:16–17), Eve did not exist yet. Adam did not communicate God's prohibition to Eve clearly or Eve did not take Adam seriously. In any case, Adam had no excuse of his transgression, because God spoke directly to him. Gen 3 presents both Adam and Eve guilty of transgression, as both of them receive their respective punishment from God—heavy labor for survival and death for Adam (17–19) and child-bearing and submission to the husband (16). Third, Hassan's claim that, according to the Hebrew Bible, "woman was created not only *from* man, but also *for* man" demands clarification. Hassan's claim seems to have Gen 2:20 in mind, "The man gave names to all livestock and to the birds of the heavens and to every beast of the field. But for Adam there was not found a helper ['ēzer] fit for him."

Considering that Gen 2:20 does not indicate any gender inequality, as we argued earlier, Hassan's claim that the Hebrew Bible itself presents gender inequality is unwarranted. Paul instructs, "Wives, submit to your own husbands, as to the Lord" (Eph 5:22). Paul by no means implies that wives are inferior to husbands or wives are personal slaves of husbands, for Paul just now has encouraged all his readers to "submit to one another out of reverence for Christ" (Eph 5:21). Paul also instructs, "Husbands, love your wives, as Christ loved the church and gave himself up for her" (Eph 5:25). We see here mutual submission out of reverence for Christ, rather than any hint of gender inequality, when reading this passage in its proper literary context. Emphasizing believers' unity in Christ, Paul writes, "For as many of you as were baptized into Christ have put on Christ. There is neither Jew nor Greek, there is neither slave nor free, there is no male and female, for you are all one in Christ Jesus. And if you are Christ's, then you are Abraham's offspring, heirs according to promise" (Gal 3:26–29).

One may argue that Paul discriminates against women when he writes, "the women should keep silent in the churches. For they are not permitted to speak, but should be in submission, as the Law also says" (1 Cor 14:34; 1 Tim 2:11–15). It goes beyond the scope of this study to discuss in depth such controversial Pauline passages here. However, it is worth pointing out that there are many different interpretations of these passages.[18] For example, Craig S. Keener concludes his discussion of 1 Tim 2:9–15, "There is a universal principle in this text, but it is broader than that unlearned women should not teach. If Paul does not want the women to teach in some sense, it is not because they are women, but because they are unlearned. His principle here is that those who do not understand the

---

18. Fitzmyer, *First Corinthians*, 528–35; Garland, *1 Corinthians*, 664–73.

Scriptures and are not able to teach them accurately should not permitted to teach others."[19] In our opinion, Paul had specific groups of women in mind, who caused problems in the churches that he planted, and his comments in these passages were aiming at them, rather than all women throughout history without any qualification.[20]

Implications of Human Rights in Indonesia Today

Both Islam and Christianity in their own ways affirm human rights and acknowledge the universal freedom of human beings. The Constitution of the Republic of Indonesia recognizes six religions—Islam, Hinduism, Buddhism, Catholicism, Protestantism, and Confucianism. In its current human rights crisis, Indonesians must consider religious perspectives on human rights in addition to secular perspectives on human rights, and think about their implications.

The Socio-Political Situation of Indonesia Today

Overall, there are two main Islamic groups in Indonesia today: the traditionalists and the reformists (also known as "the modernists"). The traditionalists are characterized by their strict preservation of Muslim way of life in accordance with *Mazhab*.[21] The reformists follow the ideas of Islamic reform, introduced by Muhammad Abdul and Rashid Rida in Egypt, who promoted religious practices based on the Qur'an and the Sunnah. They emphasized the need for *Ijtihad* and leaving the *Mazhabs*, and rejected local religious interpretations and practices of Islamic traditions, and established modern schools.[22] The traditionalists are affiliated with *Nahdatul Ulama* (NU), while the reformists are associated with Muhammadiyah, the two largest Muslim organizations in Indonesia today. Jajat Burhanudin

---

19. Keener, *Paul, Women & Wives*, 120.

20. Gary G. Hoag interestingly draws fresh insights from *Ephesiaca* by Xenophon by Ephesus and suggests that, in 1 Tim 2:11–15, Paul is deliberately asking his female readers not to follow the examples of Hellenistic cult prophetesses and not to fear death in childbirth, as it was believed that mothers would lose their lives if they do not worship the goddess Artemis; Hoag, *Wealth in Ancient Ephesus*.

21. *Mazhab* is derived from an Arabic word, meaning, "to go" or 'to take as away," and refers to a commonly accepted authoritative interpreter of Islamic laws.

22. *Ijtihad* refers to the process of making a legal decision by independent interpretation of the Qur'an and the Sunnah.

describes the challenge of the complex development of the socio-religious life of Muslim in Indonesia today:

> It is true that those two Islam mainstreams in Indonesia cannot fully represent the complexity of the development of the socio-religious life of Muslims. Moreover, during the last few decades, there have been socio-political and cultural changes after the New Order modernization projects that have changed the face of Islam in Indonesia. The terms "traditionalist" and "reformist" are no longer representative. The new faces of Islam, characterized by the growing of Muslim intellectuals, exceeded the two previous terms. However, to understand the "new Islam" one needs to scrutinize the historical link of mainstream Islam. The Islam intellectual genealogy can be traced back to the period of development when two faces of mainstream Islam experienced an independent development process in the early 20th Century. To be exact, the new Islam was born as a result of re-interpretation—even, to use Hobsbawn's term "finding"—of principles that have been prescribed by those involved in the process of formulating the mainstream Islam in Indonesia.[23]

In recent years, a group of Muslim intellectuals have emerged in Indonesia and started to question the role of Islam in the pluralistic and democratic nation. These Islamic thinkers discuss the Constitution of Indonesia, democracy, human rights, gender equality, and so on. In particular, the relationship between Islam and the state has recently been a topic of heated debate among them. For example, Mujahidin Counsel of Indonesia (MMI), which seeks to implement Shari'a in every province in Indonesia strongly rejects the separation of Islam and the state. This group seeks to establish an Islamic State of Indonesia.

Indonesian Muslims have different perspectives on the topic of human rights. For example, there are two groups of the *Salafi* movement in Indonesia, which reflects diversity in attitudes towards Shari'a.[24] Jajang Jahroni states:

> First, there is a call for referring solely to the original source of Islam as practiced by the Prophet and his disciples. The second element is the political militancy that emphasizes the concept of jihad and the obligation of all Muslims to defend Islam from

---

23. Burhanudin, "Mainstream Islam In Indonesia," 11–12.

24. The *Salafi* movement in Indonesia holds that religious thoughts in the earlier periods of Islam are to be considered the most authentic guide of Islam, by using the literal interpretation of the Qur'an and the Sunnah as reliable religious documents.

its enemies. The groups that emphasize the first element are called Salafis... The groups that emphasize the second element are called Jihadists. Not all Salafi groups practice violence in fulfilling their interests, nor Jihadists depart from Salafi ideas. Thus, the Salafi group is divided into two sub-groups: *peaceful Salafi and radical Salafi*. *Jama'ah Tabligh* can be categorized as a peaceful Salafi, while Al-Qaeda—led by Osama bin Laden—is considered a radical Salafi.[25]

One of the most significant *Salafi* groups in post-reform Indonesia period is *Front Pembela Islam* (FPI) whose slogan is "Defending Islam for Its Rights and Dignity." The rise of a group like FPI is concerning because it frequently uses destructive and anarchic methods to achieve its political goals. There have been incidents in which FPI members destroyed bars, discotheques, casinos, brothels, and cafes, because they consider these places sinful. Jahroni connects their motivation with their faithfulness to Islam.[26] Groups like FPI desire to implement Shari'a as universal laws in Indonesia and remove all the non-Islamic—"Western"—values from their society.

After the fall of the New Order regime, Indonesia entered a new era of political openness. Radical Islamic groups have been waiting for a long time to implement Shari'a in every aspect of their society and establish an Islamic republic of Indonesia, since the declaration of Independence (1945). There are three political parties in Indonesia today, which explicitly support the implementation of Shari'a: Partai Persatuan Pembangunan ("United Development Party"), Partai Bulan Bintang ("Crescent Star Party"), and Partai Keadilan ("Prosperous Justice Party"). Tasman reports how these three parties seek to implement Shari'a in Indonesia.[27] However, there are also many political parties in Indonesia that reject these extreme Islamic movements, such as Golongan Karya, F-PDI Perjuangan, and F-TNI Polri. In particular, F-PDI Perjuangan explicitly states that the implementation of Shari'a would be a clear deviation from the Unitary State of the Republic of Indonesia (Negara Kesatuan Republik Indonesia/NKBI), based on the *Pancasila* and the 1945 Constitution, and no one religion could be placed in a more central position over the other five constitutionally recognized religions. Another Islamic organization, Nahdlatul Ulama (NU), also states that the idea of an Islamic state could disintegrate the nation of Indonesia, since Islam is not a political ideology today. Tasman reports that Muhammadiyah also

---

25. Jahroni, "The Salafi Movement in Indonesia," 110.
26. Jahroni, "The Salafi Movement in Indonesia," 113–14.
27. Tasman, "Contemporary Indonesian," 152–62.

emphasized the need to improve Indonesian Muslim human resources, instead of seeking to establish an Islamic state in Indonesia.[28]

Religious Rights in Indonesia Today

The Constitution of Indonesia (*Undang-Undang Dasar Republik Indonesia 1945*) Chapter 27 states, "(1) All citizens hold the same position in law and government and are obliged to uphold the law and rule without it with exception. (2) Every citizen has the right to a job and a decent livelihood fit for humanity." The Universal Declaration of Human Rights, declared and adopted by the United Nations General Assembly in 1948, states in article 18, "Everyone has the right to freedom of thought, conscience and religion; this right includes freedom to change his religion or belief, and freedom, either alone or in community with others and in public or private, to manifest his religion or belief in teaching, practice, worship and observance." We have noted earlier that, while the Qur'an permits religious rights for monotheistic non-Muslims to live peacefully among Muslims, it prohibits Muslims from converting to any other religion. The Qur'an considers any Muslim's conversion to any other religion as an act of apostasy (*riddah*) and requires severe punishment (3:90; 9:11–12, 66; 16:106). Wahid critically questions Indonesian Muslims' confusion between the priority of Shari'a and that of religious rights in Indonesia, as he discusses Indonesian Muslims' conversion to Christianity:

> Moving from Islam to embrace other religions is apostasy and deserves to be punished with death. If we apply this in our country, then more than 20 million people in Indonesia who changed their religion from Islam to become Christians since 1965 would need to be punished. Can we do that? This is a question with no answers because if this is indeed implemented, that will be a reality that shakes us deeply.[29]

We see here that the Universal Declaration of Human Rights of 1948 is in tension with the Qur'an, for Universal Declaration of Human Rights of 1948 allows "everyone"—including Muslims—to have "the right to freedom of thought, conscience and religion." In Indonesia today, religious rights are threatened by the rise of radical Islam. Anyone is welcome to convert to Islam without any problem but it is "illegal" for any Muslim to convert to any other religion and for anyone to proselytize a Muslim to his or her own

---

28. Tasman, "Contemporary Indonesian," 151–52.
29. Wahid, *My Islam, Your Islam, and Our Islam*, 122.

religion in Indonesia today. The Republic of Indonesia has its constitutional obligation to protect the religious rights of all its citizens.

In recent years, there have many instances of the violation of religious rights by radical Islamic groups against religious minorities in Indonesia. In May 2015, there was an incident in the Province of Aceh, in which hundreds of radical Muslims burnt three church buildings and local authorities demolished the ruins for the "lack of building permits." Authorities detained seven people in northern Sumatra in October 2017 on suspicion of attacking several Buddhist temples and other properties in the town of Tanjung Balai, near Indonesia's fourth biggest city, Medan. Indonesia is a Muslim-majority nation but has a sizable ethnic Chinese minority, many of whom are Buddhist. The country has a history of anti-Chinese violence. Numerous crimes were committed against Chinese Indonesians in the late 1990s in midst of the political and economic crisis at the end of Suharto's dictatorship. Religious minorities in Indonesia continue to face discriminatory regulations and violent attacks by radical Islamist groups. Impunity of security forces in the Province of Papua and West Papua also remains a serious problem and dozens of Papuans remain imprisoned for non-violent expression of their political views.

These radical Islamic groups even target those Muslims whose religious views are divergent from theirs. In March 2016, two leaders of Gerakan Fajar Nusantara (Gafatar) religious community—its founder Ahmad Moshaddeq and its president Mahful Muis Tumanurung—were sentenced to five years of imprisonment for the charge of blasphemy. Andry Cahya, its vice-president, also received a three-year sentence. On June 4, 2017, the local government in Depok, West Java, sealed a mosque belonging to Ahmadiyya religious minority, who are considered as "deviant and outside of Islam" by many Islamic groups. Authorities prevented the Ahmadis from using the mosque during Ramadan. The mayor of Depok argued that the legal basis for the closure of the mosque was a ministerial decree and a provincial regulation, both forbidding Ahmadiyya community members from promoting their activities and spreading their religious teachings. He also said that it was necessary to protect the Ahmadiyya community in Depok from violent attacks by other groups in the area. On August 21, 2016, Siti Aisyah, the owner of an Islamic school in Mataram, Lombok Island, was sentenced to thirty months incarceration for the charge of blasphemy and "strange teachings." In August 2016, municipal governments in Java took steps to effectively shut down two mosques that espoused the ultra-conservative Wahabhi strain of Islam—Al Arqom mosque in Pekalongan and the Ahmad bin Hanbal mosque in Bogor—due to concerns that they could fuel "social turmoil." In early 2017, the Ministry of Religious Affairs drafted a bill that strengthens the current Indonesian criminal charge of blasphemy and makes it difficult for religious minority groups to obtain permits to build their places of worship. The draft law, still pending at the moment of writing this chapter, would also impose excessively narrow criteria for official government recognition of a religious minority group. The blasphemy provisions in Articles 156 and 156(a) of the Criminal Code and Article 28 (2) in the Electronic Information and Transaction (ITE) law have been used to imprison those who spread any misleading information in order to create disunity among different groups and individuals in the Indonesian society.[30] Individuals belonging to religious minorities were often targeted for prosecution. Such laws intrinsically threatens an individual's religious rights in Indonesia. For instance, the former Governor of DKI Jakarta, Basuki Tjahaja Purnama, also known as "Ahok," has been charged for blasphemy, with reference to ITE Article 28 (2). Amnesty International calls the Indonesian authorities to end the use of blasphemy laws to prosecute anyone who exercises his or her freedom of expression, or religious rights.[31]

As we pointed out earlier, both Islam and Christianity provide support religious rights in their own ways. As Indonesia is a pluralistic society made of many different people groups, languages, cultures, and religions, Indonesians must love their neighbors as themselves and exercise tolerance in their civil society and respect one another with respect to religious rights. Muslims and Christians must reflect on their own rich religious traditions and find their basis for religious tolerance. Jeremiah writes to his fellow Jews in exile in Babylon and asks them to "seek the welfare of the city" and "pray to the Lord on its behalf" (Jer 29:7). Paul asks his readers to "be subject to the governing authorities" (Rom 13:1). Once again, Jesus asks his disciples, "You are the salt of the earth, but if salt has lost its taste, how shall its saltiness be restored?" (Matt 5:13). In today's human rights crisis in Indonesia, Christians can no longer practice their faith only in private but must take prophetic roles in speaking truth in love, fighting for social justice for the marginalized, and seeking the common good of the Indonesian society.

---

30. Article 28 (2) indicts "any person who knowingly and without authority disseminates information aimed at inflicting hatred or dissension on individuals and/or certain groups of community based on ethnic groups, religious, races, and inter-group (SARA)."

31. https://www.amnesty.org/en/countries/asia-and-the-pacific/indonesia/report-indonesia.

Women's Rights in Indonesia Today

As we have noted earlier, the violation of women's rights has been a serious social issue in many Islamic societies. *Human Rights Watch* reports:

> Indonesia's official Commission on Violence against Women reported that, as of August 2016, the number of discriminatory national and local regulations targeting women had risen to 422, from 389 at the end of 2015. They include local laws compelling women and girls to don the hijab, or headscarf, in schools, government offices, and public spaces. While many of these laws require traditional Sunni Muslim garb both for women and men, research by Human Rights Watch indicates they disproportionately target women.[32]

As the Constitution of the Republic of Indonesia (UDD 1945) indicates, Indonesia was established as a pluralistic society with many peoples, languages, cultures, and religions from its beginning. Radical Muslims in Indonesia must consider this seriously and stop trying to go back to the Caliphate in the history of Islam, trying to make Indonesia an Islamic state. While there are certain tensions between the Qur'an and the Universal Declaration of Human Rights, they must conduct serious and mature theological reflection with respect to how they could faithfully live out the teachings of the Qur'an in the twenty-first century pluralistic society in Indonesia, without forcing the others to join Islam by violence. Radical Muslims in Indonesia must protect and promote women's rights today. In contrast to some popular perceptions, as we have pointed out earlier, Christian Scriptures support gender equality. Both the Old Testament and the New Testament support women's rights, when we consider their socio-cultural contexts. Historically speaking, Christianity has been the primary force of any social activism for women's rights in the West. Now, more than ever, Indonesian Christians should work together to educate the others about women's rights and protect women from every kind of abuse based on gender inequality, in order to fulfill their calling as the salt and light of the world (Matt 5:13–16).

Conclusion

In this chapter, we have reflected on some aspects of Islamic and Christian understandings of human rights—religious rights and women's rights in particular. While the Qur'an allows religious rights for monotheistic

---

32. https://www.hrw.org/world-report/2017/country-chapters/indonesia.

non-Muslims who live among Muslims (2:62), it forbids any Muslim converting to any other religion (3:90; 9:11–12, 66; 16:106). Some argue that the Qur'an promotes gender equality and others disagree. Regardless of that, however, historically speaking, gender inequality has been a serious social issue in many Islamic societies. Christian Scriptures present the unique concept of *Imago Dei*. God created human beings in his image and made them his stewards of his creation (Gen 1:26–28). The original image of God is corrupted by sin; however, it did not completely vanish (Gen 2:16—3:24). The original image of God is restored and renewed by the redemptive work of Jesus Christ and one's faith in Christ (2 Cor 4:4–6; Rom 8:29). That image will be consummated, only when Jesus returns to judge both the living and the dead and there will be a new heaven and a new earth (Matt 19:28; John 5:24–27; Acts 17:31–32; 2 Cor 5:10; Rev 21:1–4). John Calvin in his *Institutes of Christian Religion* (1559) reflects on this biblical metanarrative and emphasizes that human beings were created in the image of God and originally upright (1.15.1) and, after the Fall, the image of God in human beings became corrupted but was not completely destroyed (1.15.4, 6). Calvin sees the evidence of some remaining aspects of the image of God in human beings in their innate desire for justice and civil society (*Inst.* 2.2.13). Therefore, Calvin's post-fall anthropology can be characterized by both total depravity and God's common grace towards all human beings. While there is a strong emphasis on evangelism or proselytization in the New Testament, it never promotes forceful conversion to the Christian faith in any shape or form. In contrast to some popular perceptions, Christian Scriptures, both the Old and the New Testament, strongly support gender equality in contrast to their own socio-cultural contexts.

In recent years, there have been many cases of the violation of human rights by radical Islamic groups in Indonesia. Religious minorities in Indonesia such as Hindus, Buddhists, Confucians, Catholics, and Protestants have been facing increasing violence and threats from radical Muslims who seek to implement Shari'a in every area of the Indonesian society, using their political majority. In light of this human rights crisis, both Islamic and Christian religious leaders must reflect on their spiritual traditions concerning the sanctity of human rights—religious rights and women's rights in particular—in order to provide the proper theological framework for their audiences, through which the twenty-first century pluralistic Indonesian society can be a more just and compassionate society, as their religious traditions themselves promote.

Bibliography

Ali, Abdulla Yusuf. *The Qur'an: Text, Translation & Commentary.* New York: Tahrike Tarsile Qur'an, 1988.

Berkhof, Louis. *Systematic Theology.* 2 vols. Grand Rapids: Eerdmans, 1996.

Burhanudin, Jajat. "Mainstream Islam in Indonesia." In *Islamic Thought and Movements in Contemporary Indonesia,* edited by Sukma Rizal and Clara Joewono, 11–53. Yogyakarta: CSIS, 2007.

Calvin, John. *Institutes of the Christian Religion,* edited by John T. McNeill. Translated by Ford Lewis Battle. LCC 20. Louisville: Westminster John Knox, 1960.

Daulay, Richard. M. *Agama and Politic di Indonesia.* Jakarta: BPK Gunung Mulia, 2015.

Fitzmyer, Joseph A. *First Corinthians.* AYB 32. New Haven: Yale University Press, 2008.

Garland, David E. *1 Corinthians.* BECNT. Grand Rapids: Baker, 2003.

Hassan, Riffat. "Rights of Women within Islamic Communities." In *Religious Human Rights in Global Perspective: Religious Perspectives,* edited by John Witte, Jr. and Johan D. Van der Vyver, 361–86. The Hague: Kluwer Law International, 1996.

Hoag, Gary G. *Wealth in Ancient Ephesus and the First Letter to Timothy: Fresh Insights from Ephesiaca by Xenophon of Ephesus.* BBRS 11. University Park, PA: Eisenbrauns, 2015.

Jahroni, Jajang. "The Salafi Movement in Indonesia: From Muhammadiyah to Laskar Jihad." In *Islamic Thought and Movements in Contemporary Indonesia,* edited by Rizal Sukma and Clara Joewono, 105–25. Yogyakarta: CSIS, 2007.

Keener, Craig S. *Paul, Women & Wives: Marriage and Women's Ministry in the Letters of Paul.* Peabody, MA: Hendrickson, 1992.

Mernissi, Fatima. *Beyond the Veil: Male-Female Dynamics in Modern Muslim Society.* Cambridge, MA: Schenkman, 1975.

Middleton, J. Richard. *The Liberating Image: The Imago Dei in Genesis 1.* Grand Rapids: Brazos, 2005.

Tasman. "Contemporary Indonesia Islamic Parties' Agenda." In *Islamic Thought and Movements in Contemporary Indonesia,* edited by Rizal Sukma and Clara Joewono, 148–72. Yogyakarta: CSIS, 2007.

Wahid, Abdurrahman. *Islamku, Islam Anda, Islam Kita.* Jakarta: Wahid Institute, 2006.

Warraq, Ibn. *Why I Am not a Muslim.* Amherst, NY: Prometheus, 2003.

Wenham, Gordon J. *Genesis 1–15.* WBC 1. Nashville: Nelson, 1987.

10

What *The 7 Habits of Highly Effective People* Missed

A Reflection on Leadership and Christian Worldview

———————— Fransisco Budi Hardiman

Introduction

THE 7 HABITS OF *Highly Effective People* is a popular business and self-help book—more than 15 million copies sold—by Stephen Covey in 1989, in which he presents seven universal and timeless principles of leadership.[1] Sacred books of world religions such as the Bible, the Qur'an, and the *Upanishads*, and myths and legends of human history such as the Epic of Gilgamesh, the *Mahabarata*, and the *Iliad*, highlight the spiritual dimension of leadership, as their various heroes have a strong connection with the divine, which seems to have been lost in today's general perception of leadership. This is evident when we compare and contrast the pre-modern and the modern Western philosophy of politics. In *Politics*, Plato connects the statesman's vision with eternal ideas, and Thomas Aquinas, in *De regimine Principuum*, relates leadership not only to nature and essence, but also to divine order. In contrast, Niccolo Machiavelli in his *Il Prinicipe* separates any connection between political leadership and the sacred, and regards political leadership as merely a strategic rational matter, which provided a new modern framework of understanding political leadership. There have

---

1. Covey, *The 7 Habits of Highly Effective People*.

been many popular books on the topic of leadership associated with business management or self-help. While they provide many business and behavioral insights, they tend to ignore the spiritual dimension of leadership, which a Christian worldview and the other religious worldviews emphasize. In this study, I will contrast a Christian worldview's understanding of leadership with the modern secular worldview's understanding of leadership, and discuss the implications for Christian involvement in the public and service to the public today.

The Biblical Foundation of Leadership

A Christian worldview's understanding of leadership is based firmly on Christian Scriptures. Martin Heidegger discusses *Weltanschauung* ("worldview") indirectly with respect to hermeneutics or interpretation:

> Interpretation is never a presuppositionless grasping of something previously given. When a specific instance of interpretation (in the sense of a precise textual interpretation) appeals to what "is there" ["dasteht"], then that which initially "is there" is nothing other than the self-evident, undiscussed prejudice [Vormeinung] of the interpreter which necessarily lies in every interpretive approach as that which is already "posited" with interpretation in general, namely, that which is pre-given [vorgegeben] in fore-having, fore-sight, and fore-conception.[2]

Likewise, W. Andrew Hoffecker describes worldview as "a compilation of presuppositions or beliefs about reality that represents comprehensive view about this life."[3] In this study, I will utilize the concept of worldview to explore the epistemology of the concept of leadership. As we will see, worldview can be assessed by both political philosophy and theology.

Glenn A. Moots insightfully describes the relationship between politics and religion:

> Politics and religion, at least when practiced in a community, are best understood as partners. But this is admittedly a tense partnership. Individuals may sometimes have to resolve the tension when choosing civil and religious imperatives. This is especially true in a liberal political order where individual rights and individual conscience are considered inviolable. If one takes a long view of the *Western* experience, particularly

---

2. Heidegger, *Being and Time*, 146.
3. Hoffecker, *Building a Christian Worldview*, ix.

> following the Reformation, it is the mutual respect and support between political and biblical religion (the dominant Western religion) that have encouraged liberty. To suggest dichotomous priorities of "religion" and "politics" invites paranoia and disables respectful discussion. Dichotomies that seek to divorce the civil from the religious, or to subordinate one to the other, function only in the abstract. They are contrary to political reality, which is always dictated by human nature, and human nature demonstrates itself to be both political and religious. Human nature is not either political or religious; it must be both political and religious. Furthermore, the great traditions of biblical religion are political by nature . . . As conflict within the church spilled over the civil during the seventeenth century, famous philosophers such as Baruch Spinoza, Thomas Hobbes, and John Locke tried to determine the proper boundaries for ecclesiastical and civil authorities . . . Where they make important contributions, they usually owe something to arguments made by theologians before them.[4]

I contend that the concept of worldview connects philosophy and theology. Through a Christian worldview, we can explore Christian political philosophy and Christian theology of politics simultaneously.

Leadership as a concept presupposes a particular worldview. It also assumes a certain political philosophy and a theology of politics. I will demonstrate this, as I compare and contrast the traditional and modern understanding of leadership. In a traditional society, leadership was perceived as something that belongs to rulers, which is passed on to their successors. In a traditional worldview, an individual's identity was closely linked with that of their community and each person's free will was not fully recognized. Therefore, leadership was not a matter of decision, achievement, or learning process, but a fruit of traditions and aristocracy. In contrast to the traditional concept of leadership, the modern concept of leadership is an integral part of the modern worldview that perceives a human being as a subject that is above nature and an independent moral agent in history. The word "leadership" implies that it is individual leaders who create and guide their organizations. It is an integral part of the modern concept of a human being as the one who makes and changes history. This modern concept is intrinsically anthropologically centered.

What is frequently forgotten is that the idea that a human being as a historical agent has its root in the Judeo-Christian worldview, as reflected in biblical anthropology. In contrast to many other religions, Christianity does

---

4. Moots, *Politics Reformed*, 2–3.

not perceive a human being as a product of blind forces in cosmic equilibrium but it uniquely portrays him or her as a steward of God's creation. In the Christian Scriptures, God not only reveals himself through natural laws and cycles but he also revealed himself through the person and work of Jesus Christ, the incarnate Son of God, who stepped into human history (John 1:14). The Christian Scriptures begin with a striking statement, "In the beginning, God created the heavens and the earth" (Gen 1:1).[5] God who created the universe out of nothing (*ex nihilo*) is also God of history who freed Israel from slavery in Egypt, and sent his one and only Son to this world in order to redeem the humanity from sin and death. God created human beings in his image (Gen 1:26–28)—*Imago Dei*—and called human beings by their names (Isa 43:1), which shows human dignity in God's creation. A human being is not an accidental element or substance in the universe. A human being is a person (*persona*), as each of the Trinity is a person. The God of history reveals himself to Moses, "I am the God of your father, the God of Abraham, the God of Isaac, and the God of Jacob" (Exod 3:6). Jurgen Moltmann notes, "A person. . . is the individual human being in the field of resonances constituted by his or her relationships. . . In the theological sense, the 'person' comes into being through God's summons, which calls human beings out of their relationships 'in their fatherland and among their kindred' (Gen 12:1)."[6] The Judeo-Christian worldview provides the foundation for the modern concept of leadership, which developed in the Western political philosophy. For example, the most important difference between leadership and management is that, while the word "management" generally connotes working within an established system, the word "leadership" points to working through uncertainty, showing the quality of the leader who dares to make a decision, take a risk, and make a change, as seen in many biblical characters such as Abraham, David, Jesus, and Paul.

This characteristic of leadership is elaborated thoroughly in the modern philosophy of politics, which is related to the theology of politics, as demonstrated in Carl Schmitt's concept of "sovereignty."[7] However, political philosophy detaches itself from its biblical foundation, as in the case of the concept of leadership. While Schmitt revives the Western political philosophy and reconnects it with theology, this Nazi philosopher replaces God's sovereignty with the human's sovereignty—the sovereignty of *der Führer*, when he states, "*Souverän ist, wer über den Ausnahmezustand entscheidet*" ("the sovereign one is the one who makes decision in emergency situations).

---

5. In this study, I use the ESV as the primary English translation of the Scriptures.
6. Moltmann, *God for a Secular Society*, 80.
7. Schmitt, *Politische Theologie*.

Such replacement of God's sovereignty with human sovereignty turned out to bring one of the worst chapters of the entire human history, as it gave unwarranted legitimacy to totalitarianism. I would argue that this risky tendency is not limited to Schmitt but also exists in Jean-Jacques Rousseau's concept of people's sovereignty in his *On the Social Contract* (1762), in which Rousseau accepts the possibility of using political institution to force people to obey *volonté générale*.[8]

According to the Scriptures, a human being cannot be the agent and maker of history, apart from God's calling for him or her. God is sovereign over his creation and history. God is the ultimate agent and maker of history in the universe. God created human beings to rule over his creation and, therefore, human beings' stewardship cannot exist apart from God's sovereignty. Human beings are created in the image of God (*Imago Dei*) and their identity and authority originate from who God is. They are intrinsically linked with God's calling of a human being as a person (*persona*). Modern leadership theories were formed in the context of the Enlightenment and the secularization of the Western societies. While they focus on *how* to develop an organization in practice, they fail to consider *why* anyone should develop any organization in the first place. Modern secular worldviews often focus on practical matters but neglect God's calling of humanity as the stewards of his creation.

Table 10.1 Comparison between Christian and Modern Secular Worldview on Leadership

	Christian Worldview	Modern Secular Worldview
Basis	Leadership is based on God's sovereignty.	Leadership is based on one's autonomy.
	It is one's response to God's calling.	It has nothing to do with God.
Area	Leadership is holistic and affects every area of one's life.	Leadership is a specialized skill to advance in one's career.

In the Scriptures, leadership essentially refers to one's openness to God's plan of salvation of his people, in his or her own life. This openness allows God to work in one's life. In contrast, today, as the sacred is separated from the secular, leadership is often considered only as an organizational task or a career

8. Rousseau, *Du contrat social*.

building skill. When leadership is limited to this, God is out of the picture. The Scriptures, however, portray a more holistic picture of leadership. While some parts of the Torah emphasize the distinction between the sacred and the secular, the Torah and the Scriptures overall portrays a holistic picture of worship. The entire nation of Israel, not only the Levites, is called to holiness, as the LORD speaks to the Israelites, "be holy, for I am holy" (Lev 11:44; 11:45; 19:2; 20:26; 21:8). This same verse is cited in 1 Pet 1:16 in the context of the instruction of how Christian believers should live (1 Pet 1:13—2:3). Biblically speaking, someone becomes a true leader, only when he or she submits himself or herself to God and participates in God's plan or will for his or her life. The Scriptures describe this as one having faith in God. Biblical leadership stems from one's relationship with God.

One of the essential aspects of leadership is communication. In the Scriptures, God reveals himself to someone and calls him or her to be a leader, and he or she responds to that calling in faith. Why does God call anyone? What is that calling for? We can find these answers in God's revelation. Let us consider the calling of Moses, for instance. God speaks to Moses, "I have surely seen the affliction of my people who are in Egypt and have heard their cry because of their taskmasters. I know their sufferings, and I have come down to deliver them out of the hand of the Egyptians and to bring them up out of that land to a good and broad land, a land flowing with milk and honey, to the place of the Canaanites, the Hittites, the Amorites, the Perizzites, the Hivites, and the Jebusites" (Exod 3:7–8). God called Moses and Moses did not call himself. As the story unfolds in Exodus, Moses responds to God's calling for him in faith, and leads the Israelites from their slavery in Egypt to the Promised Land. As we see in the example of Moses, biblical leadership has a vertical dimension—God's calling of Moses—which leads to a horizontal dimension—Moses' leading the Israelites in the wilderness.

Leadership theories teach about the importance of vision and envisioning. Burt Nanus understands vision as "a realistic future, trusted, and attracting for an organization."[9] Leaders are speakers, executors, and trainers for a vision. As L. Smircich and G. Morgan write, people become leaders "with mobilizing meaning, articulating and defining what was implicit or unspoken before, by figuring out images and meanings that focus on new attention, and by consolidating, facing or altering common assumption."[10] Smircich and Morgan claim that leaders manage meaning. While this makes sense, it does not show us the whole picture of lead-

---

9. Nanus, *Visionary Leadership*, 8.
10. Smircich and Morgan, "Leadership," 16.

ership. Modern authors such as Nanus, Smircich and Morgan, seem to consider that the future is entirely in the hands of a leader, and one of the abilities of a leader is to perceive the future. Once again, here, leadership is understood only in the dimension of one's personal authority over his or her life, in line with the historical evolution of the survival of the fittest. We need to ask ourselves to what extent these statements are true. Human beings are limited to time and space and cannot perceive the future. The modern secular worldview overemphasizes human beings' rationality and their scientific and technological achievements in the past and in the present, while dismissing human beings' total depravity. The future remains a mystery for human beings. Even the best science and technology often fail to predict the precise impact of a natural disaster. While a Christian worldview points to the eschaton, the new heaven and the new earth (Isa 65:17; 2 Pet 3:13; Rev 21:1), modern secular worldview only points to the present world, as we know it, relying only on science and technology. Those who have a naive optimism of the future and fully trust in human progress through science and technology should review the history of humankind, which provides ample pieces of evidence for humanity's total depravity. As we can see in the examples of National Socialism and Communism in the twentieth century, despite all the incredible scientific and technological advancements, human beings could not achieve the utopian society that they claimed in their political ideologies.

In a Christian worldview, God calls a person and, at first, he or she often is unable to understand and embrace God's calling for him or her. After God tells Moses about his plan of redemption of Israel from Egypt, Moses becomes insecure about himself and replies, "Who am I that I should go to Pharaoh and bring the children of Israel out of Egypt?" (Exod 3:11). Likewise, Jer 1:4–6 writes, "Now the word of the LORD came to me, saying, 'Before I formed you in the womb I knew you, and before you were born I consecrated you; I appointed you a prophet to the nations.' Then I said, 'Ah, Lord GOD! Behold, I do not know how to speak, for I am only a youth.'" Also, after an angel of God foretells Mary about the birth of Jesus through her, Mary replies, "How will this be, since I am a virgin?" (Luke 1:34). In the Scriptures and the past history, God calls certain individuals as leaders and gives them his vision, and he enables them to do their appointed tasks. Mary in faith responds to the angel, "Behold, I am the servant of the Lord; let it be to me according to your word" (Luke 1:38). The Scriptures identify leaders' envisioning with allowing God to work in their lives. Due to its atheistic premise, the modern secular worldview overlooks this important aspect of leadership in the Scriptures and it can only present leadership as an organizational task or a career building skill.

Leadership as God's Calling

Bernard M. Bass surveys various definitions of leadership and lists the following twelve: (1) "a focus on group processes," (2) "personality and its effects," (3) "an art to produce submission," (4) "the implementation of influence," (5) "actions or behaviors," (6) "a form of persuasion," (7) "power relations," (8) "a tool to achieve goals," (9) "an effect of increased interaction," (10) "special role," (11) "the initiator of structure," and (12) "a combination of [these] elements."[11] These twelve are useful to understand the phenomenon of leadership. Nevertheless, none of them includes the spiritual dimension to understand leadership. As I discussed so far, the Scriptures help us understand leadership more holistically and do not simply equate it with a task or a function. In this section, I will elaborate more the point that I already made, that is, Christian worldview essentially identifies leadership as God's calling.

Chris Lowney explains a view that is relevant to the concept of leadership that we are looking for. Lowney points out, "Leadership is not an action. Leadership is my *life*, a way of life . . . Leadership is a never ending process."[12] This holistic concept about leadership is becoming foreign among people nowadays, which is shown by the separation between the sacred and the secular. Such separation often results in differentiating one's leadership in the public domain and one's personal life in the private domain. This kind of dualism is unwarranted in the Scriptures. When God calls a leader in the Scriptures, God does not call him or her only in the private domain but God calls him or her in both public and private domains. The modern notion of "profession" refers to certain standards in a workplace. Unfortunately, this term has also been detached from its original meaning. The Latin word *professio* ("profession") is related to another Latin word *vocatio* ("calling"), which is rooted in the Scriptures. This Scriptural root of the word is retained in the German word *Beruf* ("profession" or "occupation"), for its related German word *Berufung* ("calling") is connected with not only one's career but also one's *Lebensform* ("way of living"). The word "profession," in its root, refers to not only one's career but also one's entire way of living. For medical doctors to be professional, they not only must be experts in modern medicine but also have right medical ethics, as their patients entrust them with the care of their health. Paul writes, "I appeal to you therefore, brothers, by the mercies of God, to present your bodies as a living sacrifice, holy and acceptable to God, which

---

11. Bass, "Concepts of Leadership," 6–11.
12. Lowney, *Heroic Leadership*, 18.

is your spiritual worship" (Rom 12:1). God is calling leaders to offer their whole bodies—their whole life—in serving God and serving others.

As we can see, the secular concept of profession lacks this holistic understanding of God's calling in the Scriptures. The modern secular concept of profession developed from the concept of secular metaphysics, which perceives social order as the result of transactional and contractual relations among human beings in their own autonomy. In contrast, the Scriptural basis of profession comes from the so-called "covenant theology" which also can be viewed in the lenses of political philosophy.

There are fundamental metaphysical and anthropological differences between the Judeo-Christian concept of covenant and the modern secular concept of contract. I will highlight three in the following. First, the modern secular concept of contract assumes that it is a transaction between human beings without God, while a covenant is between God and human beings. Second, the modern secular concept of contract assumes that all agents of a contract are autonomous beings who attempt to maximize utility for themselves (utility maximizers), while God partners with human beings in his redemptive work of the humanity. Third, the modern secular concept of contract has no concern for human beings' total depravity, while the Judeo-Christian concept of covenant presupposes the need for God's salvation because of the Fall of humanity (Gen 3) and anticipates the kingdom of God.[13] As Moots points out:

> Reformed political thought is notably absent from many anthologies, histories, and surveys of political ideas. Too few critical studies of modern political theory take its influence seriously, let alone carefully discern its role in forming what we now call 'modern' political theory. It is certainly true that many factors and philosophies came together to overcome medieval Christianity and its Aristotelian variants. But scholars in political theory largely ignore Christianity in its Protestant formulations, particularly during the period of early modernity when it was most influential. Such omission is especially negligent given the highly political nature of the Reformation and the massive subscription to Protestant doctrine by all classes of society over three centuries between 1550 and 1850.[14]

Modern political theories, including contract theory, overlook their Christian foundation such as covenant theology, removing their historically rich religious backgrounds.

13. Moltmann, *God for a Secular Society*, 38–39.
14. Moots, *Politics Reformed*, 4.

Table 10.2. Comparison between Judeo-Christian Concept
of Covenant and Modern Secular Concept of Contract

Assumptions	Judeo-Christian Concept of Covenant	Modern Secular Concept of Contract
Metaphysical	God took the initiative to connect with human beings	It only refers to relations among humans; god has no place in social contracts.
Anthropological	Human beings are created in God's image; They are God's stewards for His creation. God redeems them through Christ.	Human beings are autonomous; Everything depends on chance and merit.
Theological-Political	The state reflects and anticipates God's kingdom.	The state has no connection with \God's kingdom.

The word "covenant" (*berith*) in the Hebrew Bible refers to God's unique way of interacting with human beings. While the word "covenant" in the Scriptures can refer to a contract between two parties, it presupposes God's initiative and sovereignty over that relationship, which has at least two implications. First, God calls a leader to be a steward of his creation. Leaders are God's stewards rather than the masters of their own destiny. As Tom Marshall notes, "True authority has a spiritual origin."[15] Second, as God calls a leader to be a steward of his creation, his or her conscience is accountable to God. The author of Hebrews writes, "And just as it is appointed for man to die once, and after that comes judgment" (9:27).

True personal authority comes from one's conscience. In a Christian worldview, a leader does not own authority and power by himself or herself, but God entrusts him or her with his authority and power to fulfill his plan in this world. Martin Luther King Jr. provides an excellent example of a true leader who faithfully lived out his God-given conscience, in his fight against racial injustice and discrimination in the United States in the 1960s. The concept of calling is closely related to revelation and faith. God

---

15. Marshall, *Understanding Leadership*, 107.

calls a leader and the leader responds to God in faith and obedience. In a Christian worldview, God is not the *Deus otiosus* of Deism—an absentee god who leaves the creation to its own fate after he created it. In the Scriptures, God the Creator is also God the sustainer of his creation, and nothing happens outside of his sovereignty. God calls his people in a concrete historical context, as Isa 43:1 writes, "But now thus says the Lord, he who created you, O Jacob, he who formed you, O Israel: 'Fear not, for I have redeemed you; I have called you by name, you are mine." The God of history is also God beyond history, in that he elected his people before the creation of the universe (Eph 1:3–6). In contrast to a modern secular worldview, the Christian worldview views human life not anthropocentrically but theocentrically, as Isa 55:8–9 writes, "For my thoughts are not your thoughts, neither are your ways my ways, declares the Lord. For as the heavens are higher than the earth, so are my ways higher than your ways and my thoughts than your thoughts." God will accomplish his purpose through his word (Isa 55:11). In a Christian worldview, a leader becomes a visionary by believing in God's promises to him or her. It is not the leader's vision but God's vision for his or her life. Faith is one's existential response to God's promises. Faith allows him or her to go beyond the present and anticipate the future. Vision holds both the present reality and the future possibility—God's plan in time and God's plan beyond time.

To sum up, historically speaking, the concept of leadership in Western philosophy has its foundation in Judeo-Christian worldview in which human beings are viewed as God's stewards of his creation. However, the modern theories of leadership tend to dismiss this foundation and only focus on its practical and organizational matters. Metaphysically, a human being is considered as the center of his or her world. Epistemologically, a human being is considered as the center of his or her knowledge. Axiologically, a human being is considered as the source of his or her values. The modern concept of leadership presents a human being as an independent agent and maker of history. In contrast, the Scriptures insist that God calls each person and he or she responds to God's calling in faith and obedience, to fulfill God's purpose in his or her life and in this world, which is the essence of biblical leadership. I call this biblical leadership "redeemed leadership" and I want to make four points about it.

First, redeemed leadership has to do with one's existence. In this view, leadership concerns who we are before God before anything else. Second, leadership is not limited to an organizational skill or a career building skill but it concerns *Lebensform* ("way of living"). Third, leadership is not a one-time task but entails a lifelong process. Fourth, through the person and work of Jesus Christ, God calls every Christian believer to change his or her own world for the glory of God (Rom 12:1–21; Eph 4:17—5:21).

Redeemed Leadership

In this section, I will highlight important aspects in the development of the concept of leadership in a Christian worldview, which I call "redeemed leadership." The Scriptures portray four distinctive acts in their metanarrative. First, God created human beings in his image and made them the stewards of his creation (Gen 1:26–28; 2:15). Second, human beings were tempted to become like God and sinned against God by eating the forbidden fruit of the Tree of the Knowledge of Good and Evil (Gen 3), through which sin and death came to this world (Rom 5:12–21). Third, Jesus Christ, the incarnate Son of God, came to this world to die on the cross for the sins of the humanity, to redeem those who trust in him (John 1:14; 3:16; Rom 5:6–11; 1 Cor 1:30; 2 Cor 5:16–19). Fourth, Jesus is coming back to the world to judge both the living and the dead (2 Tim 4:1) and there will be the new heaven and the new earth (Rev 21:1–4). We can think of how to understand leadership in each act of the biblical metanarrative:

Table 10.3. Leadership in Relation to the Biblical Metanarrative

Creation	Fall	Redemption	Consummation
Human beings as the stewards of God's creation	Human beings separated from God; stewardship distorted by sin	Human beings redeemed through the work of Christ; leadership redeemed	The righteous will reign with Christ in the new heaven and the new earth

The New Testament portrays a radically different picture of redeemed leadership from the common authoritarian perception of leadership. Jesus teaches his disciples in Mark 10:42–45:

> You know that those who are considered rulers of the Gentiles lord it over them, and their great ones exercise authority over them. But it shall not be so among you. But whoever would be great among you must be your servant, and whoever would be first among you must be slave of all. For even the Son of Man came not to be served but to serve, and to give his life as a ransom for many.

Likewise, Paul writes to the Philippians, "So if there is any encouragement in Christ, any comfort from love, any participation in the Spirit, any affection and sympathy, complete my joy by being of the same mind, having the same love, being in full accord and of one mind. Do nothing from selfish ambition or conceit, but in humility count others more significant than yourselves. Let each of you look not only to his own interests, but also to the interests of others" (Phil 2:1–5). The Greek word *metanoia* that is often translated as "repentance" literally means, "a change of mind." In other words, *metanoia* is a paradigm shift from one worldview to another worldview. Jesus emphasizes a leader's role to serve others in Mark 10:35–45. The shift from a ruler to a servant involves the whole person. It also includes metaphysical, epistemological, and axiological dimensions, which I will explain in the following.

First, redeemed leadership involves a metaphysical dimension. Redeemed leadership recognizes God's sovereignty. It means that there is no other greater authority than God, and everything and everyone in this universe finds its and his or her meaning of existence only in relation to God. The modern secular concept of leadership in political philosophy since Machiavelli has given its priority to human's autonomy, refusing to recognize God's sovereignty in relation to human beings. Gen 3:1–5 writes:

> Now the serpent was more crafty than any other beast of the field that the Lord God had made. He said to the woman, "Did God actually say, 'You shall not eat of any tree in the garden?'"And the woman said to the serpent, "We may eat of the fruit of the trees in the garden,but God said, 'You shall not eat of the fruit of the tree that is in the midst of the garden, neither shall you touch it, lest you die.'" But the serpent said to the woman, "You will not surely die. For God knows that when you eat of it your eyes will be opened, and you will be like God, knowing good and evil."

God speaks to Adam in Gen 2:16–17, "You may surely eat of every tree of the garden, but of the tree of the knowledge of good and evil you shall not eat, for in the day that you eat of it you shall surely die." The serpent distorts God's words to Adam and seduces Eve by asking her, "Did God actually say, 'You shall not eat of any tree in the garden?'" Although God only spoke to Adam, Eve should have trusted in the veracity of Adam's words to her, rather than doubting it. The serpent lies again to Eve and plants a desire to be like God in her. What is ironic here is that Adam and Eve were already like God, because they were the only ones in God's creation, who were created in his image. Not knowing truly who they are, Adam and Eve fell into the serpent's lie and violated God's command not to eat the fruit of the

Tree of Knowledge of Good and Evil. Dismissing God's sovereignty and seeking to play God, humanity's total depravity is demonstrated in their self-destructive behavior throughout history. When the first human tried to take the role of God, leaving their place of stewardship and seeking their place of lordship, God called him and asked him an existential question, "Where are you?" (Gen 3:9). God created human beings in his image and calls them to be his stewards of his creation. Servant-leaders who are called by God responds to God, "We are unworthy servants; we have only done what was our duty" (Luke 17:10).

Second, redeemed leadership involves an epistemological dimension. The modern secular concept of leadership is based on the claims of modernism since Renaissance such as *homo mensura* ("man is the measure of everything") and *homo autonomous* ("one is law to oneself"). In a Christian worldview, God is the source of knowledge and wisdom. There was a radical shift in Cartesian epistemology that places human beings in the center of knowledge, which contrasts Augustinian epistemology which places God's revelation—God's Word—in the center of knowledge. Redeemed leadership perceives everything from a Christian worldview, grounded on the Scriptures.

Third, redeemed leadership involves an axiological dimension. When one understands the depth of God's grace in calling him or her, he or she becomes motivated to serve God as a faithful steward of his creation, as it was meant to be from the beginning. One's desire to rule is changed into one's desire to serve. A redeemed leader is a servant-leader.[16] Jesus himself demonstrates the perfect example of a servant-leader (Mark 10:45). Paul describes who Jesus is in the following words:

> though he was in the form of God, he did not count equality with God a thing to be grasped, but emptied himself, by taking the form of a servant, being born in the likeness of men. And being found in human form, he humbled himself by becoming obedient to the point of death, even death on a cross. Therefore God has highly exalted him and bestowed on him the name that is above every name, so that at the name of Jesus every knee should bow, in heaven and on earth and under the earth, and every tongue confess that Jesus Christ is Lord, to the glory of God the Father (Phil 2:6–11).

As Paul instructs the Philippians, although believers are not Christ, they are to follow the example of Christ in humbling themselves to serve others, to glorify God. This is possible through becoming united with Christ, as

16. Greenleaf, *Servant Leadership*.

Paul writes, "We were buried therefore with him by baptism into death, in order that, just as Christ was raised from the dead by the glory of the Father, we too might walk in newness of life. For if we have been united with him in a death like this, we shall certainly be united with him in a resurrection like this" (Rom 6:4–5).

The issue of leadership mandate arises, because the modern secular society rejects any spiritual background of leadership. In the West, this process took place to guarantee tolerance for all religions, distinguishing public and private spheres, and considering religion as an entirely private and subjective matter. Sandra F. Joireman points out, "Most Christians today, we can probably say, are Anabaptists in the sense that they contend for free churches in open societies with governments that give equal treatment to all citizens regardless of their faith."[17] Such a passive attitude could limit Christians' role in transforming their society into a more just and compassionate one, because they may shy away from their religious convictions in their political involvement. On the one hand, no one wants to go back to the medieval European society, in which the Roman Catholic Church exercised absolute political and religious authority. On the other hand, however, that does not mean that Christians should uncritically accept the dualism of the modern secular society and lose the biblical foundation of Christian worldview. Taking seriously one's religious convictions is not the same as the politicization of religion. A Christian can be a constructive citizen of his or her society, when he or she holistically understands Christian worldview and actively lives out his or her calling from God. Once again, Martin Luther King Jr. is an excellent example of this. King began his quest for racial equality and reconciliation from his convictions as a Christian believer. While the civil rights movement was definitely a political movement, King did not politicize religion. In other words, King did not use religion as a political tool to replace the Constitution of the United States. Instead, King's religious conviction that God created all people equally in his image and one needs to overcome evil by doing good—non-violence resistance—drove him and the civil rights movement. Leadership in Christian worldview cannot be considered *etsi Deus non daretur* ("as if God does not exist") but *coram Deo* ("before God"). Jesus teaches his disciples:

> You are the salt of the earth, but if salt has lost its taste, how shall its saltiness be restored? It is no longer good for anything except to be thrown out and trampled under people's feet. You are the light of the world. A city set on a hill cannot be hidden. Nor do people light a lamp and put it under a basket, but on a stand, and

---

17. Joireman, *Church, State, and Citizen*, 59.

it gives light to all in the house. In the same way, let your light shine before others, so that they may see your good works and give glory to your Father who is in heaven (Matt 5:13–16).

Both the metaphor of salt and that of light point to the leadership mandate of the followers of Jesus. Tom Marshall highlights four "essential qualities" of what he calls "redeemed power": (1) "this power has settled forever the issue of obedience to the Father's will"; (2) "with this power the distinction between means and ends has been settled once and for all"; (3) "this power has embraced the cross and in Christ has died to all self-seeking, self-glorification, and self-will, or what I refer to as 'will-to-power'"; and (4) "this power has a radically different orientation. It is wholly power for others, not power for self or power over others."[18] Redeemed power is the power demonstrated in a person who serves God and others *coram Deo* ("before God"). Jesus' metaphor of salt and light in Matt 5:13–16 signifies the fact that Christian witness is not limited to private sphere but extends to public sphere.

Historically speaking, the separation of Church and State, especially in the context of the United States, started with the nation's efforts to promote religious toleration, which parallels the case of Indonesian *pancasila*. However, the privatization of religions is not the ultimate solution for peaceful coexistence, as oppression, discrimination, and marginalization still exist today in modern democratic nations. As it has been discussed, the modern secular concept of leadership dismisses its biblical foundation, which offers a more holistic picture of leadership. Integrating Christian faith into leadership means listening to one's conscience and working for the social and political transformation of the society, compelled by God's calling and God-given conscience, as seen in the legacy of Martin Luther King Jr. Jürgen Moltmann writes, "Through that separation, religion and conscience were restricted to the church, and life's other sectors were delivered over to unscrupulous power politics pursued without conscience. The new political theology presupposes the public testimony of faith, and freedom for the political leadership of Christ, not just discipleship in private life and the church."[19] Moltmann is not promoting the politicization of religion here, but Christians reflecting on God's calling on their lives, based on the biblical foundation of their faith, and acting upon it in faith and obedience, in both private and public sphere.

Abraham van de Beek argues, "Religion is its own end, and it may not be instrumentalised to anything else. This statement seems tenable, and perhaps even self-evident, for all those who know what religion really is. But

18. Marshall, *Understanding Leadership*, 67–68.
19. Moltmann, *God of a Secular Society*, 44.

we must view the consequences of accepting this statement—and I think these logical consequences may come as a shock to many people, especially many contemporary Christians."[20] Van de Beek's statements here make us think about any stream of theology closely associated with political ideology such as liberation theology. While Van de Beek correctly points out that religion is its own sovereign sphere and it cannot be used as an instrument for something else, we also have keep in mind that the instrumentalization or politicization of religious faith is not the only valid way of association between religion and politics. Good deeds can be one's public expression of his or her faith without any hidden agenda, as Kant begins *Fundamental Principles of the Metaphysics of Morals*, "Nothing can possibly be conceived in the world, or even out of it, which can be called good without qualification, except a Good Will."[21]

In Indonesia, where the majority of the population are Muslims, Christians are a political minority. However, from the beginning of the nation's history, Christians took a vital role for the nation's independence and development of its democracy. Many Christians mobilized political parties and encouraged others to form an Indonesian national identity beyond their own ethnic heritage. Christian schools and hospitals have been providing vital public service to various parts of the nation, through which the public testimony of Christian faith is shown.

Conclusion

In this study, I contrasted a Christian worldview's understanding of leadership with the modern secular worldview's understanding of leadership in the following aspects. First, a Christian worldview presupposes God's existence and sovereignty over his creation, while modern secular worldview dismisses any notion of a supernatural being. In a Christian worldview, everyone is created in the image of God and everyone is called as God's steward of his creation. In the modern secular worldview, everyone is a completely autonomous being, a product of pure chance and his or her merit. Second, a Christian worldview perceives leadership as one's response to God's calling, which affects every aspect of one's life and is based on the biblical concept of covenant, while the modern secular worldview sees no higher calling beyond oneself and views leadership simply as a useful career-building skill, which is based on one' social contract with the others. Third, a Christian worldview holistically understands leadership in relation

20. Van de Beek, "Religion Without Ulterior Motive," 8.
21. Kant, *Fundamental Principles*, 9.

to all four acts of the biblical metanarrative (Creation, Fall, Redemption, and Consummation), while the modern secular worldview dismisses the total depravity of humanity and naively presumes the progress of humanity, based on the scientific and technological advancements of today's world. Martin Luther King, Jr. provides an excellent example of how Christians can publicly confess their Christian faith in the public sphere, without its privatization or politicization, as Jesus calls his followers to become the salt and light of their world (Matt 5:13–16).

Bibliography

Bass, Bernard, M. "Concepts of Leadership." In *Leaders and the Leadership Process: Readings, Self-Assessments, and Applications*, edited by Jon Pierce and John W. Newstrom, 5–13. Chicago: Austen, 1995.

Covey, Stephen R. *The 7 Habits of Highly Effective People: Powerful Lessons in Personal Charge*. New York: Simon & Schuster, 2013.

Greenleaf, Robert K. *Servant Leadership: A Journey into the Nature of Legitimate Power and Greatness*. New York: Paulist, 1977.

Heidegger, Martin. *Being and Time*. Translated by Joan Stambaugh. Revised by Dennis J. Schmidt. SUNY Series in Contemporary Continental Philosophy. Albany: State University of New York Press, 2010.

Hoffecker, W. Andrew, ed. *Building a Christian Worldview: God, Man, and Knowledge*. Vol. 1. Phillipsburg: P&R, 1986.

Joireman, Sandra F. *Church, State, and Citizen: Christian Approaches to Political Engagement*. Oxford: Oxford University Press, 2009.

Kant, Immanuel. *Fundamental Principles of the Metaphysics of Morals*. Translated by Thomas Kingsmill Abbott. DPC. Mineola, NY: Dover, 2005.

Lowney, Chris, *Heroic Leadership: Best Practices from a 450-Year-Old Company That Changed World*. Chicago: Loyola, 2003.

Marshall, Tom, *Understanding Leadership*. Grand Rapids: Baker, 2003.

Moltmann, Jürgen, *God for a Secular Society: The Public Relevance of Theology*. London: SCM, 1999.

Moots, Glenn A. *Politics Reformed: The Anglo-American Legacy of Covenant Theology*. The Eric Voegelin Institute Series in Political Philosophy. Columbia: University of Missouri Press, 2010.

Nanus, Bert. *Visionary Leadership*. San Francisco: Jossey-Bass, 1992.

Rousseau, Jean-Jacques. *Du contrat social ou Principes du droit politique*. Amsterdam: Marc Michel Rey, 1762.

Schmitt, Carl. *Politische Theologie*. Berlin: Duncker & Humbolt, 1934.

Smircich, L. and Morgan, G. "Leadership: The Management of Meaning." In *Leaders and the Leadership Process: Readings, Self-Assessments, and Applications*, edited by Jon L. Pierce and John W. Newstrom, 16–19. Chicago: Austen, 1995.

Van de Beek, Abraham. "Religion without Ulterior Motive." In *Religion without Ulterior Motive*, edited by E. A. J. G. Van der Borght, 7–20. SRT 13. Leiden: Brill, 2006.

11

Christian Worldview and the Transformation of Korean Society

— Yong Joon (John) Choi

Introduction

By the grace of God, Korean churches have experienced enormous revival and growth over the last 100 years. Presently, Korean churches are sending more missionaries throughout the world than any other country except the United States, and several mega-churches are located in Seoul. Therefore, from the perspective of church history, Korea will be remembered as one of the most successful and exemplary cases of the Christianity's mission.

Additionally, Korean churches have made a decisive contribution to the development of modern Korean society. Even though they were not many in number, Korean Christians were active participants in the independence movement during the period of Japanese occupation. Many Korean Christian leaders established the first modern schools, social welfare services (e.g., orphanages), and hospitals in Korea, with the latter leading to the overall improvement of public health. Furthermore, Korean society in general has benefitted from the influence of Korean churches in reducing smoking, drinking, gambling, social discrimination, and gender inequality. They also promoted a frugal lifestyle, honesty, integrity, diligence, and the idea of vocation as a calling from God. All these elements of cultural transformation became the foundation of modern Korea in the twentieth century owing to the Christian worldview.

Korean churches now, however, are facing many serious challenges as Korean society is changing rapidly in many aspects. On the one hand, most

Korean churches are witnessing a decline in membership. On the other hand, Korean churches are losing their respect and influence as a moral-religious guide in Korean society, because of various scandals of many mega-church pastors. Even though Christians make up more than 20 percent of the whole population, unfortunately, not many of them are living as salt and light in the society. Korean churches have emphasized the Christian worldview, but it has not been consistently applied to every sphere of Korean society, such as science, politics, and economy.

In contrast, we are witnessing that God is working now in a very dynamic way in China and many other parts of the world. We also see that many Korean diaspora Christians are playing a very important role in this global era. For instance, we have seen that Michael Oh, a second-generation Korean American, has become the new Executive Director/Chief Executive Officer of Lausanne Committee for World Evangelization, succeeding Doug Birdsall, on March 1, 2013.

With this situation in mind, this article first details the idea of the Christian worldview developed in the Dutch theological tradition, and how it has transformed Korean society in the last 100 years. After that, I will discuss what kind of new paradigm it should provide for the rest of this century in order to make a significant contribution not only to Korean society but also to the global community.

Christian Worldview and the Transformation of Korean Society

The Contents of Christian Worldview

It was Abraham Kuyper, a Dutch theologian and politician, who developed the biblical worldview systematically. He emphasized that the sovereignty of Christ should be manifested in every sphere of human life. In order to disseminate this worldview systematically, he even founded Vrije Universiteit in Amsterdam in 1880. He concluded his opening address of this university by saying, "There is not a square inch in the whole domain of our human existence over which Christ, who is sovereign over all, does not cry, 'Mine!'"[1] Kuyper in his well-known Lectures on Calvinism sums up the basic contents of the Christian worldview in seven headings.[2]

---

1. This is the English translation of the original in Dutch, "geen duimbreed is er op heel 'terf van ons menselijk leven, waarvan Christus, die aller Souverein is' niet roept: 'Mijn!'"; Kuyper, *Souvereiniteit in Eigen Kring*, 35.

2. Kuyper, *Lectures on Calvinism*.

The Lordship of Christ

Jesus Christ, to whom all authority in heaven and on earth is given, is the Lord of all and redeems every aspect of human life (Matt 28:18). Therefore, we have to admit the headship of Christ and should not accept the dualistic worldview which separates the sacred and the secular sphere of human life.

Creation: Cultural Mandate

Creation means that the Triune God has made this world beautifully and orderly. After making human in his image, God has given the so called "Cultural Mandate" to develop and, at the same time take care of his creation (Gen 1:27–28; 2:15). This mandate is given for a historical development and cultural unfolding.

Fall: Structure and Direction

Due to the fall of Adam and Eve, sin has affected the whole cosmos and the present world is a distorted and broken one. However, structure and direction should be distinguished. Structure means created laws and norms for creation, whereas direction denotes relative deviation or conformity to norms. While the former remains untouched by the Fall because of God's common grace, the latter depends upon the central orientation of the human heart toward or away from God.[3]

Redemption: Accomplished and Applied

God has sent Jesus Christ, His only Son, to redeem the whole universe. After Jesus has accomplished his redemptive work, the Holy Spirit came to apply this redemption into each Christian individually and every Christian community collectively until the consummation. In addition, this redemptive work of Jesus extends over all of life.[4]

---

3. Wolters, *Creation Regained*.
4. Murray, *Redemption Accomplished and Applied*.

Sphere Sovereignty

Each sphere of life (e.g., family, church, state, company, and etc.) has its own distinct responsibility and authority as designed by God and no one area of life is sovereign over another. This is called "sphere sovereignty" (*Soevereiniteit in eigen kring*). Therefore, neither the Church nor the State should seek totalitarian control over other spheres outside their limited sovereign sphere.

Antithesis

There is a struggle in history and within every person—between the serpent and the woman (Gen 3:15), between the kingdom of light and the kingdom of darkness, between submission to God and rebellion against God, and between the age to come (already inaugurated in Christ) and this present evil age (of sin). This confrontation is called *the antithesis*.

No Neutral Ground

Therefore, no theoretical thought can be religiously neutral. All thinking and practice is shaped by worldviews and religious "ground-motives" (*grondmotief*).[5] All the areas of Christian life should be guided by this biblical worldview.[6]

The Transformation of Modern Korean Society

Before the arrival of Christianity, shamanism, Buddhism and Confucianism dominated each period of Korean history.[7] During the Ancient Chosun period (2333 BC–108 BC), the Three Kingdoms period—Koguryo (37 BC–668 AD); Baekje (18 BC–660 AD); Shilla (57 BC–935 AD)—and the Unified Shilla Kingdom period (668–935 AD), shamanism was the major worldview of Korean society. By the end of the Unified Shilla Kingdom Period, it fell out of favor due to problems, such as seeking fortune through mystic magic and divination, fatalistic determinism, seeking simply earthly blessing, lacking an appropriate historico-cultural perspective and

---

5. Dooyeweerd, "La Sécularization de la Science," 138–55.
6. Naugle, *Worldview*; Goheen and Bartolomew, *Living at the Crossroads*; Wolters, *Creation Regained*.
7. Choi, *Vision for Unity*, 256–337; this book is written in Korean.

a proper ethic. The Buddhist worldview imported from China replaced shamanism and it became the state religion of the Koryo Kingdom period (935–1392 AD). When Buddhism became corrupt at the end of the Koryo period, Neo-Confucianism was introduced from China and became the major worldview of the Chosun Kingdom (Yi dynasty) period (1392–1910 AD). By the end of the nineteenth century, Neo-Confucianism could no longer lead the nation due to issues related to authoritarian hierarchy, gender discrimination, social inequality, etc. The Japanese Empire, using its superior modern technology and industry, invaded and occupied Korea until the end of World War II.

The Christian message was introduced in this situation as a new and alternative paradigm. The experiment with the previous three worldviews failed, opening a spiritual and mental vacuum among Korean people. The biblical worldview shed a new light of hope on Korean society under oppression. Therefore, most Korean national leaders at this time accepted the biblical worldview to reform the Korean nation and fight for its independence from the Japanese Empire. In the following, I will discuss several important aspects in which the biblical worldview made an impact on Korean society.[8]

The Idea of Origin

With respect to the origin of all, the Christian worldview presents God revealing himself in Christ as the personal God of the Scriptures, in stark contrast to the superstitious and polytheistic shamanism, syncretic Buddhism, and Confucian belief in a vague sky deity. The Christian worldview of the Creator of the heaven and the earth replaced all the traditional Korean ideas and beliefs concerning the origin of all things.

Human as the Image of God

The biblical view of humanity as the image of God transformed the traditional viewpoints as well. This view of the human person, as the cultural agent for the service of God and his or her neighbors, and as a responsible person *Coram Deo* made an enormous impact on Korean society. This perspective radically confronted and changed the traditional shamanistic attitude of fatalistic determinism. By proclaiming the dignity of labor and reminding people of the equality of all occupations, the view revolutionarily changed the Confucian culture which had discriminated against lower classes. According

---

8. Choi, *Vision for Unity*, 320–28.

to Christian worldview, every person can contribute to the development of the community by devoting themselves to their occupations.

The Extension of Women's Rights

The extension of women's rights was another innovative idea advocated by Korean churches. At that time, women were not treated as equals and men felt no embarrassment in publicly acknowledging their concubines. Their wives were helpless in the face of their husbands' indiscretions, because remarriage was forbidden for women. The Christian worldview, however, enacted the rights of women by stressing sexual equality and the need for women's education, arguing that educated mothers were better equipped to raise children and that the development of these human resources would eventually contribute to the general development of the country. Therefore, a school for young girls was founded to train them to be better wives and mothers, and important partners in the work of God's kingdom. Even though the rigid traditional class system was abolished by the government reforms in 1894 (*Kabo kyongjang*), true civil equality began within Korean churches in which everyone is considered as equal before God. This concept played a significant role in developing democracy in Korean society later.

Christian Worldview as the Tool for Modernizing Korea

The modernized Japanese Empire's victory over China by means of superior weapons and technologies from the West shocked Koreans. Many Korean visionaries determined to abandon conventional thought and traditional culture in favor of modernization, including a turn to Christianity as a means of modernization and disclosure (*gaehwa*) of Korean society. Through education, the missionaries brought knowledge of Western science and technology and introduced modern educational curricula. Early Korean Protestants regarded disclosure, education, and religion as one and the same, and they believed that Christianity could provide the momentum for socio-cultural reform. Many schools were established by the Presbyterian churches. Especially in the first decade of the twentieth century, it could be said that only the church had a complete educational system from the primary to the college level in the country. The old Confucian system of local academies disappeared, and the new Japanese occupying government had not yet developed its own education program. Korean Christian leaders took the initiative in establishing schools that first linked together Korean nationalism and Christian religion. Christian leaders played an enormously important role not merely as church leaders but also as national leaders in the modern history of Korea.

Medical Care and Education

Christian medical services and educational institutions left a positive impression for many Koreans. The first modern hospital was opened by an American missionary under a royal grant in 1885 and numerous other hospitals have been established by other Christian missionaries. These medical institutions functioned both as a means to improve the general health care of the country and as an important evangelistic tool. The missionaries encouraged Korean Christians to learn modern science and technology as well as to believe in the gospel. So there was little tension between faith and medical science. Additionally, women were trained to be physicians, and alcohol, tobacco, and opium were banned in an attempt to improve people's health. This accounts for the Korean churches' strong moral objection to drinking and smoking.

The Transformation of Korean Economy

The frugal lifestyle of Korean Christians helped the Korean economy free itself from Korea's financial bondage to the Japanese Empire. It is remarkable to see how quickly and strong Korean economy grew between the 1960s and the 1990s, which parallels the dramatic growth of Korean churches in the same period. The spirit of stewardship and biblical worldview influenced the development of Korean capitalistic industry, just as Max Weber famously observed the correlation between the rise of capitalism and that of Protestantism in Europe.[9] Now, the Korean economy belongs to the top G-20 in the world, transforming from an aid-receiving country to an aid-giving country in only a few decades.

The Transformation of Koreans' Worldview

The Christian worldview transformed Koreans' view of reality. Rejecting polytheistic shamanism, Korean churches began to emphasize the importance of a rational way of thinking, and of modern science and technology. Criticizing the negative view of reality in Buddhism, Christian thinkers tried to be realistic, confronting the difficult situation at that time and attempting

---

9. Weber, *Die protestantische Ethik*.

to overcome that situation rather than passively accepting it as their own fate. Against the traditional Confucian social class system, Korean Christians brought modern social values of freedom, equality, justice, peace and human rights to Korea and so served as a liberating force for those shackled to Confucian thought. It was also associated with movements for national independence and socio-political democracy, and the freedom of the press. In the 1960s and 1970s, Korean liberal Christians played a significant role in resisting the oppression of human rights, the non-democratic military dictatorship, and an authoritarian bureaucracy. They also took part in social reform movements to improve wages and the working conditions among poor urban workers. All of these movements were accelerated by the biblical view of history, namely, the sovereignty of God in history, the eschatological victory of the Kingdom of God, and the linear, rather than circular or retrospective conception of time.

The Translation of the Bible into Korean

Similar to what happened to Europe after the Protestant Reformation, the translation, publication, and distribution of the Bible in Korean became a catalyst for the widespread use of the vernacular script (*Hangul*). Many other Christian books were written in Korean, or translated into Korean. With the spread of the Korean Bible and hymnals, *Hangul* became very popular. These enterprises reduced illiteracy and played an important role in breaking down the privilege of traditional elite class who held onto Confucianism and used Chinese in their learning and communication. The truth found in the Bible was easily available to the common people, which sharply contrasts with Korean Buddhism and Confucianism, because their scriptures, written in Chinese, were almost inaccessible to the general public.

The Christian Worldview as a Liberating Power

The prestige of this biblical worldview was reinforced by the presence of many Christians among the nationalists. While some Christians collaborated with the Japanese imperialists at the end of the colonial period, Korean Christianity never became associated with the Japanese Empire. Many Koreans, humiliated and frustrated by Japanese aggression, accepted Christianity, because they associated it with deliverance from Japanese imperialism. They sought a solution to the nation's dilemma in Korean churches. They were also known for their activism and organizational capacity. After liberation and economic growth, Korean churches began to help other underdeveloped countries by sending missionaries and by supporting North Korean refugees throughout the world.

The Christian worldview has been a powerful driving force in the development of modern Korean Society, making a crucial contribution in overcoming the shortcomings of all the traditional religions and worldviews in terms of their ideas and cultural structures. It blossomed modern Korean culture by directing it with its biblical perspective. This does not mean, however, that it has always been right in every aspect. Korean Christians have made some serious mistakes and still have many shortcomings that need to be addressed. Due to these problems, Korean churches are now facing great challenges that require serious and critical reflection.

The Current Crisis of Korean Christianity

Today, Korean churches are facing a serious crisis: decline in membership and influence. Furthermore, Korean Christians have often become the object of criticism rather than respect, with a number of factors contributing to this phenomenon.

Materialism

As most churches pursue growth, materialistic and shamanistic worldviews have crept into the outlook of Korean Christians. The prosperity gospel was introduced to justify material success as a blessing from God regardless of the means. Furthermore, due to new church building projects, the financial burden became heavy on church members to financially contribute. As a result, many disappointed Protestant Christians converted to Catholicism.

Division

Korean churches have experienced numerous divisions due to the political power struggle over trivial debates within local churches, synods, and general assemblies. Even in a single Presbyterian denomination, there are numerous sub-divisions. This problem has been the Achilles' heel of Korean churches, not only in Korea, but also Korean diaspora churches in the other parts of the world, and it has resulted in the Korean churches losing their credibility within Korean society.[10]

---

10. Choi, *Vision for Unity*.

Immorality

For many Christians, both leaders and lay people, their lives are not integrated with their confession of faith. Many leaders are guilty of sexual immorality, plagiarism, and financial conflicts of interest. Furthermore, young people oppose the Confucian-like authoritarianism exercised by many senior church leaders.

The Secularization of Christian Schools and Universities

Most Christian schools and universities in Korea have lost their Christian identity due to their commercial interests. Many Christians today naively suppose that education is simply for academic and career success and there is no difference between Christian and secular education. Government schools are regarded as neutral rather than as secular. Even in the textbooks and curriculum of some Christian schools, a worldview is promoted that God is not relevant to how students learn about the world and their roles in it. This absolutely goes against the gospel and to Kuyper's claim about the centrality of Christ in all of life. Most Christian schools and universities in Korea have lost their unique identity and forgotten the biblical worldview as their educational framework. Those once Christian universities gradually compromised with marketplace economy, even hiring non-Christian professors. Science and faith are not properly integrated by a Christian worldview, but they are separated from each other. Therefore, they fail to produce future Christian leaders and cannot make any significant and unique contribution to Korean society. While secular schools and universities obviously bring many important contributions to the society, Christians schools and universities lose their own unique identity and fail to fulfill their mission, when they dismiss the integration of Christian worldview in their curricula.

The Challenge of Islam

The power of Islam is expanding worldwide, now reaching to Korea. It threatens even Korean churches through various ways such as international marriage, recruiting students by giving full scholarship when they go to the Middle East to study Islam, building many mosques in major South Korean cities and promoting many cultural exchange programs. However, Korean churches are not yet properly prepared for this challenge. The most serious danger of Islam is its non-tolerant attitude toward other worldviews. It limits the freedom of religion especially for Christians and oppresses those who do not belong to Islam.

Postmodern Pluralism

Postmodern pluralism and relativism are gaining more support so that homosexuality, premarital sex, and transgender issues are regarded as natural. Any kind of regulation is criticized as dogmatic and intolerant. Korean churches have become, therefore, more defensive than before. At the same time, Korean Christianity has not developed an effective multi-cultural ministry to serve various kinds of increasingly multi-cultural families in Korean society. Rather, it still maintains traditional ministries for mainly ethnic Koreans.

The Problem of Dualism

The dualistic worldview of Korean Christians has made a false distinction between the sacred and the secular. It has produced so many Sunday church-goers who live like non-believers during the week days. The confinement of the gospel out of the "public" space and into a so-called "private" sphere, which is a part of the Enlightenment agenda, has hugely influenced contemporary Korean Christian lifestyle. This has happened to such an extent that, while most Korean Christians are passionately concerned about world missions, they see little relationship between their faith and their vocation or the rest of their lives—family, politics, economic life style, recreation, and etc. They have, therefore, failed to be the true light and salt in the society. As a result, Korean churches are facing severe criticism and are losing their integrity. Consequently, Korean churches are now facing a serious crisis and are at a tipping point where they can either progress to further development or go backward and lose their impact in both Korean and global society.

New Paradigm for the Future

Based on the above analyses, the following items are a collective proposal to provide a new paradigm for Korean churches for the future.

Restoring Biblical Stewardship

The Christian worldview should criticize the danger of materialism in Korean churches. Pointing out the shamanistic way of thinking and lifestyle, we have to emphasize that we cannot worship God and *mammon* at the same time (Matt 6:24; Luke 16:13). Instead, the biblical worldview can promote the spirit of Jubilee and the communal life model of the ancient Christian community described in Acts 2. Bob Goudzwaard, a retired Dutch professor of economics, argues that we should not merely seek economic growth anymore, but rather emphasize the lifestyle of stewardship and so pursue the "economy of care."[11] It means that instead of merely accumulating wealth, we should practice sharing what extra we have.

Peter Hahne, a German journalist and Christian, wrote his best-selling book, *Schluss mit lustig! Das Ende der Spaßgesellschaft* ("Stop extra desire! The end of the fun society") in which he emphasizes that Christians should control their desires and live a sober and thrifty life.[12] Appreciating the fruit of labor as God's blessing, Christians should fear the LORD (Ps 128) and take care of those in need with Christian love.

In relation to this, Christians can think of using church buildings with a new paradigm, for instance as a multiple complex space not only for worshipping God but also for serving the local community. Contemporary society needs the social involvement of evangelical churches. The Cape Town Commitment, the official document of the third Lausanne Congress on world evangelization also admits this and emphasizes that the whole church should take the whole gospel to the whole world, which has various problems. In this sense, John Stott suggests that Christian churches should emphasize the Protestant work ethic (diligence, honesty, stewardship, frugality) in order to resolve the problem of unemployment, and that each local church can execute many community activities, such as child-care programs, kindergarten, elderly care, coffee shop outreach, work training, and etc. He even suggests that one might change the name of the church into "Christian Center.[13]" Figuratively, new wine should be poured into new wineskins (Matt 9:17; Mark 2:22; Luke 5:37–38). The Korean church should go beyond secular materialism and the prosperity gospel and take the full mission of evangelism and social responsibility in balance. In order to do that, the Christian worldview should be able to provide a new alternative in this postmodern age without losing the essential elements of Biblical truth.

---

11. Goudzwaard et. al., *Hope in Troubled Times*, 205.
12. Hahne, *Schluss mit lustig!*
13. Stott, *Issues Facing Christians Today*, 177–81.

Restoring Christian Unity

In contrast to Roman Catholic Church, Korean Protestant churches have deep and frequent divisions. This problem should be seriously dealt with because Jesus prayed so desperately for the unity of Christians (John 17:21). In order to overcome this problem of schisms, Korean churches should attempt to restore and build unity, if they share the same biblical worldview, not only in Korea, but also globally. Similar denominations with the same confession of faith can start discussing how they can restore unity. If they cannot, due to the significant difference in the confession, they still can work together more closely in such areas as helping the poor, supporting North Korean refugees, etc. Then, perhaps, Korean society will take Korean Protestant churches seriously as a prophetic and moral voice among them.[14]

Restoring the Biblical Morality

The ethical corruption of Korean church leaders today proves that the Christian worldview has not been embodied in the daily life of Korean Christians. We need to thoroughly repent and practice discipleship at individual, local church, synod, and general assembly levels. Korean Christian leaders should first be role-models of holy, honest and transparent lives. When an issue has been discovered, they should be ready to take full responsibility. Only then can Korean churches regain respect from Korean society, which they had once before. One example might be removing all the chairs in the church where altar and pulpit stand. Most Korean pastors sit behind the pulpit or next to the altar for the whole service. In contrast, in German Protestant churches, for instance, there is no chair for the preacher at the altar area. The preacher simply sits in front row together with other members of the church. The preacher goes forward only for preaching. In Korean churches, however, the chairs for pastor or elder look like thrones in a royal court. It may misrepresent God and the gospel message. It may also promote a kind of unbiblical ecclesiastical hierarchy related to the priesthood of all believers, due to which Protestant churches separated themselves from Roman Catholic Church five hundred years ago.

---

14. In this context, I have written a book, *Vision for Unity* (Choi: 2006), on the basis of my ministry experience in Cologne, Germany, where four different churches were united into one body of Christ and diverse denominations tried to work together. Furthermore, I have explained in this book how the Christian solidarity and unity between the West and the East German churches played the crucial role in reunifying two Germanys into one. The same miracle of unification can happen, I would argue, if Korean Christians began to restore the true unity in Christ.

Restoring Balanced Ministry and Preaching

The church calendar should be respected so that congregations might understand the whole stream of God's redemptive plan throughout history. In connection with this, for instance, the day of Christ's ascension should be celebrated, considering its significance of the redemptive work of Jesus Christ. The biblical texts for sermons are quite limited in Korean churches. The whole Bible should be preached in three years for instance so that the congregation might hear the Word of God in balance. At the same time, Korean churches have lost the blessing of the Lord's Supper because they have emphasized the preaching ministry too much, and so it should be observed as often as possible (1 Cor 11:25–26). In this way, the balanced ministry and preaching can help restore the true spirituality of Korean churches and this might improve Korean society's perception of Korean churches.

Restoring Christian Education and Scholarship

In order to prevent the secularization of Christian schools and universities, Christian teachers and professors should make a concerted effort to restore the biblical worldview and to integrate their teaching and scientific research with Christian faith. Furthermore, their faith and scholarship should go hand in hand with their a lifestyle of authenticity. In this way, they can show an example to students and train leaders for the next generation.

In addition, the whole education system—from kindergarten to university, and lifelong learning—should be integrated with the Christian worldview. Korean Christian schools should demonstrate that students do not need any additional, cost-prohibitive, private education. Through holistic educational reform, Korean Christians should be the catalysts for the transformation of Korean society and culture for the future. Furthermore, we need to urgently re-educate pastors and Christian parents into the totality of the Lordship of Christ, and encourage them to provide elementary and secondary schools for our children that look at various disciplines from the biblical perspective. This is not an optional extra, but is an absolute necessity in order to preserve the identity of the Christian schools and universities.[15]

---

15. Edlin, *The Cause of Christian Education.*

Response to Islam

Against the challenge of Islam to Korean society, Korean churches should develop comprehensive strategies. For instance, they can develop Sunday school textbooks that teach what Islam is, and highlight its differences from Christianity. Furthermore, various seminars or training programs can be developed to teach pastors and lay people about the Islamic worldview and its dangers together with an effective way to confront Muslims with a loving attitude and the biblical worldview.

Response to Postmodern Pluralism

The postmodern worldview is another great challenge to Korean society these days. Postmodern relativism and religious pluralism with tolerance seem to be the present *Zeitgeist* and are critical to the conservative attitude of Korean Christians. As a response to this trend, the Christian worldview has to show the weaknesses of postmodernism(s), such as the contradictory nature of absolute relativism. Christians must present clear biblical standards and criteria as an alternative. Such a worldview should help Korean churches give a strong voice to a sensitive issue like homosexuality. The Christian worldview warns Korean Christians not to be too aggressive and radical toward the other worldviews or religions, but instead to engage in a critical dialogue with them. The Christian worldview is a comprehensive system which can validate even some aspects of the other worldviews in terms of God's common grace, instead of complete rejection of their worth.

Nonetheless, the biblical worldview should strongly affirm a multicultural ministry and society as the expression of God's abundant creation. Korean society has been transformed from basically one ethnic community to a diverse, multi-cultural one. Unfortunately, however, Korean churches are still focusing primarily on the Korean ethnic group. Although some churches have English/Chinese/Japanese service for each ethnic group, they rarely have an integrated ministry. The Bible clearly states that there is no favoritism in God (Acts 10:34–35; Col 3:25). Abraham was chosen to be a blessing to all nations (Gen 12:1–3). Therefore, the Israelites should love Gentiles and foreigners (Exod 22:21, 23:9). The book of Ruth clearly shows that Gentiles could participate in the blessings of God. Even the genealogy of Jesus includes Gentile women (Matt 1:3–6). The Pharisees admitted that Jesus was not swayed by men, because he paid no attention to who they are (Matt 22:16b). In addition, almost every congregation in the New Testament demonstrates unity and diversity in Christ, in which both Jewish and Gentile believers worshipped Jesus Christ as one family of God (Gal 3:28).

In order to be a global church and to make disciples of all nations, Korean churches need to transform their worship services to meet the needs of the *entire*, diverse, multi-cultural congregations. In this way, Korean churches can be "a house of prayer for all nations" (Mark 11:27). Then, Korean churches will be a global church in the true sense of the word and be a channel of blessing for all nations.

All of Life Redeemed[16]

The Christian worldview stresses that all of our lives should be redeemed. All kinds of professional Christians need to realize that they are called to serve God in their own areas for his kingdom. Furthermore, they need to gather together in order to share how they can realize and achieve the will of God in their spheres to make contributions not only in Korean society but also in the global community. In this way, Korean Christians should not fall into the error of dualism but rather reveal the sovereignty of Christ in every domain of their lives to redeem it. Then, Korean society will be transformed by this kind of authentic and integrative effort of Korean Christians based upon the Christian worldview.

One example would be the area of business life. Christian businessmen should try not only to evangelize other colleagues in the workplace but also integrate their faith with business ethics so that through their vocations they might witness the gospel and transform Korean society by more transparent, honest and fair business practices. In this context, the *Nuremberg Declaration* of the Christian business leaders in Germany can be a good example:[17]

> A society is only efficient and socially at the same time, if it is "under the responsibility before God and men," as stated in the preamble of the German constitution. We are convinced that economic action needs Christian values with which you can take the lead. Who is guided by God's standards: (1) is committed to integrity, honesty, diligence, reliability, compassion and fairness in all aspects of life; (2) rejects corruption, fraud, unfair wages, excessive salaries and severance pay off as much as greed, envy, avarice and slander; (3) advocates for the protection of property, the environment and of Sunday as a day of rest,

16. www.allofliferedeemed.co.uk.
17. http://www.zukunftbrauchtwerte.de/ruckschau/nurnberger-erklarung.

and is committed to the public good; (4) encourages marriages, families and children as the basis of society; (5) encourages his fellow citizens to live in union with Jesus Christ. We strive to live according to God's standards, as found by way of example in the 10 Commandments.[18]

Of course, there might be more suggestions. We should be open for all other possibilities and be ready to reform ourselves first because the church of Christ is reformed and should be always reforming (*Ecclesia Reformata et Semper Reformanda*).

Conclusion

The Christian worldview has been a powerful driving force in the development of modern Korea, making a crucial contribution to overcoming the limitations of the traditional Korean worldviews in terms of their ideas and cultural structures. It played a crucial role in building the foundation of modern Korean culture by directing it via its biblical perspective. However, this does not mean that Korean churches do not have problems in the past and in the present. Korean churches are facing many challenges today. For instance, some shamanistic elements have crept into Korean Christianity so deeply that worldly success is still emphasized as the sign of God's blessing. In addition, some Confucian aspects such as authoritarianism have made another serious impact on Korean churches. Furthermore, materialism has been a serious threat to Korean Christians, making them more secular and corrupt. The dualistic lifestyle of some Korean Christians has been criticized as hypocritical. These problems should be continuously assessed as unbiblical elements and obstacles to the proper development of Christian culture in Korea. They must be overcome by emphasizing a Christian worldview, the biblical spirit of responsible stewardship, and the principle of redeeming all

---

18. The German text of Nürnberger Erklärung is "Eine Gesellschaft ist nur dann leistungsfähig und sozial zugleich, wenn sie „unter Verantwortung vor Gott und den Menschen" geschieht, wie es in der Präambel des deutschen Grundgesetzes heißt. Wir sind überzeugt, dass wirtschaftliches Handeln christliche Werte braucht, mit denen man in Führung gehen kann. Wer sich an Gottes Maßstäben orientiert, (1) bemüht sich um Integrität, Ehrlichkeit, Fleiß, Verlässlichkeit, Barmherzigkeit und Fairness in allen Bereichen des Lebens; (2) lehnt Korruption, Betrug, unfaire Löhne, überzogene Gehälter und Abfindungen genauso ab, wie Habsucht, Neid, Geiz und üble Nachrede; (3) setzt sich für den Schutz des Eigentums, der Umwelt und des Sonntags als Ruhetag ein und engagiert sich für das öffentliche Wohl; (4) fördert Ehen, Familien und Kinder als Basis der Gesellschaft; (5) ermutigt seine Mitbürgerinnen und Mitbürger zu einem Leben in Verbindung mit Jesus Christus. Wir bemühen uns, nach den Maßstäben Gottes zu leben, wie sie sich beispielhaft in den 10 Geboten finden."

of life spheres. Then, Korean Christianity can continue to transform Korean society and give a new vision and light as the hope for the future.

Bibliography

Choi, Yong Joon. *Vision for Unity*. Seoul: InterVarsity, 2006.
Dooyeweerd, H. "La Sécularization de la Science." *La Revue Réformée* 5 (1954) 138–55.
Edlin, Richard J. *The Cause of Christian Education*. 4th ed. Sioux Center, IA: Dort College Press, 2014.
Goheen, Michael W., and Craig G. Bartolomew. *Living at the Crossroads: An Introduction to Christian Worldview*. Grand Rapids: Baker, 2008.
Goudzwaard, B., Mark Vander Vennen, and David Van Heemst. *Hope in Troubled Times: A New Vision for Confronting Global Crises*. Grand Rapids: Baker, 2007.
Hahne, Peter. *Schluss mit lustig! Das Ende der Spaßgesellschaft*. Lahr: Johannis, 2009.
Kuyper, Abraham. *Lectures on Calvinism*. Grand Rapids: Eerdmans, 1983.
———. *Souvereiniteit in Eigen Kring*. Amsterdam: Kruyt, 1880.
Murray, John. *Redemption Accomplished and Applied*. Grand Rapids: Eerdmans, 1995.
Naugle, David K. *Worldview: The History of a Concept*. Grand Rapids: Eerdmans, 2002.
Stott, John R. W. *Issues Facing Christians Today*. Rev. ed. London: Marshall Pickering, 1990.
Weber, Max. *Die protestantische Ethik und der Geist des Kapitalismus*. Tübingen: Mohr, 1934.
Wolters, Albert M. *Creation Regained: Biblical Basics for a Reformational Worldview*. Grand Rapids: Eerdmans, 2005.

Part 4

Christian Higher Education

12

Athens, Rome, Amsterdam, and Karawaci

Historical and Theological Basis of Christian Worldview-Based Liberal Arts Education

HENDRA THAMRINDINATA

Introduction

IN RECENT YEARS, THERE has been a growing interest in liberal arts education in Indonesia, indicated by the number of seminars, conferences, and publications on the topic. A few Indonesian universities include liberal arts education as their core curriculum, such as Universitas Pelita Harapan (UPH) and Universitas Pembanguan Jaya (UPJ). Universitas Pelita Harapan, located in Lippo Karawaci, Tangerang, Indonesia, has been the pioneer of providing its students a Christian worldview-based liberal arts education in the nation, in which I served as the Executive Dean of the Faculty of Liberal Arts for four years (2013–2017). In this chapter, I will briefly discuss the historical background of liberal arts education in general and the historical and theological background of Christian worldview-based liberal arts education.

Liberal Arts Education

Liberal arts education has historical roots in Greek classical education. In *Politics* 8.4.10 [1338 a], Aristotle describes what he calls *eleutheros paeda* ("education given to free men"). Ancient Greece consisted of many city-states and each city-state (*polis*) had its own government. Every city-state had two categories of citizens—free men and slaves. Free men, as citizens, had a role that was contemplative in nature, while slaves, non-citizens, had a role that was laboring in nature. Free men's contemplative role included their political and social leadership to attain "the highest good" (*summum bonum*) of their city-states. To enable free men to do their contemplative duty well, Greek city-states needed to provide them with proper education. Aristotle explains the significance of the involvement of government in public education in *Politics* 8.1.1 [1337 a II]:

> All would agree that the legislator should make the education of the young his chief and foremost concern. In the first place, the constitution of a state will suffer if education is neglected. The citizens of a state should always be educated to suit the constitution of their state. The type of character appropriate to a constitution is the power which continues to sustain it, as it is also the force which originally creates it. The democratic type of character creates and sustains democracy; the oligarchical type creates and sustains oligarchy; and as the progression ascends each higher type of character will always tend to produce a higher form of constitution. In the second place, every capacity, and every form of art, requires as a condition of its exercise some measure of previous training and some amount of preliminary habituation. Men must therefore be trained and habituated before they can do acts of goodness, as members of a state should do. The whole of a state has one common End. Evidently, therefore, the system of education in a state must also be one and the same for all, and the provision of this system must be a matter of public action.[1]

Aristotle explains here that public education contributes to the common good and, therefore, the government has to provide any necessary education to equip its citizens. The essence of education provided by the government is to shape its citizens in accordance with its essence, purpose, and characteristics.

In *Politics* 8.2.1 [1337 a II], Aristotle states, "Two things are now evident. The first is that there ought to be laws to regulate education. The second is that education ought to be conducted by the state. We have to consider now the nature of liberal arts education, and the methods by which it ought to be given." In *Politics* 8.2.3–6 [1337 b], Aristotle notes:

---

1. In this study, I use Barker's English translation of Aristotle's *Politics*.

There can be no doubt that such useful subjects as are really necessary ought to be part of the instruction of children. But this does not mean the inclusion of every useful subject. Occupations are divided into those which are fit for freemen and those which are unfit for them; and it follows from this that the total amount of useful knowledge imparted to children should never be large enough to make them "mechanically" (*banausos*) minded... A good deal depends on the purpose for which acts are done or subjects are studied. Anything done to satisfy a personal need, or to help a friend, or attain goodness, will not be illiberal; but the very same act, when done repeatedly at the instance of other persons, may be counted menial and servile.[2]

As Arthur F. Holmes states, "To educate people as responsible agents requires attention to their critical thinking and their values."[3] In addition to one's capacity to think rationally and making fair judgment as well as decisions, Holmes adds one more item to the goals of liberal arts education, what he calls "historical perspective on our sociopolitical institutions and values."[4]

There were a number of core subjects in liberal arts education in ancient Greece. Aristotle mentions reading, writing, physical training, and music, as four core subjects of liberal arts education in *Politics* 8.3.1–2 [1337 b]. Holmes states, "Cicero suggested that liberal education is the education of free men for the exercise of their freedom rather than of slaves."[5] Its focus is on the formation of human beings as human beings, not human beings in their function, profession, or what they can do. Holmes argues, "If one is to be anything more than a specialist or technician, if one is to feel life whole and to live it whole rather than piecemeal, if one is to think for himself rather than live secondhand, the liberal arts are needed to educate the person."[6] This corresponds with the fact that those subjects that Aristotle lists as four subjects of instruction focus on the foundational cultivation of human beings as human beings in relation to what they think about, hope

---

2. Barker comments on his footnote, "In something of an English fashion—at any rate as that fashion went in the eighteenth century—Aristotle feels, that the freeman or 'gentleman' ought to preserve an amateur character. Even in the liberal arts—such as music, painting, and literature—he must be a dilettante, with a find edge of appreciation, but with an edge of execution which is not too precious or virtuoso"; Aristotle, *The Politics of Aristotle*, 393.

3. Holmes, *Idea of a Christian College*, 38.
4. Holmes, *Idea of a Christian College*, 39.
5. Holmes, *Idea of a Christian College*, 27.
6. Holmes, *Idea of a Christian College*, 27.

for, and feel. They are not directly related to technical skills for workforce. This kind of cultivation intrinsically aims at transcendental truth, beauty, and goodness which are objects as well as sustainable goals of thoughts, hopes, and affections of human beings themselves. As Holmes points out, "Liberal education is an open invitation to join the human race and become more fully human. Its general goals include the ability to read and write and thereby think independently, an appreciation of lasting values coupled with the ability to make sound value judgments and live by them, a critical appreciation of the past and responsible creative participation in the future."[7] Since the focus of this education is the holistic formation of a person, Aristotle calls it *enkyklios paedea* ("circle of learning") (*Politics* 8.2.4–6 [1337 b]). This focus on intrinsic values did not ignore instrumental (or practical) values but complemented them. Each city-state sought to prepare its future leaders to achieve *summum bonum* in the governance of their city-state. They need to understand life-values and the purposes of their lives as human beings in order to become competent citizens of their city-states. With its historical roots in ancient Greece, we can define liberal arts education as holistic education in search for truth, goodness, and beauty, in order to actualize potential intellectual and moral virtues in human beings.

Worldview

I will introduce briefly five European philosophers who contributed to the development of the concept of worldview. First, David K. Naugle points out, "Immanuel Kant was a towering figure, and there is virtually universal recognition that this notable Prussian philosopher coined the term *Weltanschauung* in his work Critique of Judgment in 1790."[8] Kant writes:

> If the human mind is nonetheless to *be able even to think* the given infinite without contradiction, it must have within itself a power that is supersensible, whose idea of the noumenon cannot be intuited but can yet be regarded as the substrate underlying what is mere appearance, namely, our intuition of the world [*Weltanschauung*]. For only by means of this power and its idea do we, in a pure intellectual estimation of magnitude, comprehend the infinite in the world of sense *entirely under* a concept, even though in a mathematical estimation of magnitude *by means of numerical concepts* we can never think it in its entirety.[9]

---

7. Holmes, *Idea of a Christian College*, 35.
8. Naugle, *Worldview*, 58.
9. Kant, *Critique of Judgment*, 111–12; emphasis is Kant's.

Kant uses the word *Weltanschauung* simply as sensory intuition without any intellectual association.

Second, according to Martin Heidegger, Friedrich Wilhelm Joseph von Schelling further developed its concept and defined it as "a self-realized, productive as well as conscious way of apprehending and interpreting the universe of beings."[10]

Third, G. W. F. Hegel in *The Phenomenology of Mind* describes what he calls "the moral view of the world":

> Starting with a specific character of this sort, there is formed and established a moral outlook on the world [*moralische Weltanschauung*] which consists in a process of relating the implicit aspect of morality and the explicit aspect. This relation presupposes both thorough reciprocal indifference and specific independence as between nature and moral purposes and activity; and also, on the other side, a conscious sense of duty as the sole essential fact, and of nature as entirely devoid of independence and essential significance of its own. The moral view of the world [*Die moralische Weltanschauung*], the moral attitude, consists in the development of the moments which are found present in this relation of such entirely antithetic and conflicting presuppositions.[11]

Naugle notes, "It [*Weltanschauung*] carries the force of a practical perspective on life, a conscious attitude that is permeated with the tension of moral concern and obligation... 'ways of living and of looking at the universe.'"[12] Hegel's unique contribution to the idea of *Weltanschauung* lies in his explanation of the *raison d'être* for coexistence of different *Weltanschauungen* in this world by employing his concept of historical dialectics. Naugle comments, "Hegel played a significant role in the promotion of *Weltanschauung* as an incisive concept in the nineteenth century European intellectual scene."[13]

Fourth, Søren Kierkegaard further developed the concept of worldview. Kant introduced *Weltanschauung* philologically to the world of thought, and Schelling translated it from sensory perception to intellectual one, and Hegel explained the *raison d'etre* of the various coexistence of various *Weltanschauungen*. It was Kierkegaard who underscored its existential aspect. Kierkegaard used the Danish word *livsanskuelse* ("life-view") with

---

10. Heidegger, *The Basic Problems of Phenomenology*, 4.
11. Hegel, *The Phenomenology of Mind*, 615–16.
12. Naugle, *Worldview*, 70.
13. Naugle, *Worldview*, 73.

reference to the German word *Weltanschauung* ("worldview"), and explains, "A life-view is more than a pure idea or a sum of propositions held fast in abstract neutrality; it is more than experience which as such is always atomistic, it is namely the transubstantiation of experience, it is an unshakable certainty in oneself which has been won by all [of one's] experience" (*Samlede Værker* 5.13.68).[14]

Fifth, Martin Heidegger discusses *Weltanschauung* indirectly in its relation to hermeneutics or interpretation. Heidegger states:

> Interpretation is never a presuppositionless grasping of something previously given. When a specific instance of interpretation (in the sense of a precise textual interpretation) appeals to what "is there" [*dasteht*], then that which initially "is there" is nothing other than the self-evident, undiscussed prejudice [*Vormeinung*] of the interpreter which necessarily lies in every interpretive approach as that which is already "posited" with interpretation in general, namely, that which is pre-given [*vorgegeben*] in fore-having, fore-sight, and fore-conception.[15]

These five European philosophers whom we have briefly explored provide us with a working definition of worldview—an individual's point of reference by which he or she understands and interprets his or her universe and his or her existence and involvement in it.

Christian Worldview-Based Liberal Arts Education in Medieval Europe

The idea of worldview is foundational for liberal arts education. A particular worldview evidently defines the meaning, value, and purpose of liberal arts education. There can be no liberal arts education without a particular worldview as its foundation. Without a worldview, liberal arts education cannot have any purpose behind its curriculum and teaching methodology. A worldview provides a framework of reference for liberal arts education so that its meaning, value, and purpose can be defined holistically. It is a crucial basis for integration of learning and living. The public liberal arts education that Aristotle refers to in *Politics* 8.1.1, cited earlier, is based on the worldview of Greek city-states. In the case of medieval Europe, the Roman Catholic Church supervised liberal arts education, which was broadly

---

14. McCarthy's translation; McCarthy, *Phenomenology of Moods in Kierkegaard*, 145.

15. Heidegger, *Being and Time*, 146.

categorized as philosophy. Alcuin (ca. 735–804 AD), a medieval scholar in the Carolingian period, describes, "the seven liberal arts [grammar, rhetoric, logic, geometry, arithmetic, music, and astronomy] are *septem philosophiae gradus* ['seven degrees of philosophy']; they therefore constitute philosophy as a whole" (*Disputatio de vera philosophia* PL, 101, 854A).[16] Ulrich G. Leinsle explains that philosophy was the foundational education in medieval Europe that "did not provide any specialized training, but rather the general scientific skills needed to address the questions of the individual specialties (law, medicine, theology)."[17] In medieval Europe, liberal arts education was based on a Christian worldview and offered in the paradigm of faith seeking understanding. Roger E. Olson notes:

> All of the great Christian scholastic thinkers [in medieval period] agreed that human reason must operate at its best within the realm of faith and upon the foundation of divine revelation through Scripture and the church's tradition. In varying degrees, however, they attempted to build great "cathedral of ideas"—architectonic edifices of propositions about God, the world, and salvation-to stand at the center of the curricula of medieval universities. Theology was to be enthroned as the Queen of the Sciences so that all the disciplines (*scientia*) of the universities would be guided if not ruled by it . . . The motto of most scholastics would be "faith seeking understanding" or "I believe in order that I may understand."[18]

Thomas Aquinas suggested the use of philosophy in teaching and writing about theology, which provides a good example of the importance of Christian worldview–based liberal arts education in medieval Europe. Aquinas writes in *Commentary on Boethius' Book on the Trinity* 2.4, "those who use philosophical texts in sacred teaching, by subjugating them to faith, do not mix water with wine, but turn water into wine."[19] Aquinas explains in his sermon *Attendite a falsis prophetis*, "Faith can do more than philosophy in much; so that if philosophy is contrary to faith, it is not to be accepted."[20] According to Mark D. Jordan, "'subjugating' philosophy to theology seems to mean several things"—(1) "the theologian takes truth from the philosophers as from usurpers"; (2) "theology serves as a corrective to philosophy"; and (3) "the impure motives of philosophy—vanity, contentiousness,

---

16. Miller's translation; Leinsle, *Introduction to Scholastic Theology*, 36.
17. Leinsle, *Introduction to Scholastic Theology*, 37.
18. Olson, *The Story of Christian Theology*, 312.
19. This translation is from Jordan, "Theology and Philosophy," 235.
20. Jordan, "Theology and Philosophy," 235.

arrogance—be transformed into the motives of the Christian believer."[21] Jordan elaborates the last point, "Philosophical inquiries ought always to serve a theological end. Applied to texts, this rule would seem to require that philosophical argumentation be begun and carried forward only from the believer's motive of the twofold love of God and neighbor."[22] Christian worldview was the soul and foundation of liberal arts education in medieval Europe, which was the foundation of all the specialized education.[23]

Christian Worldview-Based Liberal Arts Education in Modern Europe

Christian worldview–based liberal arts education diminished in Europe after the Enlightenment and the modernization and secularization of the European societies. James Eglinton and Michael Bräutigam point out, "In the Netherlands, the Higher Education Act (1876) legally required Dutch universities to replace theology with religious studies (whilst retaining the title *theology*). The success and progress of the natural sciences that followed, especially in the latter half of the nineteenth century, contributed to a gradual marginalisation of theological departments across Europe."[24] Eglinton and Bräutigam focus on the Dutch neo-Calvinist dogmatician Herman Bavinck (1854–1921) and the Swiss Reformed theologian Adolf Schlatter (1852–1938), who "provide an interesting alternative to perhaps the most prominent nineteenth century Roman Catholic defence of theology within the university: *The Idea of a University* by Cardinal John Henry Newman."[25] Eglinton and Bräutigam describe Bavinck's and Schlatter's contributions:

> In addition to their rejection of a dualistic separation of theology and science, both of these theologians claimed that theology was necessary within the academy precisely to prevent the fragmentation of its various faculties and departments. Their common assertion is that theology alone is able to serve as an integrative force among the academic disciplines, as only theology provides a coherent framework that enables them to function properly and collaborate in harmony. They foresaw

21. Jordan, "Theology and Philosophy," 235.

22. Jordan, "Theology and Philosophy," 236.

23. Schaff, *History of the Christian Church*, 292–94.

24. Eglinton and Bräutigam, "Scientific Theology?," 28–29; Schlatter, "Atheistische Methoden in der Theologie," 227–50; Bavinck, *Reformed Dogmatics*, 25–58.

25. Eglinton and Bräutigam, "Scientific Theology?," 29; Newman, *The Idea of a University*.

the university as becoming a cacophony of arbitrarily associated faculties when deprived of theology. Bearing in mind that the theme of academic fragmentation (whereby one ponders what, for example, the biology department has to do with the English literature class) has become a prominent feature in discussion on the current academy, it seems that one must at least consider their claims.[26]

Abraham Kuyper (1837–1920), perhaps the most well-known Dutch neo-Calvinist theologian, was contemporary with Bavinck and Schlatter. Joel R. Beeke summarizes Kuyper's contribution as an educator:

> Kuyper was deeply concerned about establishing quality Christian education at all levels for all classes of people. Dissatisfied with the apostasy in the government-controlled universities, he set out to promote and establish a Christian university free from government control. After much labor on his part, the Free University of Amsterdam, designed to affirm a biblical and Reformed world-view throughout its entire curriculum, was established on October 20, 1880. Kuyper organised it as a school freed from government or ecclesiastical control, operated as a parental institution, and supported by the prayer and gifts of Reformed Christians.[27]

Kuyper in *Lectures on Calvinism* concludes his chapter "Calvinism and Science":

> We must have systems in science, coherence in instruction, unity in education. That is only really free, which, while it is strictly bound to its own principle, has the power to free itself from all unnatural bonds. The final result, therefore, will be, thanks to Calvinism, which has opened for us the way, that liberty of science will also triumph at last; first by guaranteeing full power to every leading life-system to reap a scientific harvest from its own principle;—and secondly, by refusing the scientific name to whatsoever investigator dare not unroll the colors of his own banner, and does not show emblazoned on his escutcheon in letters of gold the very principle for which he lives, and from which his conclusions derive their power.[28]

Beeke reports, "The Free University departed far from Kuyper's teachings in the twentieth century. By 1960, many of its 12,000 students expressed no

26. Eglinton and Bräutigam, "Scientific Theology?," 30.
27. Beeke, "Life and Vision of Abraham Kuyper," 31.
28. Kuyper, *Lectures on Calvinism*, 141.

allegiance to the Christian faith. The institution declared in 1971 that it had abandoned its commitment to Calvinism though it would retain the gospel for its basis of teaching."[29] Sadly, in recent decades, many traditionally Christian universities all around the world have abandoned Christian worldview as their foundation of education, as in the case of the Free University. However, as I argue throughout this chapter, Christian worldview provides the most comprehensive and integral framework of liberal arts education, as I myself have witnessed while in a university leadership role.

Theological Basis of Christian Worldview–Based Liberal Arts Education

Thus far, I have introduced the historical basis of liberal arts education in Classical Greece, the development of the concept of worldview, and Christian worldview-based liberal arts education in medieval Europe. In this section, I will discuss the theological basis of Christian worldview-based liberal arts education. Bavinck in *Reformed Dogmatics* notes:

> Thus we have discovered three foundations (*principia*): First, God as the essential foundation (*principium essendi*), the source, of theology; next, the external cognitive foundation (*principium cognoscendi externum*), viz., the self-revelation of God, which, insofar as it is recorded Holy Scriptures, bears an instrumental and temporary character; and finally, the internal principle of knowing (*principium cognoscendi internum*), the illumination of human beings by God's Spirit. These three are one in the respect that they have God as author and have as their content one identical knowledge of God.[30]

I agree with Bavinck that the Bible provides the most important framework of Christian worldview-based liberal arts education. In particular, Deut 4:10 demonstrates a biblical pedagogical paradigm, "how on the day that you stood before the Lord your God at Horeb, the Lord said to me, 'Gather the people to me, that I may let them hear my words, so that they may learn to fear me all the days that they live on the earth, and that they may teach their children so.'"[31] Three verbs—"hear," "learn," and "teach"—and the purpose clause—"so that they may learn to fear me all the days that they live on the earth"—have pedagogical significance. This passage

---

29. Beeke, "Life and Vision of Abraham Kuyper," 31.
30. Bavinck, *Reformed Dogmatics*, 213.
31. In this study, I use the ESV as the primary English translation of the Scriptures.

indicates that the goal of teaching and learning is to know and fear God. Deut 6:4–5 explains what it means to know and fear God, and the essence of that knowing, "Hear, O Israel: The Lord our God, the Lord is one. You shall love the Lord your God with all your heart and with all your soul and with all your might." To know and fear God as the only God refers to loving God holistically—"with all your heart," "with all your soul," and "with all your might." These phrases signify the importance of holistic education—integration of learning and life.

I find the same emphasis in the New Testament. Paul writes in Eph 6:4, "Fathers, do not provoke your children to anger, but bring them up in the discipline and instruction of the Lord." As in Deut 4:10; 6:4–5, the emphasis here is the holistic training and learning for the cultivation of mind and morals. Parents have to aim at raising their children "in the teaching and exhortation of the Lord" in a holistic way. Both in the Old Testament and in the New Testament, teaching and learning have a comprehensive goal in life, and they are never meant to be acquisition of impersonal esoteric knowledge, that has nothing to do with one's life. Nicholas P. Wolterstorff makes a similar point, "education is unavoidably pointed toward a way of being in the world within the classroom and outside it, today and for the future."[32] Wolterstorff continues, "Frequently, educational debates in our societies are presented as if they were just debates about method: How can children be taught to read more effectively? How can the American child be brought up to the Japanese child in mathematical knowledge and skills?... But the deepest educational debates are debates over how a human being appropriately lives in the world."[33]

Christian worldview-based liberal arts education holistically invites and nurtures human beings, who are created in the image of God, to live as active participants in the kingdom of God, actualizing their potentials with respect to their intellectual capabilities and moral virtues. The ultimate goal of Christian liberal arts education is to know, fear, and love the Trinitarian God. Paul writes in Eph 2:19–22, "So then you are no longer strangers and aliens, but you are fellow citizens with the saints and members of the household of God, built on the foundation of the apostles and prophets, Christ Jesus himself being the cornerstone, in whom the whole structure, being joined together, grows into a holy temple in the Lord. In him you also are being built together into a dwelling place for God by the Spirit." The Greek word for "fellow citizens" is *sympolitai* and it has a root in a Greek city-state *polis*. Similarly, Paul also writes in Phil 1:27–28a, "Only let your

---

32. Wolterstorff, *Educating for Life*, 93.
33. Wolterstorff, *Educating for Life*, 94.

manner of life be worthy of the gospel of Christ, so that whether I come and see you or am absent, I may hear of you that you are standing firm in one spirit, with one mind striving side by side for the faith of the gospel, and not frightened in anything by your opponents." The Greek word used here is *politeuesthe* ("to live one's life as a citizen"), which indicates that Paul perceived the Philippians as the citizens of the kingdom of God, when instructing them to live a life worthy of the kingdom of God. As Wolterstorff emphasizes, Christian liberal arts education is "unavoidably pointed toward a way of being in the world as citizens of the Kingdom within the classroom and outside it, today and for the future."[34]

Christian worldview-based liberal arts education focuses on the essence of Christian life in the kingdom of God and seeks to be faithful to its goal. This is related to the process of what theologians call "sanctification"—the life-long process of Christian believers who are justified by their faith in Christ, by the grace of God alone, more and more imitating Christ's righteousness and glorifying God by their faithful obedience to him. In both the Old and the New Testament, God's work of redemption always precedes this process. Israel's exodus from its slavery in Egypt typologically parallels Christian believers' redemption from sin and death by God's grace (*sola gratia*) and through faith in Jesus Christ (*sola fide*). The Old Testament and the New Testament demonstrate the same framework of God's salvation, that can be described as "from indicative to imperative." God by his sovereign grace has chosen Abraham, Isaac, and Jacob (Israel) to be a blessing to the nations (Gen 12:1–3) and "a kingdom of priests and a holy nation" (Exod 19:6). This new identity calls the Israelites to be holy—set apart—and follow God's covenant with Israel. Israel never earned their title by the works of law, or by being morally perfect. They became God's people, set apart from all the other nations, by God's gracious and unmerited election and their faithful obedience to God's calling.

Likewise, Christian believers are chosen by grace and, through their faith in Jesus Christ, have become the eschatological people of God (Eph 1:3–10; 2:1–22), by God's unmerited grace. God calls Christian believers "a royal priesthood" and "a holy nation" (1 Pet 2:9), which leads to a radical change in their lifestyle. Deut 10:12–13 writes, "And now, Israel, what does the Lord your God require of you, but to fear the Lord your God, to walk in all his ways, to love him, to serve the Lord your God with all your heart and with all your soul, and to keep the commandments and statutes of the Lord, which I am commanding you today for your good?" Moses emphasizes here that what God wants from the Israelites is not their blind and mechanical

---

34. Wolterstorff, *Educating for Life*, 93.

obedience—obedience out of ignorance and fear of judgment—but their joyful and willing obedience (*imperative*) flowing out of their intimate personal knowledge of God, gratitude towards God, and love for God, being firmly grounded in God's gracious redemption of Israel from its slavery in Egypt (*indicative*). The words used here such as "fear," "walk in all his ways," "love," "serve," and "keep" all refer to one's holistic ways of life, based on the profound understanding of God's undeserved grace, demonstrated in his works of redemption. This is the foundation of God's covenant with Israel and God's covenant with all those who believe in Jesus Christ, the new eschatological people of God that include both Jews and Gentiles, through the gospel of Jesus Christ. Christian worldview-based liberal arts education is firmly grounded in the truth of the gospel of Jesus Christ.

In addition to becoming God's people (sanctification), another essential component for the kingdom of God for God's people is experiencing its shalom ("well-being," or "wholeness"). Isa 11:6–9 envisions a messianic age:

> The wolf shall dwell with the lamb, and the leopard shall lie down with the young goat, and the calf and the lion and the fattened calf together; and a little child shall lead them. The cow and the bear shall graze; their young shall lie down together; and the lion shall eat straw like the ox. The nursing child shall play over the hole of the cobra, and the weaned child shall put his hand on the adder's den. They shall not hurt or destroy in all my holy mountain; for the earth shall be full of the knowledge of the LORD as the waters cover the sea.

In this vision for the new world for God's people, the prophet Isaiah experiences God's shalom in harmonious relationships, even between the prey and the predator. This is the outcome of the messianic figure's character as a righteous ruler, as "righteousness" and "faithfulness" describe him (Isa 11:3–5). Isa 32:15–18 writes, "until the Spirit is poured upon us from on high, and the wilderness becomes a fruitful field, and the fruitful field is deemed a forest. Then justice will dwell in the wilderness, and righteousness abide in the fruitful field. And the effect of righteousness will be peace, and the result of righteousness, quietness and trust forever. My people will abide in a peaceful habitation, in secure dwellings, and in quiet resting places." This coexistence of shalom and justice characterizes the initial state of creation, which was disrupted by sin. Although the first coming and redemptive work of Christ initiated this cosmic restoration, it will be completed only in the second coming of Christ. Shalom is relational harmony and Lev 19 elaborates this harmony in detail through the concept of "holiness." The core of this harmony is God's calling of his people to embrace holiness in their relation to God (Lev 19:4–8, 30), themselves (Lev 19:12, 26–29, 31, 35–37), others (Lev 19:9–11, 13–18, 20–22, 32–34), and the environment (Lev 19:19, 23–25). Therefore, we can conclude that the kingdom of God is realized, when and only when God's people embrace and seek shalom and justice as the manifestation of God's rule through them in this world, in relation to God, themselves, others, and the environment.

Wolterstorff offers an insightful definition of shalom, "[shalom] incorporates right, harmonious relationship with God and delight with God's worship and service . . . with other human beings and delight in human community . . . with nature and delight in our physical surroundings."[35] Wolterstorff understands shalom not only as something enjoyed by God's people but also as something to be manifested by God's people in four particular relations—with God, themselves, others, and the environment. Wolterstorff associates shalom with God's calling for his people:

> When students discuss with me what might be their calling, usually they have in mind what their occupation should be. And it seems to me that too often once they have found that occupation to which they feel God has called them, they sink into it, pretty much accept it as presented to them, and do not inquire whether the fulfillment of their calling may not require the reshaping of that occupation . . . Yet how far has the mighty idea of calling fallen when this is all it comes to. God asks of us that we commit ourselves to shalom. He calls us to this. This is our vocation, the vocation of all of us.[36]

God calls all God's people with their unique gifts and callings to bring this shalom into reality in this world. Wolterstorff continues, "It [vocation to shalom] becomes a differentiated call. God asks of each of us that we take up specific roles in society . . . What He asks is in the light of our talents and training, the needs of the church, the state of society. The call to commit oneself to shalom is always a differentiated, articulated, particularized call."[37] Christian worldview-based liberal arts education aims to inspire and equip God's missionary people to make God's shalom in Jesus Christ realized in this broken world, through its Biblically based and Christ-centered holistic education.

---

35. Wolterstorff, *Educating for Life*, 102.
36. Wolterstorff, *Educating for Life*, 128.
37. Wolterstorff, *Educating for Life*, 128.

Conclusion

In this chapter, I briefly discussed the historical origin of liberal arts education in Classical Greece, the development of the concept of worldview (*Weltanschauung*) from Immanuel Kant to Martin Heidegger, the example of Christian worldview-based liberal arts education in medieval Europe, that in modern Europe, and its theological basis. Aristotle in his *Politics* Book 8 carefully argues how Greek city-states should educate their citizens in basic liberal arts in order to equip them to become the effective leaders of their states in the future. Kant used the German word *Weltanschauung* ("worldview") for the first time and a series of philosophers developed its concept in their works. In medieval Europe, the Roman Catholic Church supervised liberal arts education and offered it in the paradigm of faith seeking understanding. Abraham Kuyper established the Free University of Amsterdam, to provide Christian worldview-based liberal arts education to all citizens, free from government and ecclesiastical control, and argues in *Lectures on Calvinism* that Calvinism provides the most comprehensive system in which a university can freely pursue its disciplines in harmony. Herman Bavinck highlights three foundations of Christian worldview-based education—(1) "God as the essential foundation"; (2) the Scriptures as "the external cognitive foundation"; and (3) "the internal principle of knowing," that is, "the illumination of human beings by God's Spirit" (*Reformed Dogmatics* 1:213). In today's postmodern world where everything is perceived as relative and socially constructed, there are many challenges for Christian higher education. Many historically Christian universities in their financial struggles have compromised their original mission of providing Christian worldview-based liberal arts education and focus only on the profitable and career-building programs, claiming Christian heritage but not Christian identity. Today, the mission of Christian universities around the world is more crucial than ever before. They must continue to take a prophetic role in their societies, offering holistic, biblically-centered, liberal arts education to equip the next generation of Christian leaders who make real differences for the kingdom of God in the world today.

Bibliography

Aristotle. *The Politics of Aristotle*. Translated by Ernest Barker. Oxford: Oxford University Press, 1950.

Bavinck, Herman. *Reformed Dogmatics*. Vol. 1. Edited by John Bolt. Translated by John Vriend. Grand Rapids: Baker, 2003.

Beeke, Joel R. "The Life and Vision of Abraham Kuyper." *Christianity & Society* 14 (2004) 24–30.

Eglinton, James, and Michael Bräutigam. "Scientific Theology? Herman Bavinck and Adolf Schlatter on the Place of Theology in the University." *JRT* 7 (2013) 27–50.

Hegel, G. W. F. *The Phenomenology of Mind*. Translated by J. B. Baillie. 2nd ed. London: Allen & Unwin, 1961.

Heidegger, Martin. *Being and Time*. Translated by Joan Stambaugh. Revised by Dennis J. Schmidt. SUNY Series in Contemporary Continental Philosophy. Albany: State University of New York Press, 2010.

———. *The Basic Problems of Phenomenology*. Translated by Albert Hofstadter. SPEP. Bloomington: Indiana University Press, 1982.

Holmes, Arthur F. *The Idea of a Christian College*. Rev. ed. Grand Rapids: Eerdmans, 1987.

Jordan, Mark D. "Theology and Philosophy." In *The Cambridge Companion to Aquinas*, edited by Norman Kretzmann and Eleonore Stump, 232–51. Cambridge Companions to Philosophy. Cambridge: Cambridge University Press, 2005.

Kant, Immanuel. *Critique of Judgment: Including the First Introduction*. Translated by Werner S. Pluhar. Indianapolis: Hackett, 1987.

Kuyper, Abraham. *Lectures on Calvinism*. 8th ed. Grand Rapids: Baker, 1987.

Leinsle, Ulrich G. *Introduction to Scholastic Theology*. Translated by Michael J. Miller. Washington, DC: The Catholic University of America Press, 2010.

McCarthy, Vincent A. *The Phenomenology of Moods in Kierkegaard*. Boston: Martinus Nijhoff, 1978.

Naugle, David K. *Worldview: The History of a Concept*. Grand Rapids: Eerdmans, 2002.

Newman, John Henry. *The Idea of a University Defined and Illustrated*. London: Longmans, 1899.

Olson, Roger E. *The Story of Christian Theology*. Downers Grove, IL: InterVarsity, 1999.

Schaff, David S. *History of the Christian Church*. Vol. 5. Grand Rapids: Eerdmans, 1981.

Schlatter, Adolf. "Atheistische Methoden in der Theologie." *BFCT* 9 (1905) 227–50.

Wolterstorff, Nicholas P. *Educating for Life: Reflections on Christian Teaching and Learning*. Edited by Gloria Goris Stronks and Clarence W. Joldersma. Grand Rapids: Eerdmans, 2002.

13

True Knowledge, Faith in Christ, and Godly Character

Christian Worldview-Based Liberal Arts Education at UPH

— Gunawaty Tjioe

Introduction

INDONESIA IS A PREDOMINANTLY Muslim nation in Southeast Asia. However, not everyone knows about the existence of many vibrant Christian churches in Indonesia. Many Christian parents send their children to private Christian schools for various reasons. In fact, there are a number of Christian universities, growing in student population and the quality of education, in addition to many Christian primary and secondary schools throughout Indonesia. Unfortunately, this phenomenon was unnoticed in *Christian Higher Education: A Global Reconnaissance* (2014), for none of the eleven studies covers Christian higher education in Indonesia in particular or Southeast Asia in general.[1] In this study, I will introduce Christian worldview-based liberal education at Universitas Pelita Harapan, where I am currently serving as the Provost. UPH has been the pioneer of liberal arts education in Indonesia in many ways, for most Indonesian universities traditionally neglected the significance of liberal arts education and only focused on practical and career-building courses and programs. However, the trend has been gradually changing and, now, more Indonesian universi-

---

1. Carpenter, Glanzer, and Lantinga, *Christian Higher Education*.

ties are recognizing the necessity of liberal arts education as the foundation for developing students' critical thinking skills and core values.

Christian Worldview–Based Liberal Arts Education

In *The Ideas of a Christian College* (1987), Arthur F. Holmes writes, "Education has to do with the making of persons, Christian education with the making of Christian persons. Since this is what God's creative and redemptive work is about—the making of persons in his own image—it follows that an education that helps make us more fully persons is especially important to Christians."[2] Holmes also notes:

> Liberal education provides an opportunity to steward life more effectively by becoming more fully a human person in the image of God, by seeing life whole rather than fragmented, by transcending the provincialism of our place in history, our geographic location, or our job. Provincialism isolates us from our past, isolates us from segments of the human race; cultural provincialism isolates the American way of life from anyone else; vocational provincialism limits the horizon to a certain kind of task. But liberal education is an opportunity to become whole and to see life whole rather than provincially fragmented in one way or another. It is an opportunity to find meaning for everything I am and do. Christian liberal arts education is concerned that we do this in the light of God's self-revelation, so that we learn to think Christianly, to value as Christians should, and so to act responsibly. I would think it worthwhile if a student, when asked what he learned in college, could reply, "I learned what it is to see and think and act like the human person God made me to be."[3]

In *Engaging the Culture, Changing the World* (2011), Philip Eaton, the President of Seattle Pacific University, addresses many difficult challenges that Christian universities in the United States are facing at the time of his publication.[4] In a more recent publication, John W. Wright concludes:

> Returning to the origins of the university in the monastic transformation of the medieval schools through re-centering the university around worship allows us to have formed in us and our students a habitus of Wisdom, a means of ordering goods in light of the Good that is God amid a world that would pull

---

2. Holmes, *The Idea of a Christian College*, 25.
3. Holmes, *The Idea of a Christian College*, 36.
4. Eaton, *Engaging the Culture*, 11–20.

us into an agonistic struggle between hegemony and resistance. It will take the faithfulness of the martyrs, witnesses who did not lose confidence in the face of receiving the full brunt of violence for refusing to play by the faith, the allegiances of the society around them.[5]

Christian higher education in Indonesia has a different set of challenges from that in the United States. Due to the rapid globalization of the world through technology and communication, however, the socio-cultural shifts of the postmodern, relativistic, and materialistic culture of the West has been affecting the entire world. More than ever, Christian universities must think about their root, purpose, and identity, in order to envision their future in the face of many challenges. As Holmes and Wright hint at, Christian worldview provides the foundation of Christian higher education. Recently, there have been many fruitful studies on Christian worldview that provide important insights for Christian worldview-based liberal arts education.[6] The Reformed tradition in particular provides a basic framework for such an education. James D. Bratt highlights four tenets of Calvinism, relevant to Christian higher education: (1) "The Glory of God and Creation"; (2) "Sin and Common Grace"; (3) "Law and Redemption"; and (4) "Order and Public Life."[7] These themes of the Biblical worldview play important roles in the Christian worldview-based liberal arts education at Universitas Pelita Harapan (UPH).

Christian Worldview-Based Liberal Arts Education at UPH

UPH is a Christian university founded in 1994 by the Yayasan Universitas Pelita Harapan (YUPH). Its Indonesian name means "the University of Light and Hope."[8] UPH envisions being "a Christ-centered university founded upon and promoting true knowledge, faith in Christ, and godly character, aiming to develop future leaders who are God-fearing, competent, and professional through excellent, holistic, and transformational education." UPH has the following missions: (1) "to provide holistic transformational learning rooted in Scripture and a Reformed theological framework"; (2)

5. Wright, "Beyond the Disciplines," 182.
6. E.g., Anderson, Clark, and Naugle, *An Introduction to Christian Worldview*; Bartholomew and Goheen, *Living at the Crossroads*; Smith, *Desiring the Kingdom*; Naugle, *Worldview*; Walsh and Middleton, *The Transforming Vision*.
7. Bratt, "What Can the Reformed Tradition Contribute?," 125–40.
8. The word *yayasan* in Indonesian means, "foundation."

"to contribute to the advancement of knowledge and culture guided by a biblical Christian worldview"; and (3) "to participate redemptively in the development of individuals and society for the glory of God." UPH seeks to produce graduates who have been "exposed to the liberal arts education taught from a biblical Christian worldview" and are equipped "to serve God, his country and his neighbors." UPH holds to the YUPH Statement of Faith which affirms the centrality of the person, work, and glory of Jesus Christ. It begins with the following statements:

> As a confessionally Christian educational foundation, YUPH is committed to the Reformed confessions and the tradition and practice of historic biblical Christianity. . . Although there are many historic Reformed confessions and creeds that are good and helpful, YUPH has selected one as a more detailed clarification of the doctrinal position of YUPH and of the system of doctrine taught in Scripture: the Westminster Confession of Faith and Catechisms.

The Statement of Faith also explicitly declares what the institution believes about the Bible, the Triune God, God the Father, Jesus Christ, the Holy Spirit, Human Beings, Salvation and Judgement, the Church, the Return of Christ, and Satan. UPH vision, mission, and goals, together with the YUPH Statement of Faith, provide the foundation of Christian worldview-based liberal arts education at UPH.[9]

As an institution, UPH is a Christ-centered university, however, it accepts all students with different religious backgrounds, such as Muslims, Hindus, Buddhists, and Confucians, and it offers courses at four campuses: Tangerang, Jakarta, Medan, and Surabaya. In this academic year (2017–2018), UPH currently has about 16,300 registered students in its 33 undergraduate programs and 10 graduate programs under 13 Schools and Faculties.[10] Undergraduate students are required to complete 144 credit hours, including Indonesian government-mandated courses in religion, civics, Indonesian, and the *Pancasila*. In order to provide undergraduate students with a Christian worldview-based liberal arts education, UPH established the Faculty of Liberal Arts (FLA) in 2009. The Dean of FLA,

---

9. All of the information about UPH and YUPH can be accessed from the website (www.uph.edu).

10. (1) Teachers College & International Teachers College; (2) Business School; (3) School of Design; (4) School of Hospitality and Management; (5) School of Information Science and Technology; (6) Faculty of Science and Technology; (7) School of Law; (8) Faculty of Medicine; (9) Conservatory of Music; (10) Faculty of Nursing; (11) Faculty of Psychology; (12) Faculty of Social and Political Science; (13) Faculty of Liberal Arts.

Dr. Matthew R. Malcolm sums up the calling and purpose of the faculty as follows:

> Our calling within UPH is to provide Christ-centered foundations for the education of students from all fields of study. Our conviction is that all students need to learn how to think critically (that is, to engage in philosophy), how to reflect on God knowledgeably (that is, to engage in theology), how to use language articulately (that is, to engage in linguistics), and how to relate maturely in community (that is, to develop life skills). We therefore provide educational foundations in our three departments of philosophy, theology, and language and life skills. . . . Humans are created by God, and called to cultivate God's creation as God's beloved image bearers; humans are fallen, being marred and influenced by sin; humans are offered redemption through Jesus Christ, who died for our sins and rose as Lord over all creation; we look forward to the return of Jesus at the time of his consummation of human history. We attempt to teach these foundations in a way that maintains a constant connection both to the lives of the students, and to their educational majors. Our hope is that by providing rigorous Christ-centered foundations in these areas, we will be contributing to the formation of graduates who are not merely proficient, but truly good.[11]

When the Faculty of Liberal Arts was established in 2009, all undergraduate students were required to take thirty-nine credit units of FLA courses which include *Christian Religion* (introduction to the Bible), *Christian Worldview 1–3*, *World Religions, Philosophy of Science, Ethics, History of Thoughts, Indonesian, Civics, Leadership, Critical Thinking, Character Development, Learning and Communication Skills, English*, and one elective course (*Philosophy; Literature; Humanities; Art; Music; Sports; Mathematics; Science*). In particular, Teachers College (TC) students who pursue a Bachelor of Education with a minor in Theology must complete 40 credit units of liberal arts: (1) 7 courses of *Systematic Theology*; (2) *Christian Apologetics*; (3) *Spiritual Formation*; (4) *Philosophy*; (5) *Psychology*; (6) *Civics*; (7) *English*; (8) *Indonesian*; and (9) one elective course (*General Science; Sociology and Anthropology; Introduction to Indonesian Literature; Theory of Reading and Writing*). I include here the UPH liberal arts curriculum in 2016 as a sample.

---

11. Check the FLA website (fla.uph.edu).

UPH Liberal Arts Curriculum in 2016

No.	Christian Track	Non-Christian Track	Credits
1	Christian Religion	World Religions	4
2	Christian Worldview 1	Philosophy of Science	4
3	Christian Worldview 2	Ethics	4
4	Christian Worldview 3	History of Thoughts	4
5	Indonesian Language	Indonesian Language	2
6	Civics		2
7	Critical Thinking		2
8	Pancasila		2
9	General English (3 Levels)		2
10	One Elective Course (Natural Sciences; Social Sciences; Aesthetics and Arts; Literature; TOEFL IBT Prep)		2
11	Academic Skills (Non-credit Requirement)		0
12	Health and Wellness (Non-credite Requirement)		0
	Total FLA Credits		28

UPH Students' and Alumni's Experience of Liberal Arts Education

In order to survey how UPH liberal arts education impacted students and alumni, I conducted a qualitatively grounded theory research, using focus group discussion. The participants of this survey included twenty-five senior undergraduate students and twenty-six alumni (graduates from 2004 and 2018) from various UPH programs. Nine focus group discussions were held in April, 2018. On the one hand, the limited size of the number of the participants would not represent the overall response of UPH students and alumni. On the other hand, however, It still provides a valuable sample of UPH students' and alumni' feedback on Christian worldview-based liberal arts education. For each FGD session, the goal of the research was explained to the participants, and they were told that their participation in the research were completely voluntary. Informed consent forms were obtained from each participant, and they were told that their identities would not be revealed in the report. The duration of each focus group was approximately twenty-five to sixty minutes, depending on the dynamic of the discussions. The three research questions during the focus group discussions were: (1) "How has UPH liberal arts education impacted your life?," (2) "Which aspects of UPH liberal arts education helped learning?," and (3) "Which aspects of UPH liberal arts education hindered learning?" As a reminder to all participants especially for alumni who had graduated for many years, the course names of the liberal arts classes were mentioned to them during the focus group discussions. With the participants' permission, all the focus discussion groups were recorded.

After each focus group discussion, I attentively listened to the recording and transcribed it. I analyzed the transcription using King and Horrocks' methodology, using three stages of thematic analysis—(1) descriptive coding, (2) interpretative coding, and (3) overarching themes.[12] For the descriptive coding process, I read through the transcripts and highlighted relevant materials with short key phrases for every focus group discussion, later creating a list of the key phrases. In my interpretative coding process, I analyzed the key phrases as descriptive codes and I categorized them in a number of groups. I interpreted the meaning of the groups in correspondence to each research question, and I applied the interpretive codes to my data. Corbin and Strauss state, "findings should be presented as a set of interrelated concepts, not just a listing of themes. It is the overall unifying explanatory scheme that raises findings to the level of theory."[13] Thus, I worked carefully to identify a number of overarching themes among the interpretative codes, and tried to present a set of interrelated concepts among the overarching themes. In the following section, I will list the overarching themes with some quotations from the participants, in response to each research question.

How Has UPH Liberal Arts Education Impacted Your Life?

Many participants mentioned that, during their first year at UPH, they did not understand why they had to take liberal arts classes, but they registered for those classes simply because they were mandatory. As UPH alumni, however, they look back and realize the benefits of having a liberal arts education, and they acknowledge its impact on their life and work.

12. King and Horrocks, *Interviews in Qualitative Research*, 61–78.
13. Corbin and Strauss, *Basics of Qualitative Research*, 104.

From the responses of the participants to Research Question 1, I have identified four overarching themes with respect to how UPH liberal arts education impacted them: (1) understanding of the Biblical worldview; (2) leadership development; (3) personal identity formation; and (4) critical thinking skills.

Understanding the Biblical Worldview

The first overarching theme of the responses to the first research question was understanding the Biblical worldview. UPH senior students and alumni acclaimed that *Christian Religion, Christian Worldview 1–3,* and *World Religions* helped them to have deeper understanding of the Biblical worldview, which produced personal spiritual growth, including the topics of the Triune God, the total depravity of human beings, salvation by God's grace alone and through faith in Christ alone, *Imago Dei,* Christian discipleship, the authority of the Scriptures, and God's calling for Christians in this world. I include here selected responses from the participants:

> "If I did not take *Christian Worldview* classes, I would have never learned about God, the Bible, and salvation."

∼

> "My doubt [about my salvation] is gone now. The followers of Jesus Christ are saved, because he died for us on the cross. Because we have been saved, we have to live out our faith."

∼

> "Because of total depravity, we cannot do anything good by ourselves. Grace in Jesus Christ is the greatest gift from God in our lives. Because of God's grace through Jesus Christ, now we can do everything for God."

∼

> "My lecturers inspired us to study the Bible carefully, and think about what God wants for us in our lives."

∼

> "My *Christian Worldview* lecturer encouraged us to read the Bible, and I learned how to interpret the Bible."

∼

"*Christian Worldview* classes helped me to know more about the Bible and theology, and I can share my knowledge with my church friends."

∼

"Through *Christian Worldview* courses, I have been growing in my knowledge of Jesus, and become more aware of his salvation. I shared about this with my non-Christian family members. I also encouraged them to read the Bible, because it is God's truth."

∼

"*Christian Worldview* classes really helped me to see who God is and who we are, and that we live to glorify God."

∼

"I heard for the first time that Jesus is 100% God and 100% man in *Christian Religion* class. So, I got the solid and clear teaching of the Bible, which I could not get from my church."

∼

"Learning theology systematically was really helpful in knowing God. I used to know bits and pieces about the Bible, but now I understand it more comprehensively."

∼

"*Systematic Theology* classes very much prepared me for my teaching in the class."

∼

"Learning theology has equipped me with respect to how to critically engage in the local community and culture, where I work as a teacher."

∼

"Through *Christian Worldview* classes, I came to recognize more the beauty of the work of Christ."

∼

"Learning theology has prepared me to teach various subjects from the biblical point of view."

∼

"I have grown to know more who Christ is and what it means to have personal relationship with him."

∾

"My personal relationship with God helps me to help my students in my class."

∾

"*Christian Worldview* classes helped me grow deeper in knowing Christ, and this helped me recognize and respond to his calling for me."

∾

"Through *Christian Worldview* classes, God has a plan to save the world through Jesus Christ which is manifested from Genesis to Revelation."

∾

"The more I understand the Holy Scriptures, the more I worship God. My faith in God became stronger through *Christian Worldview* classes, I have a greater desire to be his instrument to share the gospel with others."

∾

"Because of my *Systematic Theology* classes, I have become aware of the fact that my students are created in the image of God, which helps me as their teacher to accept them as who they are."

∾

"Through *Christian Worldview* courses, I learned more about Christ's obedience, which inspires me to obey God and serve others."

∾

"My *Systematic Theology* classes inspired me to see the role of teachers as the second parents or *in-loco-parentis*."

∾

"Through my *World Religions* class, I learned to be more appreciative of other religions."

∾

> "Previously, the issue of religion was always a sensitive issue for me. My *World Religions* class taught me how to engage in a conversation about religions both critically and respectfully.

∼

As we can see in these comments, many UPH students and alumni expressed that they deepened their understanding of the Biblical worldview through UPH liberal arts courses like *Christian Religion*, *Christian Worldview 1–3*, and *Systematic Theology*. Many Christian students and alumni reported that, through these courses, they were better able to integrate their Christian faith into every area of their lives. Also, a few non-Christian students and alumni, who took *World Religions*, commented that it helped them better understand and respect other religions.

Leadership Development

The second overarching theme of the responses to the first research question concerned the participants' leadership development. In particular, this theme was the outcome of various service learning projects required for *Christian Religion*, *Christian Worldview 1*, *Leadership*, *Learning and Communication Skills*, and *Character Development*. Service learning projects require students to go out of their comfort zone and to serve those in various needs. Many students do not understand the purpose of their service projects and unwillingly prepare for them. Many of them, however, have life-transforming experience as they engage in their service projects and interact with those who have totally different background from them. I include here selected responses from the participants:

> "Service learning projects truly prepared us to serve others and touch people's lives."

∼

> "My group participated in helping a street vendor to own a kiosk. At first, I thought that it would not be so difficult for anyone to acquire a spot to sell stuff. However, as I got to know this street vendor in person, I realized that he barely broke even every day and he had no resource at all to make a long-term investment like buying a kiosk. It was an eye-opening experience for me to see such poverty."

∼

> "My service learning project was a life-transforming experience. I would like to continue to participate in such projects on my own."

Many participants expressed that, through their service learning projects, they learned how to lead others, how to brainstorm a project and discuss creative ideas, how to plan a project, how to fundraise a project, how to interact with someone whom they never met before, how to manage time effectively, how to reach out to others with compassion, and how to reflect on and report a project.

Personal Identity Formation

The third overarching theme of the responses to the first research question was personal identity formation. A number of participants expressed that they became more mature individuals and gained more self-awareness, as they learned about how God uniquely created them and discerned their learning styles, temperaments, and calling from God. In particular, this theme was the outcome of *Psychology of Self-Awareness* and *Character Development*. I include here selected responses from the participants:

> "Through my FLA class, I learned that, only when I know who I am as a person, can I grow as a person. Now, I have more confidence to make an important life decision, as I have a better sense of who I am."

> "As I reflected on how God created each person as a unique human being, I now respect someone more, regardless of his or her socio-economic status."

> "My UPH liberal arts education helped me to become authentic to myself and more dedicated follower of Christ."

As we can see here, many participants reported that UPH liberal arts education helped them to become better human beings, as they have found their authentic selves—how God uniquely created them in his image, and restored that original image—marred by self-destructive behavior—through the redemptive work of Jesus Christ. This new awareness helped them to become not only more mature Christian believers but also more responsible and respectful citizens of their society.

Critical Thinking Skills

The fourth overarching theme of the responses to the first research question was the development of critical thinking skills. In particular, this theme was the outcome of *Learning and Communication Skills* and *Critical Thinking*. Those participants who took *Learning and Communication Skills* mentioned that the mind-mapping concept and skills that they learned in class was impactful and applicable to their lives. Similar comments were made about *Critical Thinking*. I include here selected responses from the participants:

> "Mind-mapping helped me to simplify my thinking and to make a concept become practical, so I can plan something in an orderly and systematic approach."

> "Mind-mapping is really helpful. You see the bigger picture and the smaller parts. I used mind-mapping to map out what courses I want to take each semester."

> "For me, thinking logically and problem-solving is undeniably applicable to life. And I got that from my *Critical Thinking* class where we are prepared with various ways to solve a problem."

> "With *Critical Thinking* class, we are prepared to think of possible answers to different questions."

As we can see here, the participants expressed that their UPH liberal arts education helped them to develop their critical thinking skills that prepared them for their personal life and professional career.

Which Aspects of UPH Liberal Arts Education Helped Learning?

There were three overarching themes of the responses to the second research question: (1) lecturers as role models; (2) interactive and interesting teaching methods; (3) involvement in service learning project.

Lecturers as Role Models

The first overarching theme of the responses to the second research question was lecturers as role models. The participants mentioned several UPH lecturers, as they shared about their positive liberal arts education experience. Students and alumni looked up to these lecturers who served as their role models with respect to teaching. They themselves were humble and lifelong learners. They genuinely cared for students, and even spent time with them outside of class. They were passionate about the subjects they were teaching and encouraged students to actively participate in the class. One alumnus commented that the lecturers were honest with their students and, when they were not sure about the answers to students' questions, they promised their students to research the topics and get back to them with answers later, which provided the students a good example of a lifelong learner. The lecturers remembered their students' names and were approachable to them. In this way, the classroom became such a space for holistic learning and personal transformation.

Interactive and Interesting Teaching Methods

The second overarching theme of the responses to the second research question was interactive and interesting teaching methods. Students and alumni commented that some lecturers demonstrated interactive and interesting teaching methods in their classrooms. I include here selected responses from the participants:

> "My lecturer's teaching was impressive, using interesting teaching methods, always connecting his lessons to real life. He was also funny and made his lectures interesting."

∼

> "My lecturer's teaching was good and touching. He made us interested in the Bible. He was always respectful in the ways he communicated with us, allowing time for questions and open discussion without any judgment."

∼

> "My *Ethics* lecturer always gave us real life examples in his teaching. We are always encouraged to ask any question in class. As I face similar problems in life, I am reminded of the lessons that my lecturer taught me."

> "My lecturer's teaching was comprehensive and clear and well-prepared."

> "My lecturer often shared with us real life examples and case studies related to his topics."

> "We are very glad that our lecturer gave us a case study, and his teaching was in dialogue instead of monologue."

> "For *Critical Thinking* class, at first I found it to be difficult, but my lecturer taught the subject well. She was funny and flexible with us, while maintaining focus. We were encouraged to think critically and I learned a lot from this class."

Related to this theme, other participants mentioned helpful and relevant assignments, offering the practical applications of the lessons, and helping students to integrate their liberal arts education into Christian worldview.

Community Service Projects

The third overarching theme of the responses to the second research question was community service projects. I already have mentioned the impact of service learning project on the participants' leadership development in response to the first research question. Relatedly, almost all focus groups commented that community service projects required for UPH liberal arts courses helped them to get out of their comfort zone and work with others to reach out to those in need. I include here selected responses from the participants:

> "We visited some poor people's house, who collect and sell rags. One of my group members was a neat and tidy person. She complained about the project, before we went into the house. However, later on, her heart was broken for the residents and became emotional."

> "For me, the most memorable service learning project was our visit to the school for special needs students. They were so gracious to us and I was touched by them. I loved the whole experience."

∼

> "Our project was to help a child with hearing problem and we wanted to help her buy hearing aids. Our team did fundraising by selling cookies. I learned a lot from the experience."

∼

> "In *Christian Worldview* class, we were not only learning about theology intellectually but we also had an opportunity to practice what we learned in class through a community service project. This equipped us to better serve those in needs."

∼

> "Through my community service project, I learned how to reach out to others whom I never met before."

∼

As we can see here, the community service projects required in *Christian Religion, Christian Worldview 1, Leadership, Learning and Communication Skills, Critical Thinking, Ethics,* and *Character Development*, helped students to apply the lessons they learned in their classrooms to real life situations, as they worked together to serve those in needs.

Which Aspects of UPH Liberal Arts Education Hindered Learning?

There were two overarching themes of the responses to the third research question: (1) students not knowing the rationale for liberal arts education and (2) ineffective teaching and learning environment.

Students Not Knowing the Rationale for Liberal Arts Education

The first overarching theme of the responses to the third research question was students not knowing the rationale for liberal arts education. A number of students and alumni mentioned that, as freshmen coming to the university, they did not know why they needed to take liberal arts classes.

Not fully understanding the rational for liberal arts education, they lacked motivation to take liberal arts classes. I include here selected responses from the participants:

> "Students were not aware of the importance of these courses. They did not clearly see why they needed them until they graduated."

∽

> "I mistakenly considered liberal arts class as unnecessary 'extra' classes that have nothing to do with my major."

∽

> "I wish that I understood the rational of liberal arts education better so that I could have got more from my liberal arts courses."

∽

> "I regret not having full advantage of my liberal arts education, only trying to get good grades to improve my GPA."

∽

These comments suggest that UPH needs to do a better job to help the first year students better understand the rationale and importance of liberal arts education courses so that they can take full advantage of their educational experience.

Ineffective Teaching and Learning Environment

The second overarching theme of the responses to the third research question was ineffective teaching and learning environment. Participants mentioned the following items related to this theme: (1) some lecturers' rigid teaching style that is purely based on lecture without any student involvement; (2) large class sizes; (3) tests based on memorization; (4) assignments with unclear learning purposes; (5) abstract learning without sufficient practical application of the lessons learned; (6) too heavy and technical teaching of theology for non-religion major students; (7) repetitive materials in a few classes; (8) the lack of integration of students' specific majors and liberal arts classes; and (9) the lack of lecturers' guidance in planning community service projects.

Conclusion

In this study, I have introduced an example of Christian worldview-based liberal arts education at Universitas Pelita Harapan in Indonesia. In this predominantly Muslim nation, many exciting things are happening in Christian higher education today. UPH has been the pioneer of making liberal arts education the core curriculum of undergraduate programs, providing a foundation for students' respective concentrations. I surveyed the impact of UPH liberal arts education on its students and alumni, as I conducted a qualitatively grounded research, using focus group discussion, with twenty-five UPH seniors and twenty-six UPH alumni who graduated from UPH between 2004 and 2018. Nine focus groups were held in April, 2018. Although it is not a comprehensive survey in terms of its size of the number of the participants, the outcome of this report provides a valid sample of UPH students' and alumni's feedback on its Christian worldview-based liberal arts education. Three research questions included (1) "How Has UPH Liberal Arts Education Impacted Your Life?," (2) "Which Aspects of UPH Liberal Arts Education Helped Learning?," and (3) "Which Aspects of UPH Liberal Arts Education Hindered Learning?" The overarching themes of the responses of the first research questions included (1) understanding of the Biblical worldview, (2) leadership development, (3) personal identity formation, and (4) critical thinking skills. The overarching themes of the responses to the second research question included (1) lecturers as role models, (2) interactive and interesting teaching methods, and (3) involvement in service learning project. The overarching themes of the responses to the third research question included (1) students not knowing the rationale for liberal arts education, and (2) ineffective teaching and learning environment. I hope to see more case studies of Christian worldview-based liberal arts education in the context of Southeast Asia in the future.

Bibliography

Anderson, Tawa J., W. Michael Clark, and David K. Naugle. *An Introduction to Christian Worldview: Pursuing God's Perspective in a Pluralistic World*. Downers Grove, IL: InterVarsity, 2017.

Bartholomew, Craig G., and Michael W. Goheen. *Living at the Crossroads: An Introduction to Christian Worldview*. Grand Rapids: Baker, 2008.

Bratt, James D. "What Can the Reformed Tradition Contribute to Christian Higher Education?" In *Models for Christian Higher Education: Strategies for Success in the Twenty-First Century*, edited by Richard T. Hughes and William B. Adrian, 125–40. Grand Rapids: Eerdmans, 1997.

Carpenter, Joel, Perry L. Glanzer, and Nicholas S. Lantinga, eds. *Christian Higher Education: A Global Reconnaissance*. Grand Rapids: Eerdmans, 2014.

Corbin, J. M., and A. C. Strauss. *Basics of Qualitative Research*. 3rd ed. London: Sage, 2008.

Eaton, Philip. *Engaging the Culture, Changing the World: The Christian University in a Post-Christian World*. Downers Grove, IL: InterVarsity, 2011.

Holmes. Arthur F. *The Idea of a Christian College*. Rev. ed. Grand Rapids: Eerdmans, 1987.

King, Nigel and Christiane Horrocks. *Interviews in Qualitative Research*. London: Sage, 2010.

Naugle, David K. *Worldview: A History of a Concept*. Grand Rapids: Eerdmans, 2002.

Smith, James K. A. *Desiring the Kingdom: Worship, Worldview, and Cultural Formation*. Cultural Liturgies 1. Grand Rapids: Baker, 2009.

Walsh, Brian, and J. Richard Middleton. *The Transforming Vision: Shaping a Christian Worldview*. Downers Grove, IL: InterVarsity, 1984.

Wright, John W. "Beyond the Disciplines, God: The Study of the Christian Scriptures and the Formation of a Faithful Habitus for Truthful Learning." In *Beyond Integration? Inter/Disciplinary Possibilities for the Future of Christian Higher Education*, edited by Todd C. Ream et al., 165–83. Abilene, TX: Abilene Christian University Press, 2012.

Scripture Index

Genesis

1–3	75, 145
1:1—2:3	146
1:1	165
1:26–28	144, 146, 160, 165, 173
1:26–27	75
1:27–28	182
1:27	145
2–3	73
2:4—3:24	151
2:7	145
2:15	145, 173, 182
2:16—3:24	160
2:16–17	74, 146, 148, 152, 174
2:20	146, 152
2:21	151
2:22	146
3	142, 152, 173
3:1–5	151
3:5	74
3:9	175
3:11	168
3:15	183
12:1–3	194, 212
12:1	165
15:6	75
17:7–8	28n26

Exodus

3:6	165
3:7–8	167
4:22–23	31
4:22	28
6:7	28n26
15:11	21
16:2–3	21
19:5–6	21n1
19:6	26, 212
19:12–13	21
19:21–24	21
21:29	47n17
22:21	194
23:9	194
28:41	49
29:7	49
30:11–16	47n17
33:18–23	21
40:13–15	49

Leviticus

1–16	56
9:24	22
10	23
10:2	22
11	23
11:43–44	21
11:44–45	27–28, 30–31, 167

Leviticus (continued)

11:45	31
16	21, 23, 56
16:2–3	21n1
17–25	56
19:2	21, 24, 27–28, 30–31, 167
19:4–37	214
19:10	28
19:12	214
19:18	65n9, 66
19:20	47n17
19:25	28
19:34	28
20:1–8	28, 31
20:3	21
20:7–8	27, 30
20:7	28
20:8	25n21, 27, 30
20:22–26	22
20:24–26	31
20:26	24, 27, 31, 167
20:37	24
21–22	21, 28
21:8	25n21, 27–28, 30–31, 167
21:15	25n21, 27, 30
21:23	25n21, 27, 30
22:2	21
22:9	25n21, 27, 30
22:16	25n21, 27, 30
22:31–33	25n21
22:32	21n21, 25, 27, 30
23:22	28
24:22	28
25	56–57
25:8–55	55
25:9	55–56
25:10	55
25:17	28
25:24	47n17
25:51–52	47n17
25:55	28
26:1	28
26:2	28
26:12	28n26
27:31	47n17

Numbers

3:12	47n17
9:15–16	22
11:25–26	49
16:9	22
35:25	49
35:31–34	47n17

Deuteronomy

4:10	210–11
4:24	22
6:4–5	211
9:23	22
10:12–13	212
29:12	28n26
33:7	146
35:9–34	57

Joshua

24:19	21n3

1 Samuel

2:2	21n3
2:34	124
10:1	49
16:12–13	49

2 Samuel

2:4	49
7:14	28n26
16:22–23	124

1 Kings

1:39	49
19:16	49

2 Kings

11:12	49
23:30	49

Nehemiah

9:30	49

Psalms

8:3–6	144
33:6	128
70:5	146
121:1–2	146
124:8	146
128	191
146:5	146

Proverbs

3:5	112
6:35	47n17
13:8	47n17

Ecclesiastes

3:11	8n15

Isaiah

6:3	21n4
6:10	49n24
11:2	50n29
11:3–4	50n29
11:6–9	213
11:10	50n29
11:11–12	50n29
19:18	64
26:19	58
29:18	45n11, 53
32:3–4	45n11
32:15–18	213
35:4–6	42
35:5–6	45n11, 58
35:5	53
40–55	43n3, 50, 52
40:1–4	45
41:8	51
42:1–4	45–46, 52
42:1	49–50
42:4	52
42:6	50–52
42:7	49–50
43:1–13	47
43:1	165
43:3–4	48
43:5	51
44:3	51
45:13	47n17
45:19	51
45:25	51
48:16	50
48:18	51
49:1–3	49–50
49:2	50n29
49:4	50, 52
49:5–6	50n29
49:6	51–52
49:7–1	57
49:7	52
49:9	49–50
49:13	57
49:19	51
50:4–9	50
50:4–6	49–50, 52
50:6–9	52
51:2	51
52:7–10	57
52:13—53:12	xiv, 42, 44–46, 50, 52, 60
53:3–12	52
53:3–5	43–45
53:4–6	57
53:4	42–45, 60
53:5	45
53:10	46, 51
53:10–11	47, 50, 52
53:11–12	46, 48
53:11	48, 51
53:12	45
54	51–52
54:3	51
54:17	51–52
55:5	52
55:8–9	172
55:11	172
56–66	43n3, 52
56:1	52
56:6	50, 52
56:58	52

Isaiah (continued)

57:1	52
57:15	21n4
58:6	57
58:8	51
60:1—63:6	51
60:1–22	52
60:1	51, 53
60:16	57
60:21	52
61	50, 56
61:1–9	52
61:1–4	55, 60
61:1–3	49–50, 52, 57–58
61:1	42, 49–50, 57–58
61:3–4	50
61:3	50n29, 52
61:9–11	50n29
61:9	50
61:10–11	49n27
61:10	50
62:1–12	52
62:1–2	50, 52
62:3	50n29
62:11	50
62:12	57
63:17	50, 52
65:8–9	xiv, 43, 50, 52, 60
65:13–15	50, 52
65:17	168
65:23	52
66:14	50, 52

Jeremiah

1:4–6	168
11:19–21	52
11:19	49n24
18:18	52
20:10	52
29:7	158
31:33	68–69, 72, 79
34	56
38:33	69, 71–72, 79

Ezekiel

4:4–6	49n24
34:4	50
40:1	56
46	56

Hosea

13:9	146

Zechariah

7:12	49

~

Matthew

1:3–6	194
3:2	53
3:11	43n4
4:17	53
4:23	53
5–10	54
5:13–16	151, 158
5:13	158
6:24	191
6:33	151
8:1—9:38	43, 53–54, 58
8:1–15	43
8:1–4	58
8:14–17	45–46
8:16	45, 53
8:17	42–45, 53–54, 60
8:20	53
8:23—9:8	43
9:1–8	58
9:17	191
9:18–34	43
9:18–26	58
9:27–34	58
9:35—10:4	52
9:35–38	52
9:35	53, 58
9:36	53
10:1–42	43, 48, 50, 53–54, 60

10:1–4	53	7:25	35n3
10:1–2	54	10:14–15	151
10:5–42	55	10:35–45	46, 48, 174
10:5–15	53	10:42–45	173
10:7–14	54	10:45	46–48, 175
10:7	53, 58	11:27	195
10:9–10	53		
10:11–15	53		
10:16–23	53	## Luke	
10:17–22	54		
10:18	53	1:34	168
10:24–42	54	1:38	168
10:24–25	53–54	4:43	151
10:25	54	5:37–38	191
10:29–30	122	9:2	151
10:38–39	54	9:11	151
10:38	44	9:60	151
10:42	55	10:9	151
11:2	58	16:13	191
11:3	42	17:10	175
11:4–6	42	18:16–17	151
11:5–6	53		
11:5	43, 55, 57–58, 60	## John	
12:1–13	46		
12:14–16	46	1:4	129
12:18–21	43, 45–46	1:5	149
17:22	53	1:14	146, 165, 173
18:6	55	3:16–17	146
18:10	55	3:16	173
18:14	55	4:1–42	5
19:28	147, 160	5:24–27	147, 160
20:21	114	9:2	43
20:12	43n4	15:1–17	27
20:18–19	53	17:6–26	27
20:20–28	46, 48		
20:28	45	## Acts	
22:16	194		
25:40	55	2	191
28:18–20	150	10:34–35	194
28:18	182	17:16–34	5
28:19–20	46	17:28	129
28:19	128	17:29–31	77n40, 80
		17:31–32	147, 160
## Mark		22:22–29	115
		28:16–20	116
1:14	151		
2:22	191	## Romans	
5:13–16	177, 179	1–3	70
		1:8–17	67

Romans (continued)

1:16	69n17
1:17	105
1:18—11:36	67, 69, 73
1:18—3:20	68–69, 71–75
1:18–32	69–70, 73–75
1:18–23	73
1:19–20	112
1:21–32	113
1:22	113
2:1—3:8	70
2:1–16	68–69, 75
2:5	74
2:6	69, 71, 122
2:9–11	71
2:9–10	69n17
2:11	69
2:12	64n2, 69, 73
2:13–14	70
2:13	64n2, 71
2:14–16	73
2:14	64, 66, 70–73, 75, 79–83
2:15	64n2, 71
2:17	64n2
2:18	64n2
2:20	64n2
2:23	64n2
2:25–29	69
2:25	64n2
2:26	64n2
2:27	64n2
2:29	78–79
3:9–31	68
3:9	69n17
3:19–20	71
3:19	64n2
3:20–22	93
3:20	64n2, 70–71, 76
3:21—4:25	69, 75–77
3:21–26	76
3:21	64n2, 75, 77, 80
3:22–25	76
3:23	70
3:27	64, 66, 75–76, 79–80, 82–83
3:28	64n2, 71, 75–76
3:29	69n17
3:31	64n2, 75–76
4:3	75
4:10	70
4:11–12	76
4:11	75
4:13–16	75, 76
4:13	64n2
4:14	64n2
4:15	64n2
4:16	64n2
5:1—8:39	77–78
5:1	64n2, 77
5:6–11	173
5:12–24	74
5:12–21	74, 146, 173
5:12–14	74
5:13–14	64
5:20	64n2, 77
6:1–14	27, 96
6:2	54
6:4–5	176
6:14–15	77
6:14	64n2
6:15	64n2
7:1–9	77
7:1	64n2
7:2	64n2
7:3	64n2
7:4	64n2
7:5	64n2
7:6	64n2, 73
7:7	64n2
7:8	64n2
7:9	64n2
7:12	64n2, 77
7:14	64n2, 77
7:16	64n2, 77
7:21–23	77
7:21	64n2
7:22–23	77
7:22	64n2
7:23	64, 66, 77–80, 82–83
7:25	64, 66, 77–80, 82–83
8:1–17	27, 78
8:1–2	78, 96

8:2	64, 66, 77, 79–80, 82, 83	14:21	64n2
8:2–4	77	14:34	64n2, 152
8:3	64n2, 80	15:3–4	109n4
8:4	64n2	15:56	64n2
8:7	64n2, 77	15:29–34	151
8:9	80		
8:19–20	146		
8:29	160		

2 Corinthians

3:6	73
4:4–6	160
4:7	145
5:10	70n22, 122, 147, 160
5:16–19	173
5:17	147

9:1—11:36	78
9:2	92
9:24	69n17
9:31	64n2, 78
10:4	64n2, 76, 78
10:5	64n2, 78
10:12	69n17
12:1—15:13	67–68
12:1—13:14	79
12:1–21	173
12:1–2	60
12:1	96, 170
13:1	114, 158
13:8–10	76
13:8	64n2, 79
13:10	64n2
14:10	70n22
14:17–18	76
15:14–33	67

Galatians

2:16—3:24	93
2:16	64n2, 66, 76
2:19	64n2
2:21	64n2
2:20	27
3:2	64n2, 66, 76
3:5	64n2, 66, 76
3:10–12	66
3:10	64n2, 76
3:11	64n2
3:12	64n2
3:13	64n2
3:17	64n2
3:18	64n2
3:19	64n2
3:21	64n2
3:23	64n2, 66
3:24	64n2
3:26–29	152
3:28	195
4:4	64n2, 66
4:5	64n2
4:21	64n2
5:3	64n2, 66
5:4	64n2
5:13	65n9
5:14	64–66
5:18	64n2

1 Corinthians

1:18	115
1:23	113
1:30	173
2:2	113
3:8	122
3:10–15	70n22
4:1–21	151
4:1–5	73
4:5	122
9:8	64n2
9:9	64n2
9:20–21	66
9:20	64n2
10:23	71
11:7	75
11:25–26	193

Galatians (continued)

5:23	64n2
6:2	64–66, 82, 83
6:13	64n2

Ephesians

1:3–10	212
1:3–6	172
2:1–22	212
2:19–22	211
4:17—5:21	173
5:21	152
5:22	152
5:25	152

Philippians

1:27–28	211
2:1–5	174
2:6–11	175
2:17	151
3:5	64n2
3:6	64n2
3:9	64n2

Colossians

1:15	129
3:25	194

1 Thessalonians

1:9–10	77n40, 80

1 Timothy

2:9–15	152
2:11–15	152–53

2 Timothy

3:10–4:8	151
4:1	173

Hebrews

9:27	171
12:1–6	151

1 Peter

1:3–2:3	167
1:3–12	151
1:20–21	129
2:9	212

2 Peter

3:13	168

Revelation

15:4	21n3
21:1–4	147, 160, 173
21:1	168
22:1–5	147

www.ingramcontent.com/pod-product-compliance
Lightning Source LLC
Chambersburg PA
CBHW050347230426
43663CB00010B/2029